Gregory Rabassa's
Latin American
Literature

Gregory Rabassa's Latin American Literature

A Translator's Visible Legacy

María Constanza Guzmán

Lewisburg
BUCKNELL UNIVERSITY PRESS

Published by Bucknell University Press
Co-published with The Rowman & Littlefield Publishing Group, Inc.
4501 Forbes Boulevard, Suite 200, Lanham, Maryland 20706
www.rlpgbooks.com

Estover Road, Plymouth PL6 7PY, United Kingdom

Copyright © 2010 by María Constanza Guzmán

All rights reserved. No part of this book may be reproduced in any form or by any electronic or mechanical means, including information storage and retrieval systems, without written permission from the publisher, except by a reviewer who may quote passages in a review.

British Library Cataloguing in Publication Information Available

Library of Congress Cataloging-in-Publication Data

Library of Congress Cataloguing-in-Publication Data on file under LC#2010013392
ISBN: 978-1-61148-008-5 (cl. : alk. paper)
eISBN: 978-1-61148-009-2

∞ ™ The paper used in this publication meets the minimum requirements of American National Standard for Information Sciences—Permanence of Paper for Printed Library Materials, ANSI/NISO Z39.48-1992.

Printed in the United States of America

A la memoria de Amparo, mi madre, con la valentía de su dulce adiós.

Contents

Acknowledgments	9
Introduction	13
1. Why Rabassa?: Theorizing the Translator's Legacy	17
2. Rabassa's Conceptions of Translation and Language	32
3. Del lado de allá y Del lado de acá / From this Side and from the Other: Rabassa's Dialogue with His Authors	55
4. Ayer y hoy / Past and Present: Rabassa's Canon and the Reception of His Translations	83
5. Rabassa's Translations and an Imagined Latin America	110
Afterword	131
Appendix: I: Personal interview with Gregory Rabassa	135
Appendix II: List of translations by Gregory Rabassa	147
Appendix III: Copies of annotated drafts and manuscripts	151
Notes	159
Bibliography	176
Index	186

Acknowledgments

So many voices make their way into a manuscript as it is written and rewritten through the years that it is virtually impossible to mention every person who deserves to be thanked. I am deeply grateful to my professors, colleagues, family, and friends, whose support made this book possible.

I wish to express my appreciation to Gregory Rabassa for his work and for being such an inspirational figure; he supported this project from the start and was available for consultation as it advanced. I also wish to thank the staff of the Howard Gotlieb Archival Research Center at Boston University for enabling me to consult and use the materials in Gregory Rabassa's archive. Earlier versions of the individual chapters of the book were published in the journals *TTR, deSignis,* and *Forma y función*.

I learned a great deal from the graduate seminars I attended during my years of studies at Kent State University and SUNY Binghamton. I am indebted to my professors and committee members at both institutions for the time they devoted to read and comment on my work. A warm thanks to Marilyn Gaddis Rose for her continuous support. In general, I want to express my gratitude to all my translation professors both in Colombia and in the United States for having encouraged me and having engendered many of the ideas and questions that were the basis of this project.

I am grateful to my colleagues at Glendon College, York University, in Toronto, for their generosity and respect. Special thanks to Rosalind Gill and Ian Martin for their careful reading of the manuscript at different stages, and to my research assistants for their useful input as I updated the manuscript for publication. I have benefited greatly from the advice and enriching conversations with friends and peers throughout the years, as an undergraduate and a graduate student and, recently, during the first few years of my academic career as a professor. My friends from Colombia have been my ongoing interlocutors for decades; to them I am always grateful.

Thank you to my family, who taught me the value of reading and the pleasure of language. I am deeply grateful to my parents, Amparo and Antonio, for supporting me and respecting my choices. I warmly dedicate this book to my mother, a model of grace and courage, who passed away in October of 2009. I was not able to share with her the joy of bringing this project to completion. I cannot thank my sister Marcela enough: she helped me throughout my research and supported me unconditionally.

I am profoundly grateful to Joshua for commenting on my work and supporting me intellectually and emotionally, for his presence and love.

Finally, and always, thank you to literary translators for their invaluable contribution to world culture; they do not cease to inspire me.

Copyright Acknowledgements

The author and publisher gratefully acknowledge permission to reproduce the following:

An interview with Gregory Rabassa, reproduced by permission of Gregory Rabassa.

Selected unpublished images of Gregory Rabassa's materials, reproduced by permission of Gregory Rabassa and the Howard Gotlieb Archival Research Center at Boston University.

Excerpts from *Searching for Recognition: The Promotion of Latin American Literature in the United States,* copyright ©1997 by Irene Rostagno. Reprinted by permission of ABC-CLIO, LLC.

Excerpts from *If This Be Treason: Translation and its Dyscontents,* copyright ©2005 by Gregory Rabassa. Reprinted by permission of New Directions Publishing Corp.

Gregory Rabassa's
Latin American
Literature

Introduction

During the past five decades, North American translator Gregory Rabassa has translated over fifty Latin American novels from the second half of the twentieth century. To this day, Rabassa remains one of the most prominent translators of literature from Spanish and Portuguese. His first book-length translation was Julio Cortázar's *Rayuela* (1963). The first edition, *Hopscotch* (1966), won the first National Book Award for Translation in the United States in 1967. Rabassa went on to publish recognized translations of Latin American works, including *One Hundred Years of Solitude* (1970), by the Colombian Nobel Laureate Gabriel García Márquez; *Paradiso* (1974), by the Cuban author José Lezama Lima; and *The Posthumous Memoirs of Brás Cubas* (1997), by the Brazilian author Joachim Maria Machado de Assis. Rabassa has been strongly committed to the dissemination of Latin American literature to an English-speaking readership. His pivotal role in the internationalization of several Latin American writers led to the formation of a canon and, significantly, to the construction of the most prevalent images of Latin American literature from the second half of the twentieth century and into the twenty-first century. Rabassa's translations have been crucial to the way in which the Latin American literary tradition has inscribed the Western canon.

A quick glance at Rabassa's biography shows the impressive scope of his legacy. He constitutes a somewhat unique case in the history of contemporary translation given that, contrary to prevailing conceptions and representations of translators—and without having been first known as a poet or a fiction writer—Rabassa is particularly visible as a translating subject. His translations are visible works: they are widely read and recognized. Rabassa has received numerous awards and with his work has helped give Latin America the literary voice it has at present.

Rabassa began his career as a translator in the early sixties when, as one of the editors of the literary quarterly *Odyssey*, he was in charge of searching for new writing in Spanish and Portuguese. The stories he found had to be translated, and so he took on this task. After this initial experience, Rabassa was asked by the editor of Pantheon Books—Sara Blackburn—for a sample translation of a couple of chapters of Julio Cortázar's *Rayuela* (1963). Subsequently, both the editor and the Argentinean author agreed that Rabassa should translate the entire novel.

Over the years, Rabassa has translated works by prominent Latin American authors, such as Miguel Ángel Asturias, Clarice Lispector, Mario Vargas Llosa, Jorge Amado, José Donoso, Luisa Valenzuela, and Luis Rafael Sánchez, among others. Rabassa has also translated fiction by European authors, such as Juan Goytisolo and Juan Benet from Spain and Mario de Carvalho and António Lobo Antunes from Portugal. Besides translating works by authors who are already established as part of the Latin American literary canon—his translations include many works of the so-called Latin American Boom—Rabassa has always been interested in promoting the work of lesser-known writers such as Demetrio Aguilera-Malta, Dalton Trevisan, Manuel Mujica Láinez, José Sarney, or Osman Lins. In short, as a translator, he has been strongly committed to the dissemination of Latin American literature to an English-speaking readership.

Rabassa's direct participation and influence in the formation of the literary canon constitutes one of the reasons why he is a unique case and his works are visible in their own right. As Thomas Hoaksema said in the introduction to his 1978 interview with the translator, while many translators receive and are content with minimal recognition, Rabassa is accorded nearly co-creative status with the original author.[1] And this is still the case, for Rabassa has institutional importance as a translator: he writes about and reviews translations, and his status and criteria as a specialist are taken into consideration when commissioning translations. It is largely in this sense that I refer to Rabassa's visibility, in terms of his institutional role and the extent to which his work has been an integral part in the history of Latin American literature.

Rabassa's legacy is evident, given both his importance as a translator, and the significant connection between his works and the development of the Latin American literary tradition to this day. These are the main reasons why I have chosen to examine Rabassa's translating career. In this book I take the case of this North American translator and discuss his role as an agent in shaping Latin American literature. I discuss his legacy—his translations, his writings, his relationship with the authors and his position in the history of literature—in light of developments in translation theory that have taken place in the past few decades, which have increasingly recognized the importance of studying the translator's active role in the production of texts and knowledge.

Examining Rabassa's case in this light a number of questions arise: How do we articulate his role in the institution of literature? How do we speak of the translator? Or, in other words, how do we theorize the translating subject? My main goal in placing Rabassa at the center of inquiry is to explore how the question of the translating subject can be entertained critically. I believe that Rabassa's case is prototypical of the figure of the literary translator and that, as such, it offers a unique opportunity to discuss questions being addressed by theoretical approaches to translation today.

One of the main reasons that led me to study the case of Rabassa was the fact that, although his work has been widely recognized and there are several works that record his accomplishments as a translator, the extent of his work's influence and the complexity of the socio-cultural circumstances that have surrounded his practice have remained largely unexamined. Apart from a limited number of articles and book chapters in academic publications,[2] the most significant work on Rabassa's translating career is his own full-length book, *If This Be Treason: Translation and Its Dyscontents* (2005), which contains Rabassa's own reflections about his practice as well as his accounts of the stories behind the translation of some works with details about their authors. Even though there exist theoretical works that focus on individual translators,[3] most accounts of translators' histories are structured in an anecdotal and descriptive fashion; they frequently constitute records of accomplishments or—especially in the case of articles—discussions of translation "errors" and infelicitous decisions.

A number of recent publications offer a more critical—historiographic—perspective about the lives, works, and translation practices of individual translators.[4] While there seems to be an increasing interest in looking at the work of individual translators in translation studies, there are a very limited number of critical works about individual translators. Very few works about translation approach the translator—as a creator, a writer, or the agent of an intellectual endeavor—as a subject worthy of critical inquiry. With respect to Rabassa, among the works mentioned above and other minor documents, there is no in-depth analysis about his overall contribution to Latin American literature from a critical perspective. The purpose of this project is precisely to fill this gap.

My analysis has been inspired by contemporary theories of translation that do not follow a normative logic or seek to theorize translation in terms of rules or standards. Theories such as those founded in cultural and literary studies—which led to the so-called "cultural turn"[5] in translation studies—attempt to find ways of conceptualizing translation by generating spaces of reflection and exploring dynamic and interdisciplinary directions of critical inquiry. I have found of particular interest for the study of Rabassa's legacy those theoretical approaches that deal with the translator's presence and visibility,[6] the relationship between the translator and the literary institution,[7] and the translator's ethics and responsibilities.[8] My way of thinking about translation has also been marked by postcolonial accounts of translation experiences[9]—particularly inasmuch as they engage in the discussion of the power relations inherent to translation—and by reflections on the subversive potential of translation, especially in the Latin American context.[10]

This study aims to provide an alternative to a formal assessment of Rabassa's translating styles, strategies, and practices, and to move beyond a normative discourse that is limited to issues of faithfulness to an original, meaning departures, or linguistic accomplishments and impossibilities. In short, I do not focus on the question of whether Rabassa's translations are "good" or "bad." Rather, it is my belief that with a non-evaluative focus I can better portray and reflect on the plural complexity of translation and of Rabassa's legacy. On the basis of the framework used for this study I aim to outline a critical ground for a translator's "sociography."[11]

There is a series of questions I consider key to understanding Rabassa's practice and identifying the varied aspects of his legacy: How did Rabassa the translator and his work come to occupy center stage? How does his visibility manifest itself in his practice and reflection about translation? How does Rabassa construct himself as a translator? How are his translations received and judged? Have these perceptions changed? What may have caused these changes? How does Rabassa relate to others—works, authors, communities, traditions, and influences—and how is he influenced by them in his translation practice?

It is my assumption that these questions can be approached by looking at Rabassa's relationship with the translated works, as well as with *his* authors and other participants in the literary community, and with his own practice, the practice of translation itself.

1
Why Rabassa?:
Theorizing the Translator's Legacy

HISTORICALLY, AS TRANSLATION THEORY HAS STRIVEN TO ESTABLISH itself as an area of inquiry in its own right and to lay down the grounds upon which translation ought to be theorized, the translator as an object of study has received many different treatments. Depending on the theoretical approach or perspective at play, we have translators performing different tasks, responding to various "missions," and complying with differing characterizations. The most widely recognized images of the translator are those associated with absence and invisibility. Traditionally, the translator's image is associated with that of a scribe, a copier, or the neutral messenger of a stable message. In particular, the position of the literary translator is often regarded as secondary and translations as derivative.[1] According to these perceptions, translators and their works are secondary and their place in relation to the author of the original work, and to the work itself, is subordinate. These prevailing, seemingly common sense, and widely accepted conceptions of the translator pose a theoretical dilemma: if translators are invisible, any attempt to theorize them will be inescapably elusive. How to theorize an absent subject? How to place the translator at the center of critical inquiry? It is my belief that, to theorize the translator as a presence, that is, as a subject, we must begin by problematizing notions about translation that are at the core of the translator's alleged invisibility. Thus, in the following overview of recurrent perspectives about translation and translators, I will attempt to explain how the translator has come to occupy a secondary space, and in this process I will allow for a basis toward a redefinition of the translator as a subject.

For the most part, the translator has not been considered a major subject of study by translation scholars. Traditionally, and particularly from the perspective of linguistics, the study of translation has most commonly been associated with the study of languages as systems whose purpose is to communicate neutral messages. The study of translation has in fact been closely connected to linguistics. Perceptions of the translator's "persona" proposed by linguistics-oriented translation studies since the 1940s and '50s, suggest that the translator's role is that of a problem-solver and that meaning transfer is the translator's most clearly defined task. According to this perspective,[2] the central question of translation theory is the question of identity between source and target units, that is, of "equivalence," the source text being a stable, finished object, whose meaning is to be transferred and preserved in the target text.

Perspectives grounded in other schools of thought challenge the image of the translator as a mere problem-solver. They critique linguistics-oriented approaches to translation that, rather than problematizing the very notion of meaning or the subject who performs the linguistic operations that concern them, see translation as an instrumental process of message transfer in which the translator—although accomplished—comes out as a neutral mediator whose task or mission is to be the faithful messenger of a stable, finished message.[3]

Nonetheless, the possibility of total meaning recovery suggested by the linguistics-oriented concept of translation presupposes that translation *is* possible. Given that ideas that had prevailed previously saw translation mainly in terms of impossibility and loss, linguistics-oriented approaches did make a contribution in that they enabled translation theory to move beyond impossibility and take an empirical view. This view, however, conceives of language as communicative, rather than constitutive, of meaning—i.e., referential. As Lawrence Venuti notes, "linguistics addresses the issue of translatability by analyzing specific translation problems and describing the methods that translators have developed to solve them."[4] In this light, theorizing translation becomes a task of inquiring not "if" one can translate but "how" to do it to communicate meaning and how to do it well.

The ideas of linguists such as Roman Jakobson, for instance, contributed to this challenge to the "dogma of impossibility." In his essay "On Linguistic Aspects of Translating,"[5] Jakobson explains translation as a decoding operation whose product is the recoding of a particular sign or set of signs. From a similar perspective, translation scholar Eugene Nida states that since there can be no fully exact translations, "no identity in detail," the total impact of a translation is to be "reasonably close to the original."[6] Jakobson affirmed that translation should not be assessed in terms of loss, betrayal, or failure.[7] Both theorists—as well as several others—embraced a view that opens a space of possibility for translation beyond the traditional understanding of it being defined in terms of its impossibility. Generally speaking, linguistics was the first discipline to offer translation the promise of a kind of rigor and systematicity that would turn it into a discipline in its own right. Assuming that translation is possible, linguistics offered a path and a program for its study. However, it also limited its subject of study to explaining the mechanics of the translating practice. Moreover, it presupposes the existence of a clear-cut separation between languages, which leads to a sense of transparency at the core of conceptions of language, translation, and difference.

Other approaches to translation, such as those emerging from philosophical perspectives, provide a different framework from that proposed by linguistics. These approaches have generally paid more attention to the question of "the translator," and to the translator's role and mission. Often, philosophical approaches, as well as those associated with literary criticism, have been more interested in investigating the interpretive character of translation, thus offering a space to reflect on translation as a creative endeavor and on the translator as a more visible subject. One of the most influential texts about translation from this perspective is Walter Benjamin's essay "The Task of the Translator."[8] In this essay, Benjamin stresses the complexity of the study of translation: "it is necessary to found the concept of translation at the deepest level of linguistic theory, for it is much too far-reaching and powerful to be treated in any way as an afterthought."[9] Benjamin does not equate translatability with equivalence or correspondence, for he believes that a work's "translatability" is determined by its historical relevance. Translation is a necessary result of a literary work and constitutes its value. Translation is thus the "afterlife" of the work and the means through which it is inscribed in history.

The contribution of Benjamin's essay to translation is undeniable, mostly in regard to his understanding of translation as creative performance—his perspective departs from the notion or ideal of "faithfulness." According to Benjamin, the translator's "task" is not to be faithful in the sense of staying close to the original. For him translation is the necessary and expected outcome of the very existence of the work, and the translator's mission is the work's survival. In his reflections, Benjamin acknowledges the translator's existence and presents a view of translation as a practice that goes beyond the mechanical activity of reproducing or of copying. Benjamin's essay is relevant when it comes to understanding the development of translation studies because, besides being a key referent in the work of many translation theorists to this day—it is foundational to George Steiner's *After Babel,* for instance, and is also at the core of Venuti's critique—it both represents and challenges important traditional notions and theoretical positions about translation. It contributes to the recognition of translation as transformation and to the fact that translation is indispensable to enabling the passage of the works from their life to their afterlife—i.e., it is the condition for the works' very possibility of survival.

Benjamin's essay has been critiqued mainly on the grounds that it is, in other respects, founded on notions that have contributed to keeping translation in a marginal cultural space. In the essay "Des Tours de Babel," Jacques Derrida offers his reading and commentary of Benjamin's text, and questions Benjamin's understanding of the translator's performance understood as a "task":

> From the very title Benjamin situates the *problem* in the sense of that which is precisely *before oneself* as a task, as the problem of the translator and not that of translation. He names the subject of translation, as an indebted subject, obligated by a duty, already in the position of heir, entered as survivor in a genealogy, as survivor or agent of survival. The survival of works, not authors. Perhaps the sur-vival of authors' names and signatures, but not of authors.[10]

Derrida understands Benjamin's "task" as commitment, and stresses the fact that Benjamin sees this task as the translator's duty—a mission and a debt. He points out an important implication of viewing translation as a "duty," which is that translators appear to themselves and to others as indebted subjects, whose task is "to *render* that which must have been given."[11] What Derrida sees as a problem is the fact that both the original text and the mission of translation itself entail a debt, for which something must be given in return.

In Benjamin's terms, translation calls for transformation. Derrida sees how, for Benjamin, translation is creative, for "the debt does not involve restitution of a copy or a good image . . . the original gives itself in modifying itself."[12] However, Derrida also sees that, in Benjamin's terms, the translation remains secondary to the original, or rather, that the original remains "remote" in it—i.e., sacred. The notion of the sacralized original lies on Benjamin's notion of "pure language" given that, as Derrida explains, for Benjamin translation is possible also because there is a possibility for a language beyond languages, a "pure," true language that can overcome its own conventionality, that is, a possibility of language *as* truth, which, to him, takes the form of "the *pure language* in which the meaning and the letter no longer dissociate."[13] Benjamin's notion of "pure language" is based on a notion of linguistic harmony: it leaves the translator with the task—i.e., duty—to attain the "reconciliation" of languages on the basis of a promise of a language beyond the untranslatability of languages. This kingdom, according to Derrida, remains untouchable, and "in this sense the reconciliation that translation offers is only promised."[14] Although Benjamin shifts the traditional roles of the original and the version, in Derrida's reading, he still maintains the duality between the translated and the translating, which allows the original, and the author, to retain their unique (and undebatable) authority. Thus, the translator is still absent, or at best in an ambiguous position.

Derrida's choice to discuss "The Task of the Translator" is telling; as he himself explains, Benjamin's text is a "singular example, at once archetypical and allegorical, that could serve as an introduction to all the so-called theoretical problems of translation." He does not look so much at Benjamin or at his "task" in themselves but, rather, at the discourse that his essay represents as theory, in order to problematize its limits and possibilities *as* conceptualization: "No theorization, inasmuch as it is produced in a language, will be able to dominate the Babelian [sic] performance."[15] This realization constitutes an important reminder that any statement about translation is bound to the production, location, and circumstance of the statement itself. Inasmuch as the theorization stays in language, it will remain particular; thus it should not be taken as a univocal response. Derrida's commentary on Benjamin's text is a helpful critique considering the prevalence of an idealized understanding of meaning that reifies originality and authorship in reflections concerning translation. Nevertheless, Benjamin's text offers numerous readings and is insightful, particularly concerning the relevance of translation for the afterlife of literary works and its transformative potential; it is also a compelling invitation to push the conventional limits of language and to embrace the foreign.

Philosophical reflections about language and translation have constituted, for translation studies, a space to think about the translator as a present subject and about translation as an interpretive process and a form of writing. Since the cultural turn in translation studies, critical inquiry has shifted the attention from the discussion on texts and meaning as detached subjects of observation to questions of translation in culture and of the translator as a participant in complex processes of cultural production. Revisions of the notions of authorship and originality such as those emanating from the work of such philosophers as Michel Foucault and Derrida himself, and in general from cultural studies and post-structuralist perspectives, are at the core of contemporary understandings and theoretical attempts to define translators as visible subjects and texts in translation as works in their own right.

As Venuti—the most prominent advocate of the importance of the translator's visibility—explains, the implications of prevailing ideas of invisibility are complex because "the effect of transparency masks the mediations between and within copy and original and eclipses the translator's labor with an illusion of authorial presence," thus reproducing translation's cultural marginality.[16] Rosemary Arrojo also questions the traditional belief in the "conscious" authorial presence in texts by stating that, if originals are perceived as true recipients of their creators' "intentions and expression, any translation is, by definition, devalued since it necessarily represents a form of falsification, always removed from the original and its author."[17] This image contributes to the perception of translations as illegitimate copies or falsifications that, in turn, informs and conditions the translator's image and self-image. This is one of the reasons leading to the translator's invisibility: besides the need to make translation look "seamless" in writing[18]—a translation should not read like a translation, this is a question of standards and taste—translators themselves, as Arrojo states, hide to avoid being associated with the form of falsification that translation represents.

Views about translation that propose ways of radically revising the conventional notions of originality, authorship, and interpretation provide a basis on which to inquire as to what is at stake in hiding or concealing the translator. In general, these views share the belief that it is neither possible nor desirable to try to reach any pure origin that would be univocal and beyond any perspective, and that interference— i.e., writing—is inevitable. In the absence of a pure origin or true meaning, translation may rightfully be a transformative and creative practice, without entailing any inherent form of falsification. Arrojo has proposed that the revision of the relationship between the translator and the author could be done, for instance, by bringing to the realm of translation Foucault's reflection on the "author function," whereby the author is not sacred but a regulating element and a "functional principle;" similarly, the notion of the "translator function" can also be entertained.¹⁹ The questioning of traditional notions of authorship does not imply the complete disappearance of originals, but a critique of essentializing ideas of textuality and of translation as perfect equivalence. Thinking about the author as a regulating element rather than as an immutable entity carrying an essential meaning would allow for an understanding of translation as "regulated transformation," as Derrida proposed, of one language by another, of one text by another.²⁰ Such productive conceptual recognition of the dynamics of difference in language eliminates views of translation as falsifying or illegitimate, and understandings of it as a neutral reproduction of texts independent from the translator's circumstances. It constitutes a move toward validating the translator's voice as legitimate interference.

Along with the increasing scholarly attention paid to the translator in recent years, greater attention has also been paid to the importance of studying translation as an intellectual endeavor and a practice of textual production, and investigating the peculiarities of translation as writing. Douglas Robinson defines translation as a form of writing that — like most writing — has rules, limits, and possibilities. He compares authors and translators in light of the writing practice that they each perform, and asks:

> Who translates? Who is the subject of translation? Is the translator allowed to be a subject, to have subjectivity? If so, what forces are active within it, and to what extent are those forces channeled into it from without? Who translates/writes? Who controls the act of writing/translating? Whose voice speaks when we write or translate?[21]

For Robinson translation is writing and the translator is a writer. On the basis of this assumption, he problematizes common views and expectations about translators, in terms of what they are to achieve if they translate an author's work. To describe the values that commonly underlie the relationship between the translator and the author, what he identifies as the expectations imposed on the translator, Robinson proposes the metaphor of "channeling" because, according to him, the notions of faithfulness and ideal equivalence presuppose such a connection between the translator and the author; translators are practically expected to "channel" authors to know what they *wanted* to say. Although he draws mainly on cases of translators of sacred texts, this "spirit-channeling" metaphor can be extrapolated to speak about the relationship between translators and texts in general, inasmuch as original texts are understood as immutable—i.e., sacralized. Robinson's is a provocative metaphor for a reflection around the relationship between an imagined author and a translator as a real-life, organic body. He asks: if a translator in the present would claim "to be psychically channeling the dead spirit of Homer and thus to know exactly what Homer wanted to say in the target language,"[22] what would be our reaction to such claim? Probably suspicion and amusement. But as he shows, although the claim that the dead writer can "inspire" or "overshadow" the translator's work on his or her text, or that "the translation is a joint project undertaken by the translator's body and the author's spirit," may sound strange and extravagant, it turns out to be a very common claim indeed. A good translator is supposed to be able to somehow know exactly what the author "meant."[23]

Robinson aims to introduce post-rationalist reformulations of the translator's subjectivity.[24] His metaphors exemplify succinctly the hidden thought or desire to be the author's intermediary or "medium," or to "channel" the author's spirit, latent both in common-sense views of what translation is about, and in what translators themselves believe their ultimate goal to be—translators claim that they "know" or aspire to know, i.e., attain complete understanding. So perhaps this claim is a precondition of translation, for if it is not granted (or a least promised) that the "invisible hand" of the author is the same one that is writing the text, the translator is at fault. Certainly, the complicated implications of what Robinson calls the translator's "desirable subordinated or instrumentalized subjectivity"[25] turn out to be a key element in translators' awareness of themselves and of their role in the production of meaning. They underscore the ideology behind the reluctance to recognize translation as writing. Along with the question of invisibility, this type of problematization—which associates translation with the expectations that surround it and with the translator's self-awareness—as well as the exploration of the translator's "task," can inform a reflection on the translator's role framed in terms of ethics.

These views[26] confront us with the conflicts and contradictions that the figure of the translator embodies and that are embedded in the practice of translating as a "task." In turn, such conflicts and contradictions seem to be at the core of the elusive character of the translator's figure that has prevailed in theories of textuality. But why exactly is rendering the translator present—and not only the translation—so important? And why should the translator be rendered as a creative subject and not as a faithful scribe or as a subservient messenger?

Contemporary concepts of translation that challenge the translator's invisibility and problematize process-oriented views of translation seek to frame the practice by endorsing and working through notions of texts in which the originals are not sacralized. They do not attempt to replace other frameworks; rather, they serve to diversify and expand theoretical boundaries and contextualize reified ideas of texts and subjects, by constantly emphasizing the need to recognize that translation is exchange, not a one-person enterprise, and that it occurs in and among collective spaces. Umberto Eco offers an instance of this type of theoretical move when he proposes to modify Jakobson's definition of "translation proper"—i.e., interlingual translation (between languages)—and add the notion of "negotiation" to it. Although he endorses Jakobson's definition, Eco believes that such a definition ought to include such elements as law (e.g., copyright), trade, and general institutional and commercial criteria.[27] With this characterization, Eco underscores the fact that the translator participates in an inherently collective exchange, which ought to be called a "negotiation" so as to mark it as an act that is never disinterested.

The study of translation must involve the study of attitudes and gestures that are inherently ideological and political. According to Venuti, to unveil the real negotiations and disparate interests that may be at stake in the translating exchange, it is necessary to speak of the translator's invisibility. Furthermore, in any revision of the translator's figure, it is key to place the translator as a subject that exists *in* history. It is thus of crucial importance to historicize conceptualizations and practices of translation. Venuti positions himself clearly and explicitly in his spatial-temporal context; his thinking is rooted in the position of the translator in contemporary Anglo-American culture. His views about translation also presuppose that translation is much more complex than what is conventionally called a "communicative act." Translation inevitably inscribes the original text with the values of the receiving culture. It "never communicates in an untroubled fashion because the translator negotiates the linguistic and cultural differences of the foreign text by reducing them and supplying another set of differences." This other set of differences is "basically domestic, drawn from the receiving language and culture."[28]

Venuti speaks most of the time of "the translator"—rather than focusing on "language" or "texts" alone—because, for him, the study of translation is inseparable from the study of the translating subject. He insists on the importance of historicizing translation also to reveal the relationships involved in translating experiences and among particular communities and individuals. Venuti's own preference is for translation strategies that displace standard linguistic values and defy the canon of fluency by preserving the foreignness of the text—"foreign" designating both what is geographically or linguistically remote and what is socially or institutionally marginalized. Following this interest, he proposes translation as a site to displace language and literature by means of strategies that introduce variations from the privileged forms of standard language—regional or group dialects, jargons, archaisms, neologisms, and so on—to find and/or create analogues of foreign forms in rewriting the text in translation. For Venuti translation is always ideological: "it releases a domestic remainder, an inscription of values, beliefs, and representations linked to historical moments and social positions in the domestic culture."[29] Venuti's views, like Berman's and those of other theorists who exhibit analogous concerns, are illuminating for thinking about translation as a practice that is not—and cannot be seen as—produced, practiced, or consumed by ahistorical subjects, but one that should be studied, instead, in relation to the community or communities in which it is produced, occurs, and circulates. They lead us to see the power tensions embedded in the relations between the communities that interact in translation, to see how these communities not only assign a text-translation its meanings but also determine its value, and even allow for its very existence. Translation is revealed as conditioned by public and institutional perceptions, taste, and standards that will, in turn, inform translators' ways of seeing, reading, and writing, and the way their versions are to be consumed—i.e., authorized. In this light, given the ethical, political, and ideological variables that determine the translating practice, the finished product—a completed translation—is a testimony.

There is a strong relationship between translation and community formation. Venuti has asserted that, besides belonging to one or several communities, the translator also *creates* communities or helps to bring them into existence. Besides being a product and a participant in a given community, the translator participates by helping potential narrative and interpretive communities unfold:[30]

> The communities fostered by translating are initially potential, signaled in the text, in the discursive strategy deployed by the translator, but not yet possessing a social existence. They depend for their realization on the ensemble of the domestic cultural constituencies among which the translation will circulate.[31]

Such potential to open up the "local" language and take it to unfamiliar or unprivileged places and forms has an ideological function. A translation thus marked by domestic interests is, potentially, a means to challenge existing domestic values. In this sense Venuti sees translation (both translating, in terms of practice and strategies, and translated texts) as utopian, a possibility to create imagined communities around that which is considered foreign.

The relationship between translation and community has an impact on the translator's self-understanding and self-awareness; a translator who is aware of its potential may engage it actively and consciously. It is also relevant when it comes to articulating the ideological basis of the choices made in translation at all levels; for instance, choosing one translation strategy or another may have the effect of producing translations that will establish a common understanding between domestic and foreign readers, but it can also have the opposite effect of blocking this understanding. The work of a self-aware translator will be informed and regulated by such type of questions and reflections. Venuti recognizes that, although he calls this community-formation projection "utopian," it is not inconsistent with the social realities and circumstances that surround translating: the "inscription" of translation cannot be so comprehensive or total as to create a "community of interest without exclusion or hierarchy" and "the asymmetry between the foreign and domestic cultures persists even when the foreign context is partly inscribed in the translation."[32]

Despite the fact that Venuti's ideas are controversial and often contested, the ways in which he thinks about the translator as a subject placed in history are a radical departure from idealized or unrealistic images of the translator's performance. Critical approaches to translation that derive from or respond to Venuti's work help us find ways to "name" the translator and underscore the translator's role as an active agent who is part of communities and their interactions, working in the context of the socio-political hierarchy of languages and of all the variables and implications that lie behind what has often been characterized as simple decision-making.

As I noted earlier, when thinking of the translator's self-understanding and awareness and of the translator's subjectivity and historical agency in particular, the question of ethics comes to occupy center stage. Speaking of the translators' agency leads us to articulate an image of the translator as an ethical subject and look at translators in terms of the social implications of the writing practice they perform, of the texts they produce, and of the effects they produce in and through discourse. As Arrojo has indicated, partly as a result of idealized notions of equivalence and authorship, the ethical position of the translator is often conflicted and seen with suspicion. As they are sometimes seen as unwelcome intermediaries, "translators generally agree to practice an activity which perversely associates excellence with invisibility." This belief fosters the sense that "a successful translator is allegedly the one who gives readers the illusion of his or her non-interference in the writing he or she actually produces."[33]

We can say then, that if translators are seen as producers of texts, it follows that they are responsible for the translating/writing they perform. If it is true that translators cannot escape their own presence and inevitably inscribe the text with their own selves, their texts result from the conceptions of language and of translation according to which they operate, and the translation will bear the ideologies that underlie these conceptions. Are translators unaware of their circumstance? Do they act with an aim or a purpose? To which structures and laws do they conform? Which ones do they challenge? The notions of translation underlying these questions contribute to an articulation of the translator in terms of presence and raise the question of translation in terms of ethics. They ascribe greater importance to the nature of the translator-author relationship, the translator's motivations and self-awareness, and the tensions caused by the power asymmetries at play in the translating encounter. In that context, it becomes possible and legitimate to discuss, for instance, how someone's translations have influenced particular standards of rhetoric and taste or affected the literary canon in a certain place and at a certain time. Moreover, these questions are relevant if we realize that, however contradictory or vague its nature is commonly believed to be, translation is a key instrument in history, as can be seen, for instance, in the way it has been rightly and explicitly associated with (oft times unequal and conflictive) encounters of peoples and communities, as is the case, for instance, of (post)colonial contexts.

Michael Cronin suggests that one necessary step toward rethinking perceptions about translation would be to stop looking at it as a detached object of study—about which we ought to speak in factual terms—and instead recognize it as embedded in our everyday experience, so that we can face the fact that translation matters.[34] If we understand translation as "mediation," says Cronin, and given that mediation, understood as a presence that is not disinterested, has far-ranging consequences in local and global dynamics, the translator's presence stands out, especially if we think, as he puts it, in terms of contemporary "global" politics.[35]

Translation is by definition the enactment of language and culture contact. It is an instrument in people's invested interactions and relates to our ideologically-bound relationship—or dialogue—with our living space and with the world at large, what Cronin calls our "active sense of global citizenship."[36] Cronin relates an individual's experience of translation with collective historical and spatial experiences. He speaks of historical and political circumstances, such as "processes of conquest, resistance and self-definition"[37] as guiding translation in its relationship with power and history. He also speaks of spatial relationships, often in relation to minoritized languages and the redrawing of maps and boundaries—i.e., to the negotiation of territories—as determinant of the asymmetric position of one language in relation to another. This underscores the relational nature of both temporal and spatial relationships of language contact. Thinking translation along these lines we may say that, if translation is (like) dialogue, then what happens in "real-life" translation is similar to what happens in "real-life" dialogue: there are misunderstandings, silences, interruptions, refusals to understand, distortions, and voices that impose themselves over one another. Translation entails relation, contact, tension, plurality, conflict, and (again) negotiation. It may even be a site to understand why we may *not* particularly like or be inclined to understand what the other has written, said, or produced. It may well reveal who is invited to speak and who is not, or even who is allowed to have a voice. This perspective expands the critical potential of the study of translation since, as Rose believes, translation exhibits realities about cultural and political history at large and about the "oscillations" of cultural history, and it should be seen in its organicity and as part of the (human) cultural continuum.[38]

Thinking of translation as invested mediation in everyday experience "forces" us—translators, readers—to remain aware of our presence; it does not let us feel removed from the socio-cultural position and from the responsibility we hold as we speak/write/translate, nor from that which results from that position:

> Our narrative imagination—our ability to try to imagine what it is like to be someone else from another language, another culture, another community or another country—is itself a mere figment of the imagination if we have no way of reading the books, watching the plays, looking at the films produced by others. In other words, if citizenship is seen as no longer exclusively defined by nationality or the nation-state.[39]

If we relate Cronin's views to the translator's "task" in order to derive ideas about the translator's responsibility or "mission," we see that it offers a radically different perspective from the kind of "task" that can be found in Benjamin's essay. In Cronin's terms—as well as in Venuti's—the translator's mission is determined by the collective space and time in which the translator exists and interacts. As a consequence, the translator becomes defined also as one of the agents involved in the writing and circulation of the narratives that construct culture in very concrete ways—whether that results in enabling the circulation of those narratives or in obscuring or blocking them. In any case, translation is never innocent and cannot be—understood merely as enabling neutral or transparent communication. Whether endowed with "positive" or "negative" social powers, translators are participants in the construction of the narrative imagination of which they are themselves a part.

At this point I must ask: what are the critical possibilities of the changing ideas about the translator that contemporary theories have been developing, and the theoretical implications of seeing translation as writing, rendering the translator visible, and historicizing the translating practice, when it comes to theorizing Gregory Rabassa? This study about Rabassa's legacy is framed in terms of the influence of his work and of the complexity of the socio-cultural circumstances that have surrounded his translating practice, which, as I noted in the introduction, are aspects that have remained largely unexamined. The theoretical approaches discussed move the translator from a peripheral position to a central one, thus providing a relevant context for the study of Rabassa's legacy.

Placing Gregory Rabassa at the center of inquiry is itself a project founded on the assumption that the translator does exist as a subject and that a translator's work constitutes a cultural legacy. As a translator for several decades, Rabassa himself has been a particularly active agent in the traveling of Latin American narratives as they exist in the English-speaking world. Therefore, to understand the insertion of these narratives in literary and cultural history it is essential to ask questions about the negotiations in which Rabassa, as a translator, has participated—and continues to do so.

What theories of language have underlain Rabassa's ideas about translation? With what image of the translator does Rabassa identify himself? How does he relate to the authors whose works he has translated? How has he participated in the insertion of their works into the literary institution? How have these writers and their works participated in making Rabassa visible? How does he interact with the interpretive community he inhabits? To what extent has Rabassa conformed to Anglo-American translation standards and to what extent has he—consciously or unconsciously—contributed to displacing them? Has he participated in the realization of any potential reading or interpretive communities? What does Rabassa see as his "task" or "mission" and what means has he chosen to accomplish it? These questions are complex in nature and the angles from which they can be addressed are multiple. In the following chapters I intend to propose some possible ways to entertain them.

Returning to the original question of why and how to theorize Rabassa in particular, Suzanne Jill Levine—another well-known translator of Latin American literature—comes to mind; her ideas about the relationship between translation and Latin American literature are particularly relevant for Rabassa's case. Levine wonders what it means to be a translator in the context of "the formal and linguistic complexities of twentieth-century fiction," and asks: How is it determined that (a certain) literature, or a certain work, is worthy of translation? Why? Do the problems involved in translating it deserve our attention?[40] We may say that, posing these questions, Levine is looking for ways to speak of the translator's "task" or "mission" in a way that Cronin—to take one example—would probably endorse, for she relates the practice and role of translators of Latin American literature to "the complex political history of the big American continent," and says that it is important for the readers of English-speaking America "to understand *how* Latin American writing is transmitted to them, and *how* differences and similarities between cultures and languages affect *what* is finally transmitted."[41] If we believe that translation has such far-ranging sociocultural implications as the ones Levine suggests, then the question of the history of the translation of Latin American narrative—e.g., of the sixties and the Boom—and of Rabassa's role in it, yet to be written, becomes legitimate.

2
Rabassa's Conceptions of Translation and Language

Things have a built-in ambiguity about them.

—Gregory Rabassa

If this be treason, make the most of it.[1]

—Patrick Henry

IN THE INTRODUCTION TO HIS RECENTLY PUBLISHED BOOK, *IF THIS BE Treason: Translation and Its Dyscontents*[2] Gregory Rabassa affirms that "the facelessness imposed on the translator, so often thought of as an ideal, can only mean incarceration in Segismundo's tower in the end."[3] This statement, which characterizes "facelessness" as "imprisonment," illustrates Rabassa's impulse—as far as it is recognizable in his writings—to affirm that translators are writers, that is, subjects who are visible and present in the texts that they translate. Nevertheless, despite Rabassa's admission of the translator's visibility, as we look closely at his reflections on the practice of translating, there appear to be tensions, at times contradictions, among his conceptions and statements about translation. Venuti finds in his comments some of the self-effacement attitudes common to most translators; he shows evidence of this self-effacement in Rabassa's belief that it is necessary to re-translate literary works:

> The fact is that there is a kind of continental drift that slowly works on language as words wander away from their original spot in the lexicon and suffer the accretion of subtle new nuances, which result from distortions brought about by time and the events that people it. The choice made by an earlier translator, then, no longer obtains and we must choose again. Through some instinct wrought of genius, the author's original choices of word and idiom seem to endure.[4]

Venuti argues that Rabassa's view that the original endures, that it is "eternal," whereas a translation dates, reveals the perception that the original is a form of self-expression appropriate to the author, a copy true to his personality or intention, which is the authorized copy, to be distinguished from the translation, a simulacrum that deviates from the author;[5] and because of this, "translation provokes the fear of inauthenticity, distortion, contamination."[6] Venuti explains that these notions of originality are problematic, not only at the level of the social status of translation, but also at the level of the particular strategies according to which texts are translated. That is to say, when the self-effacing attitude of translators is performed in language, it results in discursive strategies that privilege fluency and erase "any textual effect, any play of the signifier, which calls attention to the materiality of language, to words as words, their opacity, their resistance to empathic response and interpretive mastery."[7]

Venuti maintains that despite the fact that Rabassa recognizes the transformative character of translation and acknowledges that the translator's experience is expressed in the text he produces, we can still see a self-effacing impulse in his articulations of his practice. There are in fact contradictions in his statements: while on the one hand Rabassa seems to view translation as a form of writing, on the other he has remarked, for instance, that translation is the "lazy man's writing."[8] Besides, Rabassa does not grant a translation the originality that would make it a text of the same order of the original or "the authorized copy."[9] However, the assumption that his general perception and understanding of himself and what he does is self-effacing is debatable. In fact, we can begin to contest it with Rabassa's analogy between the faceless translator and the imprisonment of Prince Segismundo.

For decades, Rabassa has been one of the most renowned and influencial translators into English. In Sara Blackburn's article about the translator from 1974, for instance, it is evident that Rabassa was already well-known and established at the time. As she put it, given the increasing acceptance of Spanish-language literature in the seventies and Rabassa's own reputation, he could choose which works he wanted to translate; he was also able to recommend to the publishers new writers or authors he admired.[10] Hoaksema described Rabassa's status along the same lines in an introduction to his interview with the translator in 1978: "at a time when many translators receive and are content with minimal recognition, Rabassa is accorded nearly co-creative status with the original author."[11] From the seventies to this day, Rabassa's recognition has continued to increase.

Venuti chooses to use Rabassa's name precisely because it is a proper name that is recognizable in a similar way that an author's name is also recognizable. He has chosen a translator who is not anonymous, at least among English-language readerships. Precisely because of his visibility and status, Rabassa's remarks must be viewed in the context in which they are expressed, for they are articulated in relation to the cultural community—or communities—to which he belongs and where he is a visible cultural agent. Taking into account Rabassa's location, the tensions and contradictions of his statements may suggest, for example, that besides being influenced by the way theories and discourses about translation have traditionally treated and constructed authors, translators, and originals, Rabassa's statements are also conditioned by the discursive space in which he operates at a certain time and under particular circumstances. It is, therefore, necessary to contextualize his statements to understand to what extent, as a totality, they can be said to represent a self-effacing attitude on the part of Rabassa. This may, in turn, shed light on whether Rabassa's practice, experience, ways of representing himself, and also his legacy at large, in fact reflect or reproduce conceptions, beliefs, and expectations about language and translation that advocate the invisibility of the translator or that see translation as transparent reproduction or as mediation without interference.

Words as Metaphors: on the Conventionality of Language

A key to understanding Rabassa's conceptions of translation (i.e., of writing and language) is the notion of the arbitrariness of language. Rabassa recurrently articulates the character and functioning of language as performing a metaphoric function. He believes that a word is nothing but a metaphor for an object or for another word.[12] He often cites the way Dean Swift describes, in the third part of *Gulliver's Travels*, a project at the school of languages in the Academy of Lagado, whereby, in order to do away with "the bothersome intermediary of words" and with oral communication, and to avoid the necessity of words and their dangerous nuances, *all* humans would have to carry around the things themselves in a sack.[13] Rabassa's views of language echo Nietzsche's views on the conventionality of language. From a Nietzschean perspective, the relationship between things and their designations is arbitrary, and the idea that language has a true relationship to things is a human illusion. Nietzsche affirmed: "we believe that we know something about the things themselves when we speak of trees, colors, snow, and flowers; and yet we possess nothing but metaphors for things—metaphors which correspond in no way to the original entities."[14] He calls this quality of language the "legislation of language."[15]

Nietzsche's reflections about language—influential to post-structuralist theories of language and texts—point to the fact that the lack of access to the original "thing" (i.e., a single original text, meaning, origin, etc.) is part of the nature of language:

> We may say that words relate to things only inasmuch as we determine this relationship which is established by means of the metaphors we create for them; this in turn means that these designations are man-made, arbitrary, and provisional. The *correct perception* is inaccessible, for it would belong to a criterion that is *not available*.[16]

Both the inaccessibility of some true, pristine meaning, and the arbitrariness of the "correct perception" lead to a displacement of the notion of equivalence, which affects significantly the way we see the figure of the translator, who then becomes a rightful writer of a text on the basis of a perception that is, at all times, provisional, and who therefore participates in the ongoing process of making meaning.

From a Nietzschean perspective the arbitrariness of the relationship between words and their meanings also permeates the quality of language contact in interlingual translation: "The various languages placed side by side show that with words it is never a question of truth, never a question of adequate expression, for the designations, assignments, and differentiations are in themselves arbitrary from the start."[17]

Rabassa's understanding of equivalence, like that of words, resembles these statements. In his playful and ironic way, Rabassa, as a translator-theorist, puts forth his understanding of language as arbitrary: "Wishful thinking and early training in arithmetic have convinced a majority of people that there are such things as equals in the world. A more severe examination of comparisons, however, will quickly show us that all objects, alive or otherwise, are thoroughly individual in spite of their resemblances."[18]

In numerous instances, Rabassa addresses the conventionality of language and the reader's meaning-making role; when he reflects on language, he de-emphasizes the focus on perfect equivalence, seeking to explore the limits and possibilities of translation. When he attempts to document his decision-making process, Rabassa often speaks of the notion of "voice" and of the complexities of the interplay of voices in translation: "more important than the words themselves are the characters, their status and their circumstances."[19] Rabassa believes that translators must have a good "ear" for what their authors are saying and also for what they themselves are saying, and that it is important to identify who is speaking; according to him, translators have the responsibility to listen to what is written and then to listen to the text that they are producing.[20] Here again, regarding the interplay of voices and the plurivocal nature ever present within and among texts, Rabassa addresses the difficulty of speaking of a single, unified, original meaning. He has been quoted as saying that translation is "easier" than writing, that it is a "lazy man's writing." He expands on this point as follows:

> I think translation is the easiest form of writing because you don't have to worry about plot, character, background, all you have to think about is words, and if you come right down to it writing is really about words. When you translate you are writing. To tell a story about the clouds you think of the story. The difference is that in translation somebody has already told the story about the clouds, but you still have to write it. Translation is a rewrite.[21]

When he speaks of his translations, Rabassa often focuses on words and expression, rather than on the content of what is narrated in them. Thus, his "lazy-man's writing" statement should be seen in light of the value he gives to crafting language; by stating "all you have to think about is words," he does not mean to say that the translator is left the easiest part. Rabassa grants translation great importance at a personal level and at a socio-cultural one and does not really embrace the idea that translation is a matter of "laziness" in any serious way. Rather, in regard to this statement, the aspect of translation that needs to be underscored is, to Rabassa, the materiality of the act of translating. As he puts it, "perhaps the main difference between the art of fiction, for example, and that of translation is that the translator's prime task is concerned with words, the tale and the ideas all having been received."[22] This is Rabassa's way of making sense of the distinction between the practice of translating and that of writing, from which it does not follow that he considers one to be lesser than the other.

In sum, assuming that Rabassa's thinking about translation stems from his way of looking at language, it may be concluded that Rabassa's image of the translator is that of a subject who engages with the author's and characters' voices and with her or his own in order to transform:

> We have the personal word of the author's to be transformed into a personal word of the translator's. As always with translation, this calls for a choice among synonyms. Ideally the author's choice among the synonyms in his own language was made in a purposeful and conscious way. In most cases, however, and as it should be, it is made quite naturally and instinctively. . . . Nevertheless, the translator must be alert and aware of the fact that both he and the author have their "own" words.[23]

Here again, Rabassa opposes what he conceives of as "ideal" to what takes place in the translator's practice. Following his views, translation exists within the realm of language and operates according to it. Therefore, if translation "fails" it does so because language also fails.[24] When asked if he really believes that translation is impossible, Rabassa replies that it depends of how it is seen. He states that what is impossible is to reproduce, when reproducing is seen as "cloning": "You can't clone from one language to the other because of the sound. Take *'Les sanglots longs des violons de l'automne.'* You can't do it because French is French and Spanish is Spanish."[25] He thinks translation is possible if understood from the territory of the reader, because nobody reads the same book: "When you read a book you are translating it, even if you read it in the same language."[26]

Rabassa uses the analogy of music to speak of the question of sound, or tone, in translation; he explains that, since languages sound different, the process of translating is a matter of interpretation, it is analogous to the transposition of a melody from one instrument to another.[27] He speaks in a similar way of the so-called "untranslatable" words: "Portuguese abounds in them, with such entries as *jeito* and the over-stressed *saudade*. These words are really only impossible when the concept behind them is hard to find in the second language, and this is really what the translator is up against most of the time."[28]

Translating as the "Narrow Act": Translation, Originality, and Writing

From the start, Rabassa opposes a representation of translation as a practice of invisibility and subservience. In the article "If this Be

Treason: Translation and its Possibilities," first published in *American Scholar* in 1974, it is evident that he places translation alongside writing, and that he accords translation similar characteristics to those of writing. While it is true that Rabassa goes along with the idea that translation is a difficult search for balance, a "narrow act,"[29] that has its limitations compared to the act of writing,[30] he nonetheless characterizes translation as a creative act, a "flux of matter" that results from a "creative urge,"[31] and that, consequently, entails transformation. Rabassa sees the translator as a writer whose practice is limited by a number of particular constraints. He notes that, as a writer, the translator has great limitations: "In many ways he can be compared to the poets of the neo-classical period, when so much had been set forth and with so many accepted ideas that their skill was often confined to a sense of beauty and accuracy in the use of language."[32] Rabassa speaks of the limits of translation as being different, albeit analogous, to those of writing. He believes the translator's space to be "narrow" and constrained, and at the same time he conceives of writing, too, as being subject to constraints of its own; he sees these constraints as a condition of writing.

Rabassa sees the translator's search for the *mot juste* as analogous to the same search on the part of the writer. This emphasis on viewing translation as writing, which prevails in Rabassa's texts, can be used as a basis to challenge Venuti's self-effacement "thesis." Thinking about the constraints of writing reinforces the analogy between translation and other writing practices, which remain creative while at the same time being confined to the limits set forth by norms and standards at various levels. As a translator of radically experimental, "untranslatable" authors—e.g., Lezama Lima, Cortázar, and more recently Lobo Antunes[33]—Rabassa does not dwell on the nostalgia for the lost original. He treats "untranslatability" as part of the regular, everyday experience of the translator (i.e., of language) and does not abide to the dogma of impossibility, nor depicts translation as failure or defeat. Translation, Rabassa states, can never be reproduction; "As the Latin root shows, it is a leading across to the other side, a setting-over, as the Germans call it."[34] Understood as a "setting-over," translation has a path and a purpose; this, however, does not contradict its creative nature. Rabassa's belief that translation is writing presupposes the presence of a writing subject who produces a text that is the result of a creative, intellectual endeavor rather than an act of mechanical reproduction.

As Douglas Robinson notes, a translator does not become *the* writer but, rather, *a* writer, who is much like the original author "because they both write, and in much the same way, drawing on their own experiences of language and the world to formulate effective discourse."[35] Inasmuch as the image of the translator-author relationship and status manifest themselves in translators' subjectivities and inform translators' ways of thinking of and representing themselves, Rabassa's characterization of translators as writers is revealing about his own self-understanding. As a translator who sees himself as a writer, Rabassa does not operate according to the desire that the "invisible hand" of the author will write the translated text—and sign it.[36] He is a participant in the ongoing meaning-making process and the rightful translator-writer of an original text whose correct perception is provisional. Undoubtedly, this view of translation has an effect on the translator's self-image. It conflicts with the complicated implications of common-sense views that underlie, as Robinson points out, the translator's "desirable subordinated or instrumentalized subjectivity."[37] As a result, it exposes the tensions associated with the expectations that surround translation and with the translator's self-awareness. It also provides a space for a reflection of the translator's "task" in terms of ethics.

If This Be Treason: From the Accusation to the Verdict

Up until 2005, most of Rabassa's writings on translation were limited to a number of articles in newspapers or literature and translation journals, a few translation prefaces, and a couple or interviews. In his writings, Gregory Rabassa often alludes to the Italian cliché *traduttore traditore*, which portrays translators "worse than unfortunate bunglers, as treacherous knaves."[38] From his early writings, when addressing this common-sense image of translation as "treason," Rabassa presents it as a proof of the stigmatization of translation; he explains that translation has traditionally been stigmatized precisely because it is a form of writing:

> Problem-seekers will find an inordinate amount of material in translation, precisely because it partakes of other, more definable aspects of writing. It is a sort of literary suburb, lacking a core or personality of its own. It is not clearly derivative, it is, then, treasonous and even treacherous, for it will be *misleading*.[39]

Here, translation is looked upon with suspicion precisely because it is not writing *stricto sensu,* but it is not neutral or innocent either; its being conceived as an "intermediary form" makes it "always vulnerable to attack."[40]

In April of 2005, Rabassa published *If This be Treason: Translation and Its Dyscontents.*[41] This book, his translator's memoir, is structured on the basis of a judicial metaphor. The book is constructed as if the translator appeared before the jury and addressed it. It starts out as follows:

> Let us submit the practice of translation to a judicial inquiry into its various ways and means and in this display seek out the many varieties of betrayal which might be inherent to its art . . . There are many spots where translation can be accused of treason, all inevitably interconnected in such diverse ways that an overall view is needed to reveal the many facets of the treason the Italians purport to see.[42]

If This Be Treason is Rabassa's statement before the jury. It is the translator's response to an accusation, that of treason. In the book, the translator places himself as the object of the accusation and, in so doing, he interrogates the very accusation—he does not endorse it. The translator is deemed accountable for a practice that is "blasphemous." What the translator does is "treasonous and even treacherous."[43] As he puts it in one of his articles:

> After the masons mumbled their different ways down from Babel's tower and went their separate ways, each to breed his one-tongued kind, God saw that his punishment was meetly condign and that it would go on to harass and hamper mankind forever after. But then there were Promethean stirrings as those of different languages attempted to be understood by one another and man's hubris was served. Translation is blasphemous by these lights, then, and it has often been treated so.[44]

The stigma of translation, according to this statement, emerges from the violation of a law of unintelligibility in an effort to share meaning. As a consequence, and given these accusations and the treatment to which translation has been subjected, instead of doing a straightforward defense, Rabassa uses the judicial metaphor to put translation "in the courtroom,"[45] setting treason as the book's premise.

For his translator's memoir Rabassa uses the title of his 1974 article, "If This Be Treason: Translation and Its Possibilities," in which he included the epigraph *"traduttore, traditore."* In his 2005 book he adds an element to that epigraph, which is Patrick Henry's phrase: "If this be treason, make the most of it." Instead of concealing the alleged treason, what the translator does is "admit" the treason, face the charge.

Following the supposed recognition of his guilt, in the book Rabassa lists the many aspects of translation that are, either potentially or actually, treasonous. He begins speaking of the betrayal translation inflicts onto words, which are "the metaphors for all the things we see, feel, and imagine."[46] Then there is a betrayal to language (in both directions), and consequently to culture, of which languages are products.[47] Then, says Rabassa, we have the personal betrayals, first to the author: "Can we ever make a different-colored clone of what he has done? Can we ever feel what the author felt as he wrote the words we are transforming?"[48] and second to the reader: "As we betray the author we betray our variegated readership and at the same time we are passing on whatever bit of betrayal the author himself may have foisted on them in the original."[49] As the list of betrayals unfolds, another set of betrayals emerges: that of language itself and its conventionality: "Words are treacherous things, much more so than any translator could ever be";[50] in addition, says Rabassa, language betrays words for, as it moves ahead, it will load them with "all manner of cultural barnacles."[51] Subsequently the author's betrayal emerges for he is a compendium of all these factors: language, culture, and individual words. These are inseparable, and the author is their product, just like his writing: "His free will and originality only exist within the bounds of his culture."[52] In turn, readers "betray" authors and texts as they make them their own in reading. Finally, Rabassa cautions in *If This Be Treason*, comes translators' betrayal to themselves. To him this last betrayal is "the saddest treason of all"[53] because translators are writers. For Rabassa translators must keep "a careful confidence in themselves," look for the "proper" words instead of using the "standard" words or norms; that, to him, would "betray the task we are set to do."[54]

As Rabassa unpacks the treasons of translation—to language, to authors, to texts, and, in turn, of language, authors, and texts themselves—what surfaces is a chain of treasonous events beyond the translation event itself and that are mutually interconnected.[55] The treason occurs as a continuum; it occurs in and because of language at large. Thus, following Rabassa, the treason in translation is a condition of language.

For his memoir Rabassa chose the metaphor of treason not because the book is deeply rooted in the Italian cliché. His writing is ironic.

From the start Rabassa interrogates the cliché, he magnifies it and displaces it—this is suggested from the initial invitation to make *the most* of the treason. *If This Be Treason* engages the translator-traitor cliché and reworks it from within. Instead of defending himself in his memoir, the translator admits his guilt (i.e., translation's guilt) and, by exposing the endless chain of treasons that precede the act(s) of translation and those that follow it, he exposes the absurdity of signaling translation out for violation. Associating treason with translation, Rabassa underscores the treason of language itself.

Rabassa mentions the treasons of language and of the author. He believes that the author's treason is not visible, for: "If he is to betray it [his culture], he betrays it from within, which connotes intimate knowledge, while the translator betrays it from without, from an acquired reflective, not reflexive awareness."[56] Thus, although translation is treasonous in a way that is similar to that in which language, and the author, are treasonous, translation is signaled out because it is not familiar or intimate enough—it embodies that which is foreign. Translation does not enjoy the kind of complicity with language and with the community or communities involved that would allow it to engage with language and text(s) in the way that the author's text enjoys; consequently, it is the complicity between the author, language, and the community, which conceals the author's treason.

Finally, Rabassa extrapolates the active "betrayal" of/to language, to experience. He relates the arbitrary, metaphoric nature of language to the experiential version of the "world" we inhabit, which we construct according to our existence in it:

> The personal aspect of language can be extended to life itself. As far as the individual is concerned, life truly exists only as he feels it and thereby ponders it. It follows, therefore, that life is an idea, a word, in short, a metaphor for conscious existence and hence a translation. We are translating our existence and our circumstance as we go along living and before we are fatally assigned the translator's lot once the treason has been done: Segismundo's tower or tomb.[57]

If we stop translating—that is, using language—we are, in Rabassa's view, doomed to return to Segismundo's tower, to give up the illusion of intelligibility. As he puts it, we may even, as Swift's project suggests, "get about rebuilding Babel."[58]

In *If This Be Treason* Rabassa uses the stigmatization of translation as treason as a rhetorical response to the common-sense, prevalent criticism of what happens to originals in translation. Instead of giving a direct response, he resorts to letting his memoir unfold in such a way that the accusation seems overly negative, unproductive, and ultimately irrelevant. By enumerating a long list of betrayals, Rabassa takes up the accusation and magnifies it to the point of rendering it absurd. He believes that, whether we call it treason or something else, translation remains a form of writing (i.e., inscribing) a text, and that this is not only true but also desirable: "The translator, who is most often adjured to be faithful, must also be inventive. Let us remember that the same language that gave us the canard *traduttore, traditore* also gave us *se non è vero, è ben trovato.*"[59] For Rabassa, what is found in the process through which the translated text emerges is legitimate and welcome.

In his memoir, Rabassa follows his reflection about the treasons of translation with stories about "his" authors and translations. He then concludes by taking the judicial inquiry to its last consequences and ends the book with the final verdict. Is translation treason? Is the translator a traitor? *A la hora de la verdad*, says Rabassa, when the time for a verdict comes, there is no "competent" juror. Who is there to determine the treason? "That is why I ended up with what they call the Scots verdict," he says; in Scottish jurisprudence the jury can come up with a third verdict, which he finds to be "very handy": neither guilty, nor innocent, but "not proven"; the treason has not been proven, but it may be there.[60]

This ambiguous, open-ended verdict could be taken as a means of putting an end to a discussion that is ultimately unresolved, in which case "not proven" would stand for "not known." The Scots verdict is consistent with the fact that the accusation of treason has, in the end, not really been deemed a legitimate charge or, if it is, it is a weak or incomplete one at most. Nevertheless, this verdict-end to Rabassa's translation "memoir" can also be read as a statement.

THE PRACTITIONER AS THEORIST

At this point it is worth returning to Venuti's self-effacement "thesis" and examining it in light of the significance of the Scots verdict at the end of *If This Be Treason*. In his memoir, as well as in several of his writings, Rabassa reinforces an image of translation as a legitimate cultural practice. The book is also an attempt to rework and resolve in and through writing the apparent tensions and contradictions of the translator's experience. An attempt to conceptualize Rabassa's self-understanding must reveal the complexity of the task itself and take into account his own history to understand how he speaks from his location and how his reflections are interwoven with his practice. When looking at Rabassa's "theories" in this light it becomes evident that, when he tries to articulate his practice—and this may apply to other translators—there is a wide and multiple range of possibilities, many of them circumstancial, that show that what may seem desirable, appropriate, or ethical, in some cases, may not be so in others. There is a tension between viewing translation as intellectual and creative and also speaking to a sense of responsibility. Rabassa sees translation as a limited writing practice—"the narrow path"—and also calls attention to the fact that writing responds to—often unacknowledged—constraints of time, rhetorical standards, and so on, which are played out and negotiated in texts in a seamless fashion. According to the translator, this negotiation is not equally seamless in translation, which is why translators are looked upon with suspicion. In sum, if as Venuti states, self-effacement as "a weird form of self-annihilation,"[61] that would not be an accurate characterization of Rabassa's understanding of himself and his practice.

Rabassa has been vocal in regard to the institutional aspects of the translating practice for decades. In 1971 he directed the PEN conference for translator's visibility and rights (co-sponsored by the Center for Inter-American Relations), which aimed to advocate for better pay, credit for the translator on the title page, book jacket, and in all publicity and advertisement, and minimum translation rates.[62] Rabassa repeatedly complains about the difficulty for non-English speaking authors to enter the U.S. mainstream readership, which in his view is due to the "provincialism" of the U.S. public: "It may have to do with the environment; the American public wants to read what is in its own backyard."[63] As Lowe and Fitz point out, being "cognizant of the political, economic, and historical particularities of the original texts, he builds these elements into his translations.[64] Rabassa stresses the need to translate so that narratives and literatures (and their narratives) continue to disseminate. From his privileged position in the cultural milieu and in academia in the United States, when he discusses the political and institutional problems that affect the practice of translation, Rabassa addresses translators' freedoms, loyalties, and responsibilities. He realizes that, as a translator, he is subject to the demands of a system that has particularly domesticating translation standards.

Rabassa is undoubtedly positioned in the Anglo-American social, economic, and linguistic context that Venuti describes, which is where he operates and negotiates; moreover, he is in a privileged position within it. It is its rules and standards that determine his choices in regard to the discursive strategies and institutional structures that mediate in the production, circulation, and reception of his translations. As Venuti notes, "the cultural dominance of Anglo-American individualism represents foreign cultures with ideological discourses specific to English-language discourses but conceals all these determinations and effects under the veil of transparency."[65] Following Venuti's logic, and his understanding of translators as historically-bound subjects related to communities, helps unveil the tensions and negotiations between the translator and the communities that assign her or his work a value.

In regard to the individual/social/ideological elements that underlie Rabassa's ideas, Venuti has found a similar attitude in relation to the study of translation in the views of literary translator William Weaver. Weaver is a somewhat analogous figure to Rabassa: he has been recognized as the major English-language translator of modern Italian literature—he has translated roughly sixty works and received a number of literary awards. According to Venuti, Weaver's views about his practice presuppose that translation is a largely "unreflective process" where the decisions a translator makes are not only unarticulated but also "unknown." Venuti questions Weaver's statements about his practice as follows:

> Although in describing one such translation process Weaver gives reasons for his choices, none of these reasons takes the form of an explanation that extends beyond a brief semantic or stylistic comment on the Italian word or on a possible English equivalent. . . . Many choices seem to be based either on linguistic and cultural values that remain unstated or on sheer personal preference. . . . Weaver's essay certainly documents his own translation process, even if he does not actually explain it.[66]

Rabassa's statements about his translation decisions are along the same lines as Weaver's; this can be seen, for instance, when he states that "the translator must have some inner instinct for what is just right,"[67] or when he explains: "I know that a translation is going well when I get the feeling that the English is sounding just the way the author sounded in the original. This is completely instinctive, and I cannot explain it in any rational way, but it is there."[68] Although in the form of explanations, these statements do not show intent to explain what goes on in the process through which the translator renders the work.[69] Like Weaver's, Rabassa's way of explaining his decision-making process is significantly different from critical perspectives that place the translator's work as part of larger structures and systems, that is, from perspectives that would consider the work of these translators themselves in terms of social and institutional practices and processes of textual and cultural production.

Venuti advocates a historicized analysis of translators and their decisions because, as he puts it, since translation creates difference, it *is* difference; therefore, we must find ways to articulate the difference that "translators" make. As he explains, although that difference is what translating is supposed to negotiate or resolve in the first place, it ultimately winds up multiplying and exacerbating it, sometimes without the translator's awareness and almost always without the awareness of the audience for whom the translation is produced.[70] We must study these differences, not in the hope of eradicating them completely—they cannot be eradicated, and some should not be, since they are necessary to see the foreignness in the foreign text. According to Venuti the goal we should set for translation studies is the "ultimately ethical one of developing methods of translation research and practice that describe, explain, and take responsibility for the differences that translation inevitably makes."[71]

If This Be Treason does not necessarily endorse self-effacing views. Rather, the book reinforces an image of translation as a legitimate cultural practice. But, is this image totally non-self-effacing? Rabassa moves across conceptual boundaries in ways that do not really allow for a framing of his viewpoint as being essentially one *or* the other. He advocates inventiveness, describes meaning as arbitrary and provisional, speaks of translators as readers, interpreters, and writers, and dismisses the ideal of perfect equivalence; therefore, although Venuti has a point in finding some of Rabassa's statements to be self-effacing, these ideas are sufficient to challenge Venuti's characterization. Rabassa's self-understanding and self-identification are complex. His writings would not be sufficient to exemplify his self-effacement attitude or that of other translators. The complexity of this situation is closely related to Rabassa's own history, to how he speaks from his location, and must be understood as interwoven with his practice. When looking at Rabassa's "theories" in this light it becomes evident that, when he tries to articulate his practice—and this may apply to other translators—there is a wide and multiple range of possibilities between having a romanticized conception of texts and having an overly confident attitude that focuses solely on visibility and self-assertion; these aspects, when it comes to particular cases, must be considered alongside the surrounding circumstances—e.g., what may seem desirable, appropriate, or ethical in some cases, may not be so in others.

Rabassa's views in regard to the role of translation in academia are worth noting. He finds that translators have some specific uses for the study of literature; they can contribute what they have done, that is, the translated text itself, and also the way they have done it.[72] He considers translation useful in various ways for academic purposes because of the translator's "unique" position in the literary world: "The translator may be the one person who exists simultaneously in two different worlds: as he works he must be both critic and writer, writer and reader."[73] This, among other reasons, is why translators, according to Rabassa, should strive for making the profession more visible: "The translator's position is what makes his presence valuable beyond the mere idea of middle-man, and is good reason for his receiving more recognition and consideration."[74] Nevertheless, according to Rabassa, beyond the realm of stylistics the study of translation is, largely, unnecessary. He claims that there are no theories to be had about translation. His position on translation theory, which Venuti also finds problematic, is clear: "I am very cautions about theories that lie outside the natural sciences, where there are fewer unknowns. . . . Having started out in physics in college, I learned to be skeptical . . . I am rather amused at the idea of a theory concerning something I do in a completely untheoretical way."[75]

If it is true that, as Venuti suggests, the translator is located in an intertextual and ideological configuration that may escape her or his consciousness to some extent and result in unanticipated consequences, like social reproduction or change,[76] limiting the study of translation to the realm of stylistics may reduce the critical possibilities of translation. It would not provide a space, for instance, to explore questions pertaining to the agency and responsibility of translators in the formation of traditions, or to the role of translation in the way cultural values are played out, reproduced, or erased. The study of translation in relation to literary studies would be mainly instrumental. Rabassa's position in relation to particular traditions and institutions may be, at least in part, the basis of his ideas about the study of translation. His critical position is also rooted in a particular understanding of the literary as a subject of study.

As I noted in the first chapter, several theorists insist on the importance of contesting statements about "instinctive" or "unconscious" decision-making as they find that some so-called instinctive choices, that some of the translator's "unconscious" (or "instinctive") decisions, and also some effects (even errors), may in fact be conscious. Others, as Venuti puts it, may exceed even the experienced translator's conscious intention, taking the form of misconstructions or misreadings that are symptomatic of an unconscious motivation. Others may be caused by the foreign text, its formal and thematic features, and yet others may be triggered by something that lies outside of the immediate context of the error but is nonetheless connected to it, the larger cultural and social situation in which the translation is produced.[77]

Conventionally, because it embodies the foreign and is thus suspect within the linguistic communities where it occurs, the writing of translation ought to be concealed. Rabassa's position against the study of translation is partly related to the very fact that translation and translators have been stigmatized—Rabassa often addresses the institutional beliefs and attitudes that lay at the basis of this suspicion. He comments, for instance, on the role of translation vis-à-vis criticism. Being an academic, he explains that his "anti-theory" attitude is partly due to how much work in literary translation has been devoted exclusively to close readings of the works *in order to* find the flaws in the translations. He finds the role of critics to be useful and important to some extent, but criticizes those who concentrate on small details, ignoring the overall result and literary value of the work. Rabassa humorously uses Alastair Reid's term "translation police," or Sara Blackburn's "Professor Horrendo"[78] to speak of this kind of critic who, Rabassa says, "will roll up his sleeves and proceed to slice into the translation"[79] and who nitpicks through the text and often arrives at the "exasperating conclusion, like those in multiple choice tests, 'none of the above.'"[80] This critic, says Rabassa, cannot see the forest for the trees.[81] Rabassa characterizes translation as an art, and it is in this light that he explains his lack of interest in theorizing, questioning, or contesting the discursive operations that take place in translation.

The Translator's Documents

A question worth posing at this point would be: What do translators do as they write about their work? How do we look at translators' writings about their practice? *What do we translators do when we write about our work?*

Rabassa's documents—his articles and reviews, his memoir, as well as drafts and interviews—are part of the totality of the translator's body of work. As a result, they must be accounted for in a study about the translator. They are also a way of rendering the translator's voice. Besides, as Suzanne Jill Levine proposes in her introduction to *The Subversive Scribe*, "self-referential inquisitions by prose translators should provide useful models for translation studies as well as models of self-questioning for all interpreters."[82] Translators' documents are symptomatic, or rather, reflexive, of the translator's practice and experience. A comprehensive, conscious, and fully self-aware account of every decision is not to be found in a translator's writings, and such an expectation would not even be desirable. It is not possible either to establish whether that is the type of account a particular translator aims for in the first place, given that translators' writings—so often paratextual—belong to particular rhetorical spaces, which affect the content, the tone, and the way in which they position themselves in relation to translation—in the case of Rabassa, for example, was he using self-effacing "wit" in order to appear humble?[83] The writing space can also pose pragmatic limitations—as is the case with prefaces or interviews; there are rules and constraints in regard to both form and content; thus, these texts can have a purpose that may not lend itself to candid self-reflection.

Reading translators' accounts does not lead to the comprehensive image that translators have of themselves. Therefore, it is important to seek a balance between engaging these texts while at the same time avoiding taking them strictly at face value. Translators' documents may be read as part of the process of translating itself, the part that has to do with an ongoing process of making sense of one's own creative process. They may also be looked at as symptoms of particular translating experiences bound to a multiplicity of complex circumstances, as examples of theories of textuality and translation at work, or as channels—both contexts and conceptual frameworks—that translators choose for self-reflection.

Translation: A Labor of Sisyphus? Between Impossibility and an Ethics of Doubt

Rabassa's reflections illustrate the tensions he faces as a translating subject. They also reveal his conceptions about language, textuality, and translation, and are indicative of the translator's ethical configuration. Rabassa repeatedly describes translation as an "ambiguous" practice — the notion of ambiguity comes up recurrently in his writings. He finds ambiguity to be a common presence in language, author-text relations, language-culture interactions, and also in the translator's space. On the one hand, the suggestion that words and translation have a "built-in ambiguity" about them is in itself a resistance to a dualistic logic, which is consonant with other ways in which Rabassa resists certain forms of dualistic ordering. Alongside the recognition that translation is writing and that, if it is treasonous, it is so inasmuch as language is also treasonous, Rabassa points to the notion of uncertainty, which he conceives of as embedded in translation, inherent to it. Rabassa emphasizes the fact that the whole process of translation is a matter of choice, and that the "proper" choice is hardly ever definable. He says that translation is "on-going," "a labor of Sisyphus, as it were," and calls it "disturbing" because translators can only have little certainty about what they are doing.[84]

As a cultural practice in a larger sense, Rabassa sees translation as an ongoing, unfinished conversation at least in two respects. As part of the process and in regard to the translator-author relationship per se, he sees it as a dialogue that fosters a sense of proximity and as a way to engage language and exchange through camaraderie — perhaps even a certain complicity — in the dynamics of meaning and understanding. As a product, translation is the logical continuation of the author's writing. Translation is part of the work, and the work itself is part of a continuum, which neither starts with the author nor ends with the translator.

Rabassa conceives of himself as a creator and does not believe he ought to occupy a position of invisibility or subordination. He still argues that the translator must be a doubter at all times.[85] Is this a contradiction? Can a translator be non-self-effacing, advocate visibility, and remain uncertain? Rabassa embraces uncertainty in a similar way in which he embraces the arbitrariness of language. For him, uncertainty does not revert into a sense of failure, neither does it lead to a nostalgia for a lost original. What to make, then, of this uncertainty? Let us look back at Rabassa's Scots verdict:

> All of this has been borne out by my ultimate dissatisfaction with any translation I have done, even the most praise-worthy. This would suggest, then, that there has been some kind of treason afoot. As judge, therefore, I must render what is called a Scots verdict: not proven. We translators will not be shot at cock's crow, but neither shall we walk about free of our own doubts that we may have somehow done something treasonable in our work.[86]

In *If This Be Treason* Rabassa acknowledges both his authority and his subjectivity, while presenting an unpretentious account of his life as a translator. According to him, the ultimate dissatisfaction is none other than the translator's. After ruling out all possible judges—out of incompetence—the translator remains his own judge. These statements are not complacent, but they are not self-condemning either (the treason is not proven, after all, though "it may be there"). In the end, from his discursive location he has chosen not to issue a univocal judgment. Thus, rather than an unresolved answer, the verdict at the end of Rabassa's *If This Be Treason* points to the question of responsibility; it is an ethical call.

First, Rabassa is speaking, here again, of ambiguity in translation alongside the ambiguity of the original:

> I don't think that any translation can really be called either definitive or final. Ambivalence and ambiguity come to the fore; words change subtly over the years; there is a sort of Doppler effect in meaning as time passes, so that *both translation and original* will present a different meaning now from what they did a hundred years ago.[87]

Second, if we look back at Rabassa's position in the world map, we see him seated at the center of power, as a member of a hegemonic social and linguistic community. In this context, given the way cultures are represented in and through translation, I find Rabassa's acknowledgment of a permanent sense of doubt and the need for caution to be pertinent. If translation were believed to be completely derivative, it would be a disinterested copy of an original. However, Rabassa is saying that it is not: it is actually a form of writing, which makes it potentially "misleading."[88] How can translators claim to be completely sure of what they are doing to a text by writing it and rewriting it? Would it be possible for translators to be aware and know (i.e., control) what will become of it? What would it mean for a translator from such a privileged position to hold definitive and conclusive opinions in regard to what ought to be done to texts in translation? Would complete certainty be desirable at all?

Rabassa's translations of Latin American literature have played a crucial role in the construction of collective narratives and representations of Latin American literature and of "Latin America" in its literature. Given the linguistic hegemony of the United States in general, as well as in the production and circulation of cultural capital, and given the cultural complexities of the Americas—the north-south divide, the neocolonial reality—it is important for translators to remember that they, along with their work, can be "misleading."[89] Thus, translators should remain aware of the potential violence of any form of cultural appropriation. As a consequence, a certainty principle may in fact be problematic. Judgment, when it comes to translation, should befit the location and position(s) of the parties—i.e., a plurality of authors, translators, languages, communities—within a set of hierarchies, privileges, and opportunities given or taken away in the context of particular power structures.

Translation occurs in a collective space of negotiation. As with any form of writing, social, political, and institutional "ambiguities" exist given the maneuvers of the institution of culture; the translator, in isolation, is not responsible for the entire translating event. Thus, since the many variables surrounding translators make it impossible for them to have full control over the event, it may be salubrious to recognize that uncertainty is inescapably part of it.

When he interrogates William Weaver's ways of representing himself as a translator, Venuti quotes Derrida in regard to the "body" or "materiality" of the text: "The materiality of a word cannot be translated or carried over into another language. Materiality is precisely that which translation relinquishes. To relinquish materiality: such is the driving force of translation. And when that materiality is reinstated, translation becomes poetry."[90] Venuti discusses this passage by explaining that, in Derrida's view, the body (*le corps*) of the foreign text, its materiality in the sense of the specific chain of acoustic or typographical signifiers that constitute it, cannot be reproduced in translation and therefore is inevitably dropped by the translator. This, according to Venuti, is the "decontextualizing" aspect of translation.[91] Derrida, says Venuti, also observes that when translation restores a body, a materiality in the sense of another chain of signifiers in another language . . . translation

2: RABASSA'S CONCEPTIONS OF TRANSLATION AND LANGUAGE 53

means displacement in that it "creates another signifying chain accompanied by intratextual effects and intertextual relations that are designed to reproduce the foreign text, but that also work in the translating language and culture."[92] This is the "recontextualizing" aspect of translation, which takes up a different body:

> The creation of a different signifying chain proliferates semantic possibilities as the translator seeks to fix a signified that answers not only to the foreign text, but to the intelligibilities and interests in the translating culture. In restoring a materiality, in creating a text, translation is radically recontextualizing and thus produces a second difference, in fact a set of linguistic and cultural differences that are inscribed in the foreign text.[93]

This difference, says Venuti, is irreducible: "Despite what may seem to be analogous linguistic and discursive structures between a foreign text and its translation, no similarity of form and meaning or of reception pre-exists the translating process."[94] Thus, contexts are dismantled, negotiated, multiplied, and articulated. Difference is not "resolved" or settled.

Rabassa's translations are famous and often considered "masterful." They have been accepted, authorized, and have become uncontested literary products in themselves. Let us look at the opening lines of his most famous translation:

> Muchos años después, frente al pelotón de fusilamiento, el coronel Aureliano Buendía había de recordar aquella tarde remota en que su padre lo llevó a conocer el hielo.[95]

> Many years later, as he faced the firing squad, Colonel Aureliano Buendía was to remember that distant afternoon when his father took him to discover ice.[96]

Shall we say that the first text *is* the second? Rabassa's translation does not look like the original text. It does not sound like it either. It is not the original. Translation is writing. One text is not the clone of another. The sound of Rabassa's translation of *Cien Años de Soledad* is an English-language sound. As Rabassa says, quoting Ortega y Gasset, he is a translator "within" his circumstance. If the translation aspect of his text is not acknowledged, the text can be "misleading." Translation, like dialogue, is populated with misunderstandings, interferences, silences (deliberate and otherwise). Consequently, within the multivalent and collective spaces of translation, Rabassa's opening to uncertainty after the verdict may be seen as a call for responsibility in relation to the potential violence exercised by translation and its mediating nature.

Rabassa speaks of "misunderstanding" as a most important word in almost any sphere of life: "We have international misunderstandings that can lead to war, although sometimes said misunderstanding is cultivated and intentional . . . every so often the misunderstanding does not come from a wrong interpretation of the words involved but, rather, from a misconception of what they stand for."[97] This, I believe, is a form of recognition that there is room for "treason" in creating and disseminating narratives in translation as much as there is room for treason in writing and in using language. Hence, the recognition of doubt, of uncertainty, as inherent to translation, may function—between impossibility and possibility—as an ethics of doubt.

I read Rabassa's verdict as a statement that, whether desirable or not, indeterminacy is part of the nature of translation; translation has a quality of ongoing questioning to it. It is a call for translators to be attentive to the circumstances surrounding the translating situation and to translate "with their eyes open."[98] Rabassa sees uncertainty, for translators, as strength. As a translator who embodies a particular experience of cultural and linguistic contact, his embracing uncertainty is significant. Rabassa's words at the end of *If This Be Treason* leave an opening to uncertainty that, if seen as an ethical stance and in light of Rabassa's thoughts about language, suggests a call for self-reflection and, also, openness to worldly fluidity, to time and space, to continuance, and to change.

3
Del lado de allá y Del lado de acá / From this Side and from the Other: Rabassa's Dialogue with His Authors

> One day one of us should write the history of this translation. I don't believe there has been anything like it in the annals of the genre.
>
> —Julio Cortázar[1]

> One should not rein in the horse too much.
>
> —Gregory Rabassa[2]

WITH THE EXCEPTION OF MACHADO DE ASSIS, GREGORY RABASSA HAS always translated works written by living authors. He has often established a personal relationship, a remarkably convivial and fruitful dialogue with them. This relationship—not always a practice for literary translators—has been very significant in the case of Rabassa. He has had a great deal of contact with several authors during the process of translating their works, and in several cases he has invited the authors to participate, in one way or another, in the translation process.

Apart from Rabassa's own account in *If This Be Treason: Translation and Its Dyscontents,* there is practically no document about the histories behind his translations or the interaction between the translator and the authors. This chapter aims to illustrate Rabassa's relationship with "his" authors, and to explore the nature of the translator-author relationship. The information discussed was gathered from various sources, including interviews and letters between Rabassa and some of the authors he translated. I begin with a brief description of the translator's background. I then recount Rabassa's relationship with some of the authors who played a major role in his career and with whom he had the most contact while he was translating their works. I examine how

Rabassa approached and entered into dialogue with these authors, and what the authors' role was in the exchange. I then discuss some patterns and general practices that can be observed in these relationships, and discuss the mechanisms of the translator-author dialogue and Rabassa's position in it. Focusing on the translator's role and expectations and looking at the translator-author interactions, I discuss the extent to which Rabassa's contact with his authors has been an attempt on the part of the translator to go to the source, that is, to look for the "truth" of the novels, or whether it was part of a process of meaning-making and of negotiation.

THE BEGINNING

Gregory Rabassa has said on several occasions that he became a translator by chance. As he puts it in *If This Be Treason*, in general, things "just seemed to fall together" and his full-fledged entry into translation came about in such a way.[3] Even though Rabassa's explanation of his beginnings as a translator as a matter of "serendipity" is somewhat accurate, it is not sufficient, for there was a series of circumstances that may account for his inclination to become a translator. He acknowledges this fact in his memoir, when he says: "Although I may have said that I sort of backed into translation without having thought about it or having set my sights on it, I do have within me certain ingredients, innate or circumstantial, that could be said to have tilted me in that direction."[4]

As stated in the introduction to *Writing Between the Lines*—a volume of critical essays about Anglophone translators in Canada—the paths that lead translators to engage in literary translation are often deeply personal; in the case of several of the translators whose lives and works are discussed in that volume, there was a "discernable presence of otherness that cannot be unrelated to their eventual commitment to translation and its role in the facilitation of intercultural communication"[5]—this can be seen, for example, in Sherry Simon's account in "William Hume Blake, or the Translator as Amateur Ethnologist." Background, circumstances, and lived experiences may generate the tendencies that lead some to translation. Frequently, translators' personal experiences lead to the "complex mixture of predisposition and circumstance" that engenders a general sensitivity to difference.[6] Levine has explored this aspect of the relationship between the translators' lives and their work. As Lowe and Fitz note, she aptly said that as a translator, one often seeks in the foreign what one is drawn to, whether consciously or unconsciously, in the familiar; "We translate to be translated."[7] Rabassa also speaks of otherness as the foundation of translation in almost every sense of the word; "the translator must become the author's other, his Doppelganger, what Julio Cortázar called his *paredros*, using a Greek term for the old Egyptian concept of otherness. At the same time the translator must turn the author into another possibility of his own existence."[8]

Rabassa was raised in a multilingual and multicultural environment. His grandparents were from Spain (Catalonia), Cuba, England, and the United States. The son of Miguel Rabassa, a Cuban sugar broker, and Clara Macfarland, from New York, Rabassa was born in Yorkers, New York. When he was young, his family lived in a number of different places on the East Coast of the United States. As he puts it, both his parents were "good-word people."[9] As a foreigner, Rabassa's father became fluent in English and "would fool around with it as only someone with an outside vantage point could."[10] The translator describes his whole family as a mixture of linguistic wit and playfulness, where the names of people and places would be turned around and reinvented constantly.

Rabassa says that with all the "diverse mannerisms" he heard around him, he developed "an ear of sounds."[11] He had an "active ear" and was always curious about other languages, especially inasmuch as they were attached to other places. Strangely, he says, he did not pick up much Spanish at home—his father spoke English most of the time.[12] In high school Rabassa studied Latin and French, and did not start studying Spanish formally until college. Then he also took up Portuguese, and then Italian, soon becoming a "language collector." He did translation through college because, during that time, translation was a particularly important part of language study.[13]

Rabassa's formal education and his environment nourished his predisposition for translation. His formation took shape in the thirties, the forties, and the fifties, a triad of decades he calls "fearsome," and that, he says, called for enormous efforts at survival and sanity.[14] Both in academia and in his private life, there was "a great awareness of language." He reflects: "I think that the seemingly somnambulistic musings of my early years have been good for my application of thought to language and from there, in reverse, to the language and thought of someone I have been translating."[15]

While Rabassa was in college, the reserves were called up and he went to serve in the United States army. He received basic military training and then was assigned to the message center to learn cryptography. Rabassa says that this was his first experience with an artificial language, although the cryptographic work itself, decoding incoming messages and encoding outgoing ones, seemed to him rather elementary.[16] After some time he was transferred to Algiers. There, he had to rewrite and paraphrase messages in English, an operation he describes as somewhere between cryptography and translation.[17] Rabassa relates his start as a translator with this experience:

> So there I was, doing what I would be doing years later, not aware that I was already doing translation. As they would say today, the parameters were narrow. You didn't have the option of simply reworking the word order; the same letters would still be there. Sometimes it was hard to find good synonyms. There are words that have none and can't be resaid in some roundabout way. This was especially true if the message concerned order of battle, as so many did. A regiment had to be a regiment, a division a division, and their identifying numbers had to remain the same.[18]

Since he was about to finish his college degree when he was enlisted in the reserves, Rabassa was awarded his diploma when he was overseas. As a result, when he finished his army service he was able to go directly to graduate school. In 1948 he became a full-time instructor at Columbia College. Soon after, Rabassa was invited by some of his colleagues to collaborate in a literary review entitled *Odyssey*. The journal aimed to publish contemporary writing from two European and two Latin American countries in each issue. Rabassa became the editor in charge of looking for new writing in Spanish and Portuguese and thus began to translate some of the Latin American short stories to be published in the quarterly—which he signed under various pseudonyms "in order to give an impression of variety."[19]

As Rabassa puts it, *Odyssey* was to become "the true forerunner" of what in the United States would subsequently be called the Latin American "Boom" and, although it ended after only six issues, it played a role in welcoming unknown authors who would later receive worldwide acclaim.[20] As I mentioned earlier, at that time Rabassa was asked by Sara Blackburn at Pantheon Books to translate a couple of sample chapters of Julio Cortázar's *Rayuela*. She then agreed with the author that Rabassa should translate the novel, and *Hopscotch*, which was first published in 1966, was the first book-length translation done by

Rabassa for a commercial publisher. Subsequently, this translation won the National Book Award and attracted considerable critical attention. *Hopscotch* set Rabassa further along in the translation path.

Rabassa has been translating ever since the publication of *Hopscotch*. As he puts it, this first translation also "led" him to *One Hundred Years of Solitude*,[21] by Nobel Laureate Gabriel García Márquez, and one of his most recognized translations. Other major works translated by Rabassa—whose authors, like the former two, were not so internationally well-known when he translated them—are *Paradiso*, by Lezama Lima, and *The Posthumous Memoirs of Brás Cubas*, by Machado de Assis. Rabassa also translated works by Miguel Ángel Asturias, Manuel Mujica Láinez, Clarice Lispector, Mario Vargas Llosa, Demetrio Aguilera-Malta, Dalton Trevisan, Jorge Amado, José Donoso, Luisa Valenzuela, Luis Rafael Sánchez, and Osman Lins.[22]

With time, several of the works Rabassa translated became established as part of the Latin American literary canon—his translations include many works of the Latin American Boom. Nevertheless, Rabassa has always been interested in promoting writers who are not internationally well-known. Moreover, he also translated fiction by European authors such as Juan Goytisolo and Juan Benet from Spain, and Mario de Carvalho and António Lobo Antunes from Portugal. One of his latest publications was *Rosario Tijeras*, by the Colombian author Jorge Franco. Some other translations, such as *Internal War*, by Volodia Teitelboim, are awaiting a publisher.

Rabassa has translated mostly novels. He has done only two works of nonfiction. The first one was Afranio Coutinho's *An Introduction to Literature of Brazil*. The translator states that, although the work is of great value, to him, doing this translation was not an example of good judgment because the language of criticism and critical theory did not offer much room for creativity.[23] He was glad to help make a piece of scholarly work from Brazil available for the English-reading audience, but decided that he would never do another scholarly book.[24] However, he was persuaded by one of his former students to undertake the translation of a second nonfiction work, *The Brazilian People*, by Darcy Ribeiro. He accepted mainly because Ribeiro was also a fiction writer; as he explains: "Darcy is also a writer of novels and his book reads like one, even with all its statistical tables."[25] Apart from those two nonfiction works, the only other genre Rabassa has explored is drama. He has translated five plays, most of which were performed by the Puerto Rican Traveling Theater between 1981 and 1983—one play is awaiting production. He finds this kind of work enjoyable, especially seeing the plays acted out: "There is always the actor, who adds his or her voice to that of the author and that of the translator."[26]

Among the list of translations done by Rabassa, which are mostly novels—clearly the genre he prefers to translate—there is a good number of "difficult works," as he himself puts it.[27] Among these are Juan Benet's *A Meditation*, Julio Cortázar's *Hopscotch*, Osman Lins's *Avalovara*, and Lezama Lima's *Paradiso*. These works are highly experimental, self-reflective, and formally challenging—Rabassa's predilection for this type of narrative is evident. From his most recent works, he says that António Lobo Antunes, for example, belongs to the large array of writers he has translated who can be called "difficult."[28] As mentioned earlier, speaking of the translation of *Que farei quando tudo arde?* while he was working on it—in 2005—he said, "this is the 'worst' one. This is good," and compared it with *Finnegans Wake*.[29] In general terms, to a greater or lesser extent all the authors Rabassa has translated into English are particularly inventive and self-reflective in their use of language.

When asked about his translation method, Rabassa explains that he likes to translate books as he reads them for the first time. He did that with *Hopscotch* and continued to do it afterward: "This would become my usual technique with subsequent books. I used the excuse that it gave the translation the freshness that a first reading would have and which ought to make others' reading of the translation be endowed with that same feeling."[30] Usually, the first draft is followed by several manuscripts.

Rabassa sometimes discusses particular challenges he encounters when translating literature, many of which he attributes to "intimate uses of language"[31]—as in the case of Cortázar's "glíglico," an invented language that, based on word sounds, evokes erotic experience. Regarding specific questions and challenges of linguistic difference, Rabassa notes that it is difficult to show the foreign language in the English text, mostly in terms of grammar, if one is to avoid producing extremely foreignized, unintelligible versions. He does not claim to have one particular approach to translate "difficult" works or to import radical innovations to the English language. He thinks, however, that "there ought to be some kind of under-current, some background hum that lets the English-speaking reader feel that this is not an English book."[32] Now, in his eighties and after several decades translating works from Spanish and Portuguese, he still writes on his "probable Olympic typewriter."[33]

Cortázar

Julio Cortázar's *Rayuela*, published in English as *Hopscotch*, marked Rabassa's start in translation. He had heard of Cortázar but had not read the novel before. Rabassa read *Rayuela* as he was translating it; it took him a year to do the English version of this important Argentine novel. This translation seemed to affect the work he did subsequently in significant ways. In his reflections about the importance of his experience with Cortázar's work in his subsequent practice, he suggests that every translation he has done since *Hopscotch* has in some way or another been its continuation.[34]

In all, Rabassa translated six book-length works by Cortázar. A long-lasting friendship developed between them. Speaking of his relationship with Cortázar, Rabassa explains that the author liked the way he handled his works: "Of all 'my authors' he was the one who came closest to what might be called collaboration. His marginal notes were well-taken and sometimes he would even alter his text to better fit the English."[35]

Rabassa worked with Cortázar through the whole process of translating *Rayuela*. The author read everything and commented on it; they commented back and forth.[36] Rabassa has said that the translation of *Hopscotch* was "shared work"[37] because the author helped him make many of the choices; he mentions the fact that Cortázar's English was very good and he was a conscientious reader. Their exchange and cooperation, which took place mainly through correspondence, continued throughout the various translations he did of Cortázar's works—most of the author's novels.[38] Although Cortázar visited New York once in a while and, when he did, he would visit Rabassa and his family, when Rabassa was working on a translation they would discuss it mainly by mail.

Rabassa and Cortázar corresponded often. The translator took the author's numerous suggestions seriously. In the three-volume collection of Cortázar's letters, published in 2000—and which provides substantial material for his literary biography—there are thirty-three letters to Rabassa. Cortázar's letters to the translator were written between 1964 and 1982. The first letter, from April 25, 1964, is Cortázar's response to Rabassa's letter right after Blackburn had asked him to translate a few chapters of *Rayuela*. Rabassa had sent the author a few translated chapters and had asked him some questions, particularly concerning expressions from Buenos Aires *lunfardo*, and Cortázar was answering some of his queries.[39] In the second letter, from the same year, Cortázar expresses great satisfaction and enthusiasm about the translation; his letter is accompanied by the first batch of annotated pages of the translation[40] — he makes a few suggestions and states that he finds the translation to be exceptionally good.[41] This would be one of the many exchanges of this kind that were to take place over the years.

During the translation of *Rayuela* in particular, Cortázar sent Rabassa letters accompanied by annotated batches of pages and detailed lists with answers to his queries and problems with suggested solutions. When the author found a problem (whether about solicited or unsolicited points) he would comment on it very directly. In addition to speaking of the general tone and approach to the translation, he would often point out what he considered to be felicitous renderings and solutions as well. This is the case particularly where there is a great deal of wordplay in the novel, such as Horacio Oliveira's deliberate spelling mistakes,[42] the characters' *juegos en el cementerio* (games played with the dictionary, or "cemetery of the language") or the translation of glíglico,[43] which is one of the most extreme attempts to transgress the laws of language in the novel. Rabassa describes the way he approached Cortázar's glíglico, for instance, by saying that he created "Gliglish" instead of using English to reproduce "this manufactured case of linguistic difference that illustrates how sometimes language is unnecessary to convey meaning."[44] In his letters, Cortázar tells Rabassa why he likes his translation choices. About the deliberate spelling "mishaps," he notes that Rabassa's rendition reproduces the effect — ironic, self-deprecating — of Oliveira's language gestures. He said Rabassa's choices for the language games of Oliveira and his friends were "a beauty!" — he used the English expression — and asked Rabassa not to "touch" what he had already done.[45] He liked the translation of "glíglico" in particular for it conveyed the atmosphere of hidden meanings that was to be sensed by perceptive, active readers.[46] Another example of a part of the translation that Cortázar praised was the translation of César Bruto's text[47] at the beginning of the novel.[48] Once in a while the author speaks of Rabassa's translation approach at large, as when he approves of Rabassa's refusal to use footnotes[49] or to stay too close — in the sense of word for word — to the original. He believes that Rabassa reaches a tone that makes it different from "boring translators (even if they are faithful)."[50] Rabassa also explains why he did not translate the French that is woven into the narration in the novel, particularly in the part "Del lado de allá," which takes place in Paris: "Had Julio wanted these spots in English he would have translated them into Spanish in the first place." He also left the Spanish intact in some places in the novel; he states that he saw no reason to dumb the book down for readers of English.[51]

The letter with the last batch of revised chapters, which was sent by Cortázar in June 1965—while the author was also working with the French translator—discusses details about publishing arrangements.[52] Later, in the last *Rayuela* letter, from July 1965, Cortázar reaffirms that he finds Rabassa's work to be exceptional, and says he is fortunate to have found a translator he can trust completely—the author recommended Rabassa to other authors, such as García Márquez and Lezama Lima, and his way of speaking to them about the translator reveals a deep appreciation of his work.

In some of his letters, Cortázar speaks of translators whose work he does not appreciate and, although respectful, he does not hesitate to state he is dissatisfied or that he does not believe the work should be published. In contrast, he was pleased with Rabassa's translations from the start. After having worked closely and intensely with Rabassa during the translation of *Hopscotch*, Cortázar told the translator that he had often discussed with his fellow writers some of his translation solutions, which he believed Rabassa had found with intelligence, sensitivity, and a sense of humour—"a rare combination." The author was grateful to have found a friend and a suitable collaborator for a task so filled with "tricks and winks."[53]

The exchange between Cortázar and Rabassa continued throughout subsequent translations. Their letters show that the relationship grew increasingly personal. Shortly after their correspondence began, Cortázar addressed the translator in a warm, humor-filled, and personal tone; it becomes clear through the letters that the relationship was no longer just academic or professional. They became close intellectual interlocutors. Rabassa and Cortázar's intellectual conversation started soon after they began to be in contact, as can be seen in Cortázar's responses to Rabassa's growing interest in Brazilian literature, for instance, or in their discussions about the Cuban literature that was emerging at the time. Through the years, Cortázar would keep Rabassa updated on other editions and translations of his works and they would discuss professional matters (e.g., publishing details, small publishers, and independent cultural brokers). They would also write to each other about music—mainly jazz—literature, and increasingly toward the end of Cortázar's life, politics. Both of them traveled regularly (Cortázar back and forth between Paris and Central and South America, Rabassa mostly between the United States and Brazil), and they would share their impressions of their trips. They would talk about their projects, their friends (the ones they had in common as well as new, recently found *cronopios*), and about their partners. At times they also shared their opinions about the "effects" of their work—they would discuss, for instance, aspects of the reception of Cortázar's work in the United States. After *Hopscotch* came out, Cortázar discussed with Rabassa the reaction some critics had to the novel. He noted that critics might have found the novel off-putting because of its non-conventional structure, or because it did not conform to their expectations of Latin American literature: it was cosmopolitan instead of being in the *costumbrista* mode.[54]

A large portion of the correspondence between Rabassa and Cortázar dealt with what the author called *la triangulación lezamiana*, in reference to the process of translating Lezama Lima's *Paradiso*—Rabassa still refers to it as the "triangulation."[55] This translation—which I will discuss in greater detail later—would not have been possible without Cortázar's participation: besides bringing Lezama medicine, pens, books, and other things he would have difficulty getting in Cuba, he would ensure that the Cuban author would get Rabassa's letters and queries and batches of pages translated. Cortázar would also make sure Rabassa would get Lezama's responses. As Cortázar wrote to the author in January 1970, soon after the translation started:

> Enviarás los capítulos de *Paradiso* que ya has corregido y por supuesto los espero para remitírselos a Rabassa. El sistema se vuelve forzosamente lento y aleatorio, pero por el momento tengo la impresión de que marcha bien. Dime sin vacilar si necesitas otras cosas, lo que sea; siempre encontraremos la persona que te lleve un oso hormiguero, un tratado de formas anamórficas o varios kilos de confitura de rosas, según tu gusto.[56]

> [I will wait for you to send the chapters of *Paradiso* that you have already corrected and then I will forward them to Rabassa. This system may be slow and fortuitous but, for now, it seems to be working well. Do not hesitate to let me know if you need other things. Anything. We will always be able to find someone to bring you an anteater, a treaty of anamorphic forms, or a few pounds of rose jam. Anything you wish.]

Rabassa also translated Cortázar's *El libro de Manuel*. The author did not want to entrust this translation to anybody else; when Rabassa confirmed he would undertake it (in 1974), Cortázar wrote to him:

3: DEL LADO DE ALLÁ Y DEL LADO DE ACÁ   65

La noticia de que vas a traducir a mi Manuelito es de esas que me reconcilian con la vida y sus alrededores. Ahora que es un hecho confirmado, puedo confesar que tuve mucho miedo. No porque los otros traductores sean malos ni mucho menos, pero es que yo contigo me siento en terreno fraternal e inmediato. Sé que me entiendes admirablemente y que yo "paso" al inglés sin esfuerzo, como si directamente hubiera escrito en ese idioma y no en mi criollo rioplatense.[57]

[The news that you will translate my little "Manuel" has helped me reconcile with life and its surroundings. Now that it is confirmed, I must confess that I was afraid that someone else would translate the novel, not because I think the other translators are not good, but because with you I feel in a terrain at once fraternal and immediate. I know that you understand me really well and that I "move" to English effortlessly, as if I had written directly in that language instead of doing it in my own Buenos Aires vernacular.]

Rabassa and Cortázar worked together to sort out the translation of the title *El libro de Manuel*, which was troublesome for them—they discussed a number of possibilities at length: "Manuel's Book" and "The Screwery," among others[58]; Rabassa says that, although they "settled" on Rabassa's own "hesitant suggestion," *A Manual for Manuel*, he still wonders about the title.[59] For *El libro de Manuel* Cortázar also suggested that Rabassa use Laure Bataillon's French translation as reference, for he had overseen it closely.[60]

The last book by Cortázar that Rabassa translated was *A Certain Lucas*. As with other works, the translator and the author discussed various drafts and also some editorial decisions. For instance, the publishers wanted to merge it with *We Love Glenda So Much*, and both Rabassa and Cortázar thought that was not a good decision. In 1981 Cortázar wrote to Rabassa: "One day we will find records that will have a Sibelius symphony alongside Armstrong's 'Mahogany Hall Stomp.' Editors are capable of doing unbelievable things if they are not closely watched."[61] The translation of *A Certain Lucas* came out in 1984, the year of Cortázar's death. Regarding this circumstance, Rabassa remarks: "There must be something deeper and more mysterious to all this because I feel that of all his books this is the most Julio one."[62]

Cortázar wrote his last letter to Rabassa on November 30, 1982, only two years before the author's death, when he was already in poor health. It is a very moving note in which he tells Rabassa that Carol Dunlop, his partner during the later years of his life and a woman he loved very much, had died. The same month she died, he wrote:

Greg, tal vez ya lo sepas, Carol se me murió el 2 de este mes, después de dos meses de hospital en que nada pudieron hacer para salvarla. No lo comprendo todavía, estoy en un pozo ciego del que no consigo salir, pero Carol los quería tanto a Clem y a vos y necesito decírtelo y abrazarlos muy fuerte.[63]

[Greg, you may know this already. Carol died on the second of this month. She was in the hospital for two months but they couldn't do anything to save her life. I don't understand; I feel as if I am in a black hole and cannot get out. But Carol loved Clem and you very much so I need to tell you and embrace you close.]

Rabassa believes that translating Cortázar put him in the proper "mood and mode" for the translations that were to come; he says that he learned to blend his words with Cortázar's[64] and that, in all the works by him that he translated subsequently, there was a natural flow of expression that he would only find when writing something personal.[65]

Although he corresponded and worked with other authors, Rabassa did not have as close a connection with any as the one he had with Cortázar. In addition to the friendship that grew between them, their relationship was the one that came closest to "collaboration." There may have been many reasons for this relationship to flourish. Besides the personal empathy they had from the beginning, *Rayuela* was the first book-length translation of Rabassa's. He believes that his relationship with Cortázar was an exception, and that their working so closely may have been due to the fact that it was his first translation. "I wanted to see what he thought. He read everything and commented on it. We commented back and forth."[66]

On the other hand, Cortázar himself was a translator. He worked as a translator at UNESCO, and from this he made a living. He was also a literary translator and enjoyed this practice greatly: "Silent interpreter in my youth, I spent many delightful hours translating works such as Marguerite Yourcenar's *Mémoires d'Hadrien* or André Gide's *L'immoraliste.*"[67] A major author he translated from the English was Edgar Allan Poe. Translating Poe enabled him to explore his language, to form his own, informed opinion about the criticism from the English and the Americans that Poe was "too baroque," and to greatly appreciate his genius.[68]

Cortázar's experience as a translator was possibly a reason for the interest, devotion, and seriousness with which he related both to translators and to the translation process. It may also be a reason for the substantial feedback and comments he provided, and for the richness of his relationship with his translators, Rabassa in particular. As Rabassa puts it, "being a translator himself, he had great respect for the translator's work."[69] Through the years, Cortázar trusted and valued Rabassa's work to such an extent that he wanted him to translate most of his novels. After Rabassa had translated several of his works, Cortázar once commented, speaking of the manuscript that was to become *A Manual for Manuel*, that it had Rabassa's signature. He praised the work by saying—in English—that it had the "Rabassa brand."[70]

Regarding Cortázar's work as a translator, Rabassa comments:

> Instead of making me quiver with insecurity under the scrutiny of a master of the trade, it relaxed me with the knowledge that Julio knew from experience what I was up against. Indeed, in some cases he would make suggestions that only a translator could make. So when I came to the documentation that he used to spice up the novel I found myself doing what he was doing for a living, faithfully translating the reports.[71]

For Cortázar, his own experience translating literature became a means to develop an acute sensitivity and awareness about translation: "All this has left me with an appreciation for the subtle transmigrations and transgressions that take place in the translation of any text when its meaning goes beyond the bridges of language."[72]

Besides the fact that he was a practicioner, translation was, for Cortázar, a matter of ongoing reflection. Translation is a recurrent theme in Cortázar's fiction—he often has translators as characters—and it is also important in Cortázar's way of thinking about language and writing. He uses translation as a means to reflect on language, for he sees language as a translation, that is, an imposition of words—and meanings—on experience.[73]

Cortázar and Rabassa did not discuss their views about translation in a more abstract way. When asked about whether he ever talked about translation with Cortázar, Rabassa answers that they never did, and that it was strange: "We would talk about the authors but not about the translations. I don't really know what he thought about translation in that sense."[74] Nevertheless, it can be argued that Cortázar shares Rabassa's views about translation to some extent. Specifically, they share the sense of anguished pleasure and productive uncertainty inherent to translating a text: "Few activities are as uncertain and constrained as translation, something that gives the calling a kind of charming madness when it is practiced with good-natured humor."⁷⁵

Lezama Lima

Even though Rabassa's eyes "glowed with pleasure" when he was offered the translation of José Lezama Lima's major novel, as Irene Rostagno puts it "he was well aware that *Paradiso* was one of the toughest challenges of his career."⁷⁶ One of the difficulties in translating the novel was communicating with the author himself. As Rostagno explains, getting through to the author was almost as sinuous an endeavor as translating the novel. Thus, the story of the translation of *Paradiso* turned out to be "as labyrinthine as the novel itself."⁷⁷ Political matters ended up obstructing the smooth flow of the translation process for, given the United States blockade of Cuba, mailing letters, queries, and comments back and forth was almost impossible. Although in this case the relationship with the author was complex and involved several mediators, Rabassa did correspond with Lezama and, to a certain degree, a relationship was established between them.

Rabassa's version of the first section was forwarded to Lezama by Susan Sontag, who in 1970 spent a month in Cuba and brought back his comments to New York. From then on, the key mediator in the relationship between Rabassa and Lezama was Julio Cortázar, who was a friend and protector of Lezama's. Cortázar knew the work well; in fact, he had helped Lezama rewrite sections of the novel. An edition of *Paradiso*, revised by him and Carlos Monsiváis, among others, was published by the Mexican publishing house ERA. This edition—along with the translations—helped bring the novel to international attention. Lezama thought that the ERA edition of *Paradiso* was carefully and generously done and said that it contained the "true" *Paradiso*. He was proud of it and described it as "impeccable."⁷⁸

In his first letter to Rabassa after he agreed to translate *Paradiso*, Lezama says to the translator that his work had been highly recommended to him and that, for that reason, he trusted the English translation would be of very high quality. He urges Rabassa to use the Mexican edition for the translation because, upon revising it closely, he believes it is the best.⁷⁹ Rabassa, who followed the ERA edition, says that, since its publication "notes and other things have turned up posthumously and changes have been spotted," but he does not see any urgency for a new translation.[80] While doing the translation, Rabassa mailed samples of it to Cortázar, who lived in Paris, and he would find someone he would trust who would be traveling to Cuba to give them to Lezama. The author would, in turn, find ways to send the work back to Cortázar.[81] Lezama would send Rabassa pages with lists of words about which he had inquired. The author would often send the letters and annotated chapters through three different routes, to ensure that at least one would reach the translator.

As the translation progressed, Lezama told Rabassa that he was glad to have the opportunity to have a "working dialogue" with him. He also told him that he had "found" his style.[82] The author was always eager to get more chapters of the translation—he said he liked it better and better. From the last letter it is evident that Lezama wanted to get the English translation published as soon as possible, particularly because two editions in French and one in Italian had already come out.[83]

When the translation process was going slowly, Cortázar would reassure Lezama. For instance, in a letter of August 1970, he wrote to him that he understood his concern about the pace of Rabassa's translation but asked him to be patient. He wrote: "I can assure, as a translator, that it is a hell of a task, especially if you put your heart into what you do." Cortázar reiterated that he trusted Rabassa and that he didn't believe anyone else could do a better job at translating *Paradiso*.[84]

In some of the letters to Rabassa in which Cortázar speaks about Lezama and the translation, he mentions the challenges that he anticipated "every paragraph" of the novel would pose for translation, and says he knows that Lezama likes Rabassa's work.[85] As is the case with most of his correspondence with the translator, these letters are serious and beautiful, as are the ones that Cortázar writes to Lezama himself and in which he also speaks about the translation. The letters show the great admiration and tenderness that Cortázar felt for Lezama, his loyalty and solidarity, and his "devotion" to *Paradiso*. Cortázar would call Lezama a different, affectionate nickname in each letter to Rabassa: "El Gran Gordo Cósmico," "el Poderoso Fumador de Cigarros Metafísicos," "Flash Gordon," "El Gran Shaman," "el Gordo Trismegístico." Likewise, he would call the "triangulation" itself a number of different ways, such as "the great LEZAMA-GREG-JULIO triangle," or "the magical New York-Paris-Havana triangle."[86] Some of the other people who helped complete the New York-Paris-Cuba link whose names appear in the letters are the poets Mario Benedetti and Roque Dalton, and the journalist Aroldo Wall.

Cortázar believed in the importance of translating *Paradiso*. He also believed in the process and thus participated in order to help it go as smoothly as possible. In a letter of 1971, Cortázar expressed to Rabassa that the value of translating the novel went beyond the value of literary translation, that it was important in a humanitarian and in a political sense. He said that, besides bringing great happiness to the Cuban author, Rabassa was enabling contact between the island and the outside world, which was so necessary and so limited because of the United States blockade.[87] When the translation of *Paradiso* was nearing completion, Cortázar became persona *non grata* in Cuba,[88] and so the contact was interrupted. However, it was really through him that the translator and the author were able to establish a connection—or "triangulation."

Rabassa says that *Paradiso* is without a doubt the most challenging novel he has translated and explains that he encountered many difficulties while he was translating it. Lezama is a creator of neologisms, as he says, and "the richness of the vocabulary was matched by the wealth held by each individual word itself."[89] The translator explains that when he was translating Lezama's *Paradiso* he was able to imagine Cuban voices by thinking of his Cuban relatives' way of talking. He says that those Proustian reminiscences were of great help—he thought at times he was translating Proust and believed he should aim for "a tropical, baroque Combray."[90] Rostagno notes that Rabassa calls this translation experience "arduous but rewarding."[91]

Rabassa's translation of *Paradiso* was finished in 1973. When it was sent to the editors, even Rabassa's translation of that "impenetrable original" was not considered to be "clear enough."[92] As Lowe and Fitz describe, "What Rabassa had labored so hard to achieve, the near matching of an idiosyncratic modern English baroque of his own creation with Lezama Lima's idiosyncratic modern Spanish baroque, was subjected to a severe editorial laundering, chiefly for reasons of 'readability.'"[93] After being edited extensively, the translation came out in 1974.

García Márquez

Colombian author Gabriel García Márquez began to achieve international recognition after the publication in 1967 of *Cien años de soledad*, a book that he says "he had been struggling to write for many years."[94] The novel won the best foreign book prize in 1969 from the Académie Française; it was followed by *El otoño del patriarca*, published in 1975, a novel that was "a continuation of his fictional investigation of solitude and its relationship to power"[95] and that received similar acclaim. Cortázar recommended Rabassa to Gabriel García Márquez for the translation of *Cien años de soledad*, and García Márquez waited until the translator was able to start working on *One Hundred Years of Solitude*. This translation was first published in 1970.

It is not uncommon to hear a statement such as: "Rabassa's *One Hundred Years of Solitude* was perhaps the most outstanding English rendering of a Latin American novel."[96] As soon as it came out, *One Hundred Years of Solitude* received a great deal of acclaim from both the critics and the public; as Alastair Reid remarked, as soon as it was released, the novel "was immediately moved by reviewers beyond criticism into that essential literary experience occupied by *Alice in Wonderland* and *Don Quixote*."[97] Rabassa recalls that, after *One Hundred Years of Solitude*, the publishers "wasted no time in going after more Gabo[98] — the success called attention also to his earlier works. *The Autumn of the Patriarch*, which was published in 1975, won the PEN Translation Award in 1977. Gabriel García Márquez received the Nobel Prize in 1982.

The problem with *Cien años de soledad*, says García Márquez, was that after writing the novel he no longer knew whom of the millions of readers he was writing for; "this upsets and inhibits me," he says. "It's like a million eyes are looking at you and you don't really know what they think."[99] Moreover, the broader audience brings increasing artistic and intellectual responsibilities: "I think that the idea that I'm now writing for many more people than I even imagined has created a certain general responsibility that is literary and political."[100]

Cien años de soledad was one of the few novels Rabassa had read without knowing he would be the one who would translate it — this was also the case with Clarice Lispector's *A maçã no escuro*, translated as *The Apple in the Dark*.[101] The relationship that Rabassa had with García Márquez was different from the one with Cortázar. "Gabo was always off somewhere or other," says the translator, "so for the translations of his works I consulted with a friend, a Colombian doctor — from either Cartagena or Barranquilla — who is also a writer and lives in Long Island. If there was a difficult word I couldn't make out I would call him immediately and he usually knew what it was."[102]

Rabassa tried to establish a conversation about the translations with

García Márquez through the mail but "Gabo is bad about answering queries and writing," he says. "It seems that someone sold a bunch of letters he'd written and it teed him off."[103] Rabassa says, however, that contrary to what people may think, from the authors he has translated, García Márquez is probably the one who translates the easiest—it took him four to five months to translate *One Hundred Years of Solitude*. Rabassa says that García Márquez gives the translator freedom and is satisfied with the final overall impression: "although hard to track down, Gabo is notorious for his acceptance of all possible interpretations of his work."[104]

When Rabassa refers to the fact that *One Hundred Years of Solitude* became so well-known, he often discusses some of his translation decisions. He explains how he decided on the title and on the beginning paragraph of the novel:

> Opening lines are often the most quoted and remembered parts of a story: Proust's *Longtemps, je me suis couché de bonne heure;* Cervantes's *En un lugar de la Mancha, de cuyo nombre no quiero acordarme;* Kafka's *Als Gregor Samsa eines Morgens aus unruhigen Träumen erwachte;* Dickens's *It was the best of times, it was the worst of times.* So it has been with this book: *Muchos años después, frente al pelotón de fusilamiento, el coronel Aureliano Buendía había de recordar aquella tarde remota en que su padre le llevó a conocer el hielo.* People go on repeating this all the time (in English) and I can only hope that I have got them saying what it means. I wrote: *Many years later, as he faced the firing squad, Colonel Aureliano Buendía was to remember that distant afternoon when his father took him to discover ice.*[105]

In his memoir Rabassa says that he stands by what he put down in this important opening sentence.[106] He says that Gabo must have liked the translation, "else he would not have made that outlandish but ever so welcome remark that he liked the English version better than his own original Spanish."[107]

Rabassa says that, although confusion "is subtly encouraged throughout the book," he took great care with the names in the novel; for example, he made sure that the old patriarch was always José Arcadio Buendía, "never any truncated version," in order to avoid confusion between father and son.[108] Also to avoid confusion, the editors decided to add a family tree at the beginning of the novel and the translator agreed to compose it. Rabassa says that, at the time, he thought it was a good idea to include the family tree because it would help readers keep in mind the names of the characters and understand the complex relationships among them. Later on he had second thoughts because if García Márquez had wanted a table or tree, the translator says, he would have included it in the first Spanish edition: "I came to think that perhaps confusion (and fusion) was meant to be a part of the novel, showing how all members of our species look to apes or horses, who would have trouble distinguishing among yahoos."[109] He believes the effect of this addition at the beginning of *One Hundred Years of Solitude* is puzzling, especially given that some subsequent Spanish editions, in particular those put together by academics—such as the one in the Cátedra series—also have a genealogical table at the beginning.[110]

Referring to the works of the novelist as a totality, Rabassa believes that there is a fabric woven from the threads of all of his work and that it is held together by theme and tenor and "style." "As I look over his collected works," he states, "I can recognize him in all the ones in Spanish and, although I am an interested party, I think I can say the same for the English."[111]

García Márquez is not a translator. He says that he has sometimes felt that he wanted to translate somebody else's work—e.g., Malraux's or Conrad's—but did not attempt to do so.[112] The few times that he did in fact try to translate literature, as was the case with the *Cantos* of Giacomo Leopardi, he did it as a "solitary pleasure" and in full knowledge that that would not be the path to glory for the author or for himself.[113] That attempt, he says, persuaded him of "how difficult, and how unselfish, is the task of the translator." As a side comment he has remarked that he does not like translators to use footnotes: "They are always trying to explain to the reader something which the author probably did not mean."[114] However, excluding the great masterpieces, he always prefers reading a translation than trying to get through a book in the original language.[115]

García Márquez recognizes the talent of some literary translators. He states that Maurice-Edgar Coindreau's translations of Faulkner and Dos Passos, for example, are "masterful," and calls him "one of the most intelligent and generous translators in France."[116] The author also recognizes the relevance of translation in intellectual history and speaks of the important role of translators in making it possible for such figures as Sartre and Camus to be known. Beyond the respect and appreciation he feels for translators, García Márquez is not interested in participating actively during the translation process. He is generous with his translators and speaks highly of them, but he does not usually read the translation of his novels in any of the three languages in which he would be capable of doing so—English, French, and Italian—because he does not "recognize" himself in any language other than Spanish.¹¹⁷ However, specifically about the English versions of his novels, he states:

> I have read some of the books that were translated into English by Gregory Rabassa and I have to admit that I found some of the passages that I liked better than in the Spanish.¹¹⁸ The impression that Rabassa's translations give me is that he hears the whole book by heart in Spanish and then writes it all over again in English.¹¹⁹

This remark about the novels being "better" in English is controversial. However, it can be seen as a tribute to Rabassa for, as Lowe and Fitz note, he also praised the translator as "the best Latin American writer in the English language."¹²⁰ García Márquez's opinion about the overall effect of Rabassa's translations is similar to Cortázar's: "his faithfulness is always more complex than simple literalness."¹²¹

Interestingly, like Cortázar—although to a lesser degree—García Márquez also participated in a translation of José Lezama Lima's *Paradiso*. He had met Lezama on a few occasions, admired him a great deal, and wanted to get better acquainted with his "hermetic novel."¹²² One summer, García Márquez's Italian translator—Enrico Cicogna—was translating *Paradiso*, and the author ended up helping Cicogna "make sense of the novel's prose." He recalls:

> Among other things, we came across a sentence the subject of which changed gender and number several times in less than ten lines, to the point that it was impossible to know for sure who it was, when, or where. Knowing Lezama Lima, it is possible that that confusion was deliberate.¹²³

García Márquez describes this translation experience as "enigmatic" and says that it was then when he understood that translating was "the deepest kind of reading";¹²⁴ he thinks that translating is "the best kind of reading, and also the most difficult and the least recognized," believes that a good translation is always "a re-creation in another language," and says that this is why he has such great admiration for Rabassa.¹²⁵

From the books Rabassa has translated, *One Hundred Years of Solitude* and *Hopscotch* are the ones that have gone through the most editions and reprints. "Even as I write this," says Rabassa in his translator's memoir, "*One Hundred Years* has suddenly appeared on the lists of bestselling paperbacks in both the *New York Times* and *Los Angeles Times*, a spot it never obtained when it first came out."[126]

LISPECTOR

Rabassa's translation of Clarice Lispector's *A maçã no escuro*, published in English as *An Apple in the Dark*, is the first one on a long list of translations he has done from the Portuguese. In the case of Lispector, Rabassa already knew the author personally and had translated one of her short stories for a magazine; he translated *The Apple in the Dark* in Rio in 1965—right after finishing Cortázar's *Rayuela*. He had read Lispector's novel before knowing he was to be commissioned to do the translation. According to Rabassa, "Clarice Lispector writes a clear, flowing, and evocative prose, and so a translator following her words should be led right along by them and have no trouble."[127] Speaking of the process, Rabassa explains that the editors asked him to write an introduction to the novel because they felt that it might be difficult for an English-speaking audience to understand it. As in the case of the family tree in *One Hundred Years of Solitude*, he agreed to do the addition but was not convinced it was a good idea: "I wondered if it really was needed or whether the novel was more arcane than I had thought."[128]

SÁNCHEZ

According to Rabassa, Luis Rafael Sánchez, from Puerto Rico, is—after Cortázar—the second author with whom he worked most closely. A student from Puerto Rico recommended to him the writing of this Puerto Rican author,[129] and he did the translation of the novel *La guaracha del macho Camacho* (1976), which gained Sánchez international recognition. During the translation of the novel, entitled in English *Macho Camacho's Beat*, the author and the translator exchanged correspondence[130] and also spent time in Puerto Rico, near Luquillo Beach, working together. They worked most closely toward the end of the translation of Sánchez's novel.

Rabassa calls the translation of *La guaracha del macho Camacho* a "challenge" and a "romp" and says that it has a great cultural value for it is a unique piece of writing that "explains" and "justifies" Puerto Rico.[131] He compares the translation challenges posed by the novel to those of

Rayuela in the sense of the importance of sound as it is interwoven with the narrative—e.g., he regrets having had to do away with the alliteration and assonance in the title *La guaracha del macho Camacho*.[132]

In the interview "De la guaracha al beat" Rabassa asks Sánchez whether the guaracha—the song—of the novel exists in real life. The author replies that it does not, but that it is a parody of the real guarachas he likes and admires.[133] Sánchez describes *La guaracha del macho Camacho* as a novel to be read out loud, and says that people consider *La guaracha* a play that has been turned into a novel, because it was conceived to be listened to, as if it had been produced as theater for the radio.[134]

Rabassa says that, precisely because of the importance of sound in the novel, while he was translating it he felt that he needed to "know" the sound of the guaracha that "pervades the book at its very essence"; however, he found that he lacked the originality needed to imagine a new melody because his head was "too crammed with the melodies of others for there to be room for anything new." He admits, however, he is not too sure how originality works in any case[135]—a remark that appears consistent with his ideas about originality and textuality that were discussed in the previous chapter.

In "De la guaracha al beat" Sánchez and Rabassa discuss the reception of *La guaracha del macho Camacho*. The translator remarks on the very different reactions critics have had to the novel, and says that Puerto Rican criticism has been significantly different from that of the rest of Spanish America and from Europe and the United States. Sánchez explains that he sees this as an example of the historical dimension of criticism. He finds the criticism about *La guaracha* to be more acute and discerning in Latin America, a fact he attributes to shared political realities. He believes that criticism does not exist in a vacuum, and that novels are interesting when they reveal and explain not only the text but also its critics and the context in which criticism is produced.[136] This is an instance of the common phenomenon of difference in reception between the Spanish language version and the response of the English-speaking readership (e.g., the cases of *Rayuela* and *Hopscotch*, and of *Cien años de soledad* and *One Hundred Years of Solitude* were analogous).

At the end of the interview, Sánchez asks Rabassa how he was able to translate the whole world of *consonancias* in *La guaracha*, that is, all the sound effects and idiomatic, vernacular expressions, which according to the author are "failed" in the most profound sense of the word in the novel itself.[137] The translator replies that it would be difficult for him to explain how he did it because it is something "natural." Rabassa says he tried to transfer the words and their meaning to the sound system of the English language.[138] In "De la guaracha al beat" Rabassa describes the process of translating the novel by saying that it translates itself, and that thus he proceeded as he did with other novels, such as those by Cortázar, García Márquez, and Vargas Llosa; the novel sets the current, says Rabassa; it is a horse galloping on its own. The translator should ride it but she or he "should not rein in the horse too much."[139]

As in the case of several other authors, Rabassa also believes that the works of Luis Rafael Sánchez deserve greater attention and that more of his work needs to come over into English.[140]

More about Rabassa's Authors

Although the abovementioned authors have been the most actively present throughout Rabassa's career, at different times and under various circumstances he worked closely with several others. He explains that, apart from Cortázar and Sánchez, his closest personal contact was with Demetrio Aguilera Malta who, like these two other authors, became his good friend. Rabassa says that, when Aguilera Malta's *Siete lunas y siete serpientes* first came out in 1970, the novel "grabbed him" so tightly he felt he had to translate it.[141] While doing the translation, entitled *Seven Serpents and Seven Moons*, Rabassa consulted with the author — he would sometimes even visit him in Mexico. This was one of the translations he did without having been commissioned by a publisher — a labor of love. When asked about the reasons that moved him to undertake the translation he explained the relevance of Aguilera's work in the context of Latin American literature and said that, as with some of the other lesser-known writers he has translated, he hoped that the American public "would be discerning enough to give Aguilera a boost."[142] Clementine Rabassa, his wife, also translated some of Aguilera Malta's short stories and both of them spent "many insightful hours" with the author.[143] As was the case for *Macho Camacho's Beat* and other novels, the Center for Inter-American Relations[144] eventually "listened to Rabassa's pleas," and promoted the publication of such an "obscure" novel as *Seven Serpents and Seven Moons*.[145]

Another author whose work Rabassa introduced to an English-speaking audience was Dalton Trevisan, first in the pages of the journal *Odyssey* and later through a collection of translations of the author's short stories, published under the title *The Vampire of Curitiba and Other Stories*. Rabassa never met the author but corresponded with him over the years. Trevisan looked over all the translations. This was a unique experience, Rabassa describes: "I had not encountered that with any other author. Dalton was never satisfied with what he had written. If we compare the first edition of one of his collections with subsequent ones, we will find all sorts of changes in the text."[146] The translator says that the author made substantial changes that had nothing to do with his translations but that carried over to them.[147] Gradually, he saw Trevisan's stories get shorter and shorter.

Rabassa compares Trevisan to Machado de Assis and says that, like his predecessor — and several other Brazilians — Trevisan has suffered from a lack of outside attention.[148] He believes there is still much in Brazil that should be brought to the attention of English-speaking readers, such as the works of Lima Barreto and others.[149]

With Mario Vargas Llosa there was not a great deal of contact. Rabassa says that he sent him "some stuff" and got some comments from the author, but not very much; he says Vargas Llosa "is helpful at times but cannot be trusted because his English is not as strong as he thinks it is."[150] In the case of the translations of Jorge Amado's works, Rabassa corresponded with his brother James, who was a translator, and he clarified his doubts.[151]

One of Rabassa's recent published translations is Jorge Franco's *Rosario Tijeras*. He says that when he first got the novel he wondered if he would be up to and adequate for the translation of a book from the "new generation."[152] He finally decided to translate the novel;[153] he did not work with Franco through the process but met the author at a reading of the book they did together in New York.

With the exception of Machado de Assis, Rabassa has translated only living authors. When asked about whether he considers Machado de Assis one of "his" authors, Rabassa replies that he is the best because he is a classic.[154] Rabassa sees his translating Machado de Assis as one of the highest points in his life as a translator: "With the welter of praise and encomia that has come my way for my work with so many fine contemporary authors, it still wasn't until I did two of Machado de Assis's masterpieces that I felt fulfillment as a translator."[155]

Rabassa's Relationship with his Authors: An Ongoing Conversation

Upon examining some of the instances in which Rabassa established a relationship with the authors whose works he has translated, I will return to the initial question, that is, to the relationship between the translator and the author. What is the nature of this relationship? Is there anything in common among the cases in which a relationship was established? What did Rabassa expect from the translator-author relationship? What were the mutual expectations? What does the gesture of "going to the source" mean in the case of Rabassa?

The section titled "Bill of Particulars," which consists of an account of Rabassa's authors and his experiences with them and with the translation of their works, comprises more than half of *If This Be Treason*, Rabassa's translator's memoir. Nevertheless, when asked whether he collaborates with his authors during the translation process, the translator suggests that he does not see the dialogue he establishes with his authors as "collaboration" in the strict sense of the term, that is, by "sitting down together and working through the works"; he explains: "I don't think there was really close collaboration in general. There are some historical cases, mostly poets, I think, who would sit down together and work through the piece. Not in my case."[156] He also states that, although his authors have been "good" to him, he does not want to rely on them, only when necessary, and that the closest he came to collaboration was with Julio Cortázar. Otherwise, he believes he has not collaborated with any author and says that he is not sure how collaborative translation works because he does not collaborate with other translators either.[157]

In any event, whether through active participation during the translation process, or through a different kind of interaction, Rabassa has a number of times established relationships with his authors that go beyond sporadic consultation. Rabassa does not claim to follow a general norm that would determine the kind of relationship he is to have with the authors whose works he translates. He explains that the relationship with each author is different and that it usually depends on him or her and also on geographical circumstance.[158] In any case, the authors' presence and participation have been prevalent in Rabassa's practice. Rabassa does state that, in general, he must have some understanding of each author's "ways";[159] having contact with the authors is one of the ways in which he seeks to understand their motivations, their style and their language.

Although in his own writings Rabassa does not explore at length the role of this translator-author relationship in his practice, he has tried to reflect on its nature:

> I've tried to figure out if this type of relationship is of any help for the translator beyond direct questions, whether a sense of nearness lets me hear the voice of these particular people as I interpret their words. If I am the translator I am supposed to be, it really shouldn't make any difference and yet I do hear their voices along with their personal pronunciations and intonations. This is that misty world of translation that is hard to describe.[160]

However difficult it may be for Rabassa to describe the translator-author relationship, as a translator who is aware of the circumstances that surround his practice, the fact that he recognizes the value of his relationship with his authors is significant inasmuch as it is important to look at the translator's self-understanding of his own relationship both with the texts and with the participants—authors, institutions—in the communities in which he performs the role of a cultural agent. If we follow a conventional reading of Rabassa's gesture of approaching the author during the translation process, we could affirm that it is an attempt on his part to go to the "source" to find pure meaning. Put in these terms, by working closely with the authors, Rabassa would be following the expectation imposed on him as a translator—or his own desire—to reach the author's "true" self—or "spirit," to use Robinson's "spirit-channeling" metaphor—in order to know what she or he meant or wanted to say. As a model translator, Rabassa would be in the ideal position to have direct access to the source—i.e., to reach true meaning.

Nevertheless, I would argue that, instead of an attempt to look for the "truth" in the text, in the case of Rabassa, establishing contact with the author has been a way to expand the scope of negotiation in translation—both in the sense of making meaning and in the context of collective, social conventions and interactions. Rabassa's contact with his authors does not take the form of a search for the ultimate source. Rather, his gesture may be better characterized by associating it with his ideas about authorship and textuality: Rabassa does not understand originals as sacred entities. We may look back at his views around the question of originality when he speaks of the translator's potential to betray himself. He says that the translator must not sacrifice or betray himself by becoming someone else as he translates, and gives the example of Miguel de Unamuno's notion that the *Quijote* and its knight were there all the time but that Cervantes just got there first.[161]

Rabassa is not seeking to get to the master to reach the origin. He acknowledges the author's value but does not see the text as the author's property. On the other hand, he does not see himself as an invisible, or unwelcome, intermediary—Rabassa does not intend to escape his own presence, or that of the author's. Thus, when approaching his authors, Rabassa seeks, instead, to establish closeness and generate a dynamic relationship with them. He engages the authors as part of the texts and of their traditions, and participates, like them, in a heterogeneous community of interest and in the process of producing the texts in translation.

Rabassa's contact with the works as well as with the authors, languages, traditions, etc., is relational. As an individual, he has engaged in a dialogue with the texts he has translated and with their authors—whether he had actual contact with them or not—seeing them, as well as himself, as elements and participants within a literary/social/cultural continuum, as social and ideological subjects involved in collective projects with(in) communities. As Venuti explains—and this is a point I discussed previously—the collective relation involves the specificity of the domestic communities, as well as the potential communities that may be realized through translation.[162] Rabassa recognizes that the translation takes place within a community and that the work does not begin with the author; the translation is part of the work, and the product of it, in turn, does not end with the translator.[163]

As a cultural practice in a larger sense, Rabassa sees translation as an ongoing, unfinished conversation at least in two respects. As part of the process and in regard to the translator-author relationship per se, it is a dialogue that fosters a sense of proximity. It is a way to engage language and exchange through camaraderie—perhaps even a certain complicity—in the dynamics of meaning and understanding. As a product, translation is the logical continuation of the author's writing. Translation is part of the work, and the work itself is part of a continuum, which neither starts with the author nor ends with the translator.

In this light, Rabassa is but one of the participants in the process through which Latin American narratives move into English. His translation practice takes place in a space that is, by definition, historically-bound, plural, and collective:

> I wonder now in my ninth decade as I watch words fade and then glimmer back into new meanings and nuances if someone will be following me at some future time into a reproduction of what Julio [Cortázar] wrote. It could go on and on, for translations have the strange progressive literary virtue of never being finished. If we have read *Hopscotch* properly we can see that it, too, was never really finished, that Cortázar is inviting us to do what he had not done.[164]

Rabassa does not expect the author's signature to be the one signing the translation. Nevertheless, he invites his authors—perhaps also his readers—to write with him. As the translator he wants to sit to the author's side so that both can listen together, approach the text and, at the same time, create it together.

4
Ayer y hoy / Past and Present: Rabassa's Canon and the Reception of His Translations

> The world was so new that many things still lacked names,
> and to mention them, one had to point with a finger.
> —*One Hundred Years of Solitude*

THE CANON OF LATIN AMERICAN LITERATURE AS IT IS KNOWN TODAY has been greatly shaped by processes of promotion and diffusion in the second half of the twentieth century. Translation has been instrumental in the internationalization of the literary works and is thus an important factor in the definition of the canon. Translation and publishing in the United States particularly influenced the formation of the Latin American Boom in literature, and Gregory Rabassa was a major figure in this process.

A Closer Look: Comments and Reactions to Rabassa's Translations

Rabassa's translations have been discussed in numerous reviews, articles, and other forms of commentary. While reviewers rarely acknowledge the fact that the book being reviewed is a translation, in the case of Rabassa many reviewers do mention his name and make a comment, even if brief, about the translation. When the translation is described in this manner—i.e., almost in passing—Rabassa's work is almost always described in celebratory terms. Some of the adjectives used to describe it are "brilliant," "superb," "magnificent," "splendid," "elegant," "excellent," "flawless."[1]

Rabassa's translation of *Rayuela* marked a turning point because of "the impact it had on American literary critics, a group hitherto oblivious to Latin American literature."² This impact had an effect in the translations to come. From the early publication of *Hopscotch*, reviewers have described his translations as "sparkling," "dazzling," "triumphant." Others use more descriptive words, such as "vivid," "spirited," "nimble" or "robust."³ When the comments are more descriptive the words are often chosen in relation to the fluency of the translation: "smooth" or "clear." In this regard—and this can be seen in the articles about his work as well—there are differing opinions. Whereas some commentators focus on the translations being "smooth" or "fluent," others concentrate on their closeness to the original. About the translation of *One Hundred Years of Solitude*, one reviewer noted the translator's "remarkable sympathy" for the language of García Márquez. Rabassa's translations of Machado de Assis are described as being "respectful of the original."⁴ The translation of *Paradiso* is described as being "skilled" and "a monumental task."⁵

Although his work is seldom talked about in negative terms, some reviews give these same characteristics (either smoothness or closeness to the original) a negative value. Sometimes Rabassa is said to have rendered the works too smoothly or to have domesticated them unnecessarily. Other times critics and commentators complain that Rabassa's translations are too foreign—non-English, not smooth enough—or "faithful to the point of adulation."⁶ One reviewer of Antunes's *The Return of the Caravels* says that, because of the fact that some words are left in the original Portuguese in the translation and others go unexplained, "Rabassa actually makes things more difficult" for the reader; he says: "the effect is of a translation in which you are never quite sure if you are concentrating furiously on Antunes's genius or Rabassa's problems."⁷ Similarly, other reviewers criticize the lack of explanations or other strategies that would make the text more accessible for the reader. For instance, in the case of Machado de Assis, one reviewer wishes there were annotations, explanations, footnotes, or an appendix.⁸ Another one, however, clearly prefers Rabassa's translating style, for according to him "Rabassa seems not to have softened and smoothed *Cubas*, or made *too* much sense of his carefree battiness."⁹

There are some instances—some reviews but mostly articles—in which critics list translation "errors." This is the case, for example, of the article "*One Hundred Years of Solitude*: Two Additional Translation Corrections," or of the following two comments: "Rabassa makes a few obvious errors, such as rendering *compromiso* as *compromise*";¹⁰ "the music descends into a monotone that undermines Sanchez's parody.

Who is to blame? Gregory Rabassa, who translated *Macho*, is also the translator of *One Hundred Years of Solitude*, a book that doesn't have one false line."[11] In some cases, after pointing out the errors, the reviewers say the translator is not to "blame," because they are due to the difficulty of the text or the impossibility of the task. The author of the second review above concludes: "I suspect that the music of *Macho* is impossible to catch in translation." Most of the time, however, Rabassa's translations are celebrated.

Some commentators discuss the translator's work in terms of the larger translation approach. Among those, there seems to be an agreement that Rabassa attempts to displace the language from its ordinary uses and conventions. Peden, a translator of Latin American fiction herself, commenting on Rabassa's rendition of *Seven Serpents and Seven Moons* by Demetrio Aguilera Malta, notes that the language most often heard in this translation is "a language that exists somewhere *between* the languages he is working with, a language that hides in the cracks between languages, a language one cannot reach or touch, but feels is there."[12] Peden suggests that what Rabassa does is let the English language suffer the "shock of the foreign language without anglizicing Aguilera Malta's unique voice."[13] She says that Rabassa absorbs the Spanish into his English, and that the new "Englishes" he creates are effective because they sound normal to an "English-trained ear." However, Peden finds Rabassa to be more faithful to the original than she would wish. She concludes, nonetheless, that in *Seven Serpents and Seven Moons*, he "met the very special problems of the text with imagination and sensitivity."[14] Blackburn maintains that, besides the "sheer abundance" of works he has translated, Rabassa is remarkable because of the "effect" of his translations.[15] She believes that the result of his English versions is almost eerie because of how close he gets to the "sense and atmosphere of the original Spanish." She explains that he has the capacity to produce what seem like literal translations on the surface, but to accomplish that "he has had to be both acrobat and inventor, creating North American equivalents for local Argentine slang, making up New Yorkese versions of Colombian street talk, and finding proper English weights for Cuban-based erotica"; she also notes that Rabassa's translations preserve perfectly "some of the best writing in the world" by taking risks creating a language of their own, and this is what makes them "works of art in themselves."[16] Levine calls Rabassa's translation of *Cien años de soledad* breathtaking. She asserts, however, that Rabassa's *One Hundred Years of Solitude* is not the same as *Cien años de soledad:* "The language of the original is an extremely potent Spanish, taut, dense, 'synthetic' meaning condensed and compressed, while the English version has a more expansive, relaxed, tall-tale tonality."[17]

In the chapter devoted to Rabassa in his book *Style and Ideology in Translation,* Jeremy Munday does a careful analysis of some of Rabassa's translations from a descriptive narratological approach and finds stylistic patterns in the translator's style, as well as common translation strategies. In *One Hundred Years of Solitude,* at the phraseological level he remarks on the identifiably American colloquialisms, and on translation strategies relying on concrete lexical realizations and syntactic amplifications "within a macro-strategy of syntactic calquing." Analysis of other texts reinforced his findings, as well as a tendency toward playful language and creative collocations partly based on sound and rhythm. He also notes explicitation and domestication of cultural lexical items. Significantly, comparing Rabassa's translations with those of others, he found less explicitation and intervention in the texts translated by Rabassa. Discussing what he calls the "psychological plane," he notes evidence of syntactic calquing, which varies according to authors. In more experimental prose such as Cortázar's *Hopscotch* and Lezama's *Paradiso,* he states, Rabassa's texts exhibit "some syntactic simplification and the fronting of space adjuncts affecting spatio-temporal point of view." He thinks that in *Hopscotch,* this may possibly be an effect of Rabassa's lexical priming.[18] Beyond his textual analysis, Munday, like other commentators and scholars, recognizes the fact that Rabassa's style of translation "conveys an image of a continent that transcends the individual author." He sees no relation between their success in an "English-speaking world that is generally resistant to translation" and any kind of ideological intervention from the translator—except for a lexical domestication that conforms to target language norms.[19]

Certainly, there are differing views about the numerous translations Rabassa has done from Spanish and Portuguese. However, looking at these comments, it can be concluded that, for the most part, Rabassa's translations meet the Anglo-American standards of taste while carrying an acceptable foreignness, a foreignness or newness that is in tension while at the same time conforming to standards of intelligibility—and acceptability—of the community for which he translates.

As a translator and scholar, Rabassa himself has written numerous pieces of criticism and commentary. In his reviews of other people's translations he does not praise a translator's work on the basis of "fluency" or "acceptability." His standards do not appear to be very clear, but his comments about the translator's work, even when they are brief, are generous and often more substantial than conventional reviews, which mention the translation only in passing. He alternates between commenting on details—e.g., style and lexical choice—and speaking of the work from a larger perspective, contextualizing it within the traditions of the literature of the Americas and referring to the relevance of the act of making it accessible for an English-speaking readership.[20]

In a review of Machado de Assis's *The Hand and the Glove*, translated by Albert Bagby, Jr., Rabassa contextualizes the work's English version by explaining that the late translation of the author makes the "non-involved American reader and critic" view him as a "new voice" and forget that he was writing in the nineteenth century. In regard to the translation work in particular, he notes that, "except for a certain vacillation in the use of contractions in order to make the dialogue grab, it reads quite well."[21] He then states that Mr. Bagby "is to be commended for bringing us Machado's minor works" and sees this as an opening for Latin American literature. He takes the opportunity to remark that, since the point of recognition of the Brazilian author has been reached and the works of Machado de Assis and Borges are appearing in English, it is time to "discover" the work of other writers. He gives the example of the Brazilian Lima Barreto, who he believes is in many ways Machado de Assis's successor.

Rabassa mentions that he disapproves of the way some critics treat translators. About Barbara Shelby's translation of Jorge Amado, for instance, he comments: "Since academics most often take delight in poking at translations, I want to stress that Barbara Shelby writes as if she were Jorge Amado's *paredros*, or double, with a tone in English that is the perfect match for the sassy style of the Portuguese."[22] As is the case with this review, in his writings he reflects on texts and their translations as being in an intertextual, dialogic—almost organic—relation with one another. In his reviews and articles Rabassa often makes connections between "his" authors, or between the work he is reviewing and that of one of the authors whose works he has translated; regarding David Rosenthal's translation of Mercè Rodoreda's *My Christina*, for instance, he says: "In his eulogy of her, Gabriel García Márquez cited her as a great influence, and the book shows why . . . Mr. Rosenthal's translation is top flight and does justice to some of the best prose that has been written in Spain in the modern era; he matches the mood as well as the meaning of each word in the original, and can therefore be forgiven his insistence upon the 1960s solecism of 'like' for 'as'."[23]

The different levels at which Rabassa discusses translations in his articles and reviews—which go from attention to detail to reflecting on the relevance of allowing the work to move across traditions—as well as the nuances he perceives in the texts themselves, are due, to a large extent, to the fact that he is a translator. Given his familiarity with the process, this generates a sense of empathy and closeness, which is based on his awareness of the materiality of the practice and also on his knowledge of the tradition.

At times, Rabassa's comments in regard to the reception, reviewing, and criticism of translations are about English translation in general and about translation at large—not necessarily about one person's work or about his own. For instance, he regrets the fact that translated books are most often reviewed as if they had originally been written in English. Other times, he says, even when the version is praised, "the translator is being told that he writes well, not that he translates well."[24] He recognizes that, although it is rarely recognized that the work the critic or reviewer is reading is a translation, this is not the case for his translations.

Rabassa acknowledges the need to have the critics' feedback and says that many translators (himself included) "fall victim" at one time or another to a kind of paranoia, the feeling that there exists a hostile host of critics out there lying in wait for the proper moment to "pounce upon [them] and savage what [they] have done."[25] Rabassa respects critics but, as mentioned earlier, he states that, at times, they concentrate too much on small details ignoring the overall result and literary value of the work.

Rabassa often addresses the fact that the translator's responsibilities "fly off in many directions,"[26] and that the narrow area of action that translators have is bound to a need to satisfy external demands. He urges translators to avoid what he calls "the silk-purse business," meaning that they should resist demands—sometimes their own temptation—to "improve" the work.[27] Rabassa states that he is somehow "responding" to those demands, and also to criticisms according to which some of his translations are "non-English"—not "smooth" enough.[28] As has been discussed previously, Rabassa sees the responsibility of the translator to be similar to that of the writer: "The author is ultimately responsible for himself, and this is also the position the translator must assume. He must reproduce a book according to his own skills and lights: buy or sell, live or die, it is his book, too, in his country and in his language."²⁹ When he translates a book, he says, he is "writing it in English" and the further "technicalities" are taken care of by copyeditors, writers who will "perfect" the work and whom he greatly respects.³⁰ Rabassa clearly believes, however, that although the translator is ultimately responsible for the translation, there is a community of participants involved in the result.

Rabassa and the "Canon of fluency"

Let us return to the question of "fluency," which comes up so frequently in reviews of translated works. The way Rabassa's translations are seen or reviewed reflects the expectations of the readers and the reading community—and of his own, as a reader. In regard to the translator's situation and activity in contemporary Anglo-American culture, it is widely acknowledged that fluency is one of the defining aspects in Anglo-American standards. Venuti associates fluency with invisibility; he characterizes invisibility as two mutually determining phenomena: the self-effacing attitude of the translator (discussed in previous chapters), and a strategy of "fluency" and "transparency" to render the translated works, which is one of the main criteria used by publishers, reviewers, and the reading public, to judge literary translations.

Venuti believes that the illusion of transparency that reduces the text's linguistic and stylistic peculiarities is an effect of fluent discourse, and that fluency dominates English-language writing and translating; he shows the way in which this becomes apparent in reviews from American and British newspapers and periodicals, both literary and for the mass-audiences, and written by critics, novelists, or reviewers. He comments:

> On those rare occasions when reviewers address the translation at all, their brief comments usually focus on its style, neglecting such other possible questions as its accuracy, its intended audience, its economic value in the current book market, its relation to literary trends in English, its place in the translator's career. And over the past fifty years the comments are amazingly consistent in praising fluent discourse while damning deviations from it, even when the most diverse range of foreign texts is considered.³¹

In his examination of reviews of translations that enjoyed considerable critical and commercial success in English, of works that "made an initial splash" and were then forgotten, comparing them with others that passed virtually unnoticed, he notes that these works were all judged by the same criterion—fluency—and explains that the fluent strategy is often equated with "accuracy." He explains that the canonization of fluency privileges a traditional domesticating method and responds to the ethnocentric impulse to reduce the foreign text to dominant cultural values in English.[32] Among his examples, he quotes a review of *One Hundred Years of Solitude:* "Rabassa's translation is a triumph of fluent, gravid momentum, all stylishness and commonsensical virtuosity."[33]

As the reviews discussed earlier in this chapter illustrate, it is in fact the case that Rabassa's translations are often praised on the basis of fluency, and criticized when there is a lack thereof. Nevertheless, Rabassa's translations show that it is difficult to determine whether a translator's versions are foreignizing or domesticating, whether they are "fluent" or "non-fluent" altogether. This assessment is more complex than it may seem. In the case of Rabassa's translations, for example, some critics assure us that they are too "smooth," that they domesticate the texts. Others affirm, as seen in the examples of *Paradiso* and *Seven Serpents and Seven Moons,* that they are too foreign.

Literary works in translation are prefigured in existing domestic forms. They are domesticated, i.e., rewritten, in such a way that they can reach and attract a wider audience. What is deemed "correct" as the work is rewritten through translation is, as Venuti points out, a domestic value: The "canons of accuracy and fidelity are always locally defined, specific to different cultural formations at different historical moments."[34] The aspect of the canon that relates to local specificity is a very important element to understanding the context in which Rabassa produced his translations, especially the Boom works.

The Boom novels were innovative; at the time Rabassa translated novels such as *Cien años de soledad* and *Rayuela,* these works were foreign in their origin, their referents, and their formal qualities, especially to non-Latin American audiences. Translation is expected to deal with the ways in which the "newness" of a new literature does not conform to certain patterns of acceptability and "correctness."[35] The innovative nature of the works renders them obscure; hence, it inevitably gets negotiatied in translation. Reviews also respond to conventional standards of taste. These standards change through time—what appears "smooth" may become "wooden" according to the audience. New forms lose their "newness" and become recognizable, familiar patterns. Before that happens, however, translation tends to be particularly attentive to conventions so as not to render the works unintelligible to a potential public, in an effort to create an audience.

Sometimes Rabassa's translations have retained the foreign to a point that has conflicted with the accepted standards, as was the case with his version of *Paradiso*, which was edited extensively for the sake of fluency. At times Rabassa employs explicative strategies, as was the case, for example, with the addition of the family tree in *One Hundred Years of Solitude*, which he did at the request of the editor. However, it is often the case that he is hesitant about the use of such strategies — often considered as the translators work with the editors. The opinions of the reviewers about these explicative strategies are mixed — some wish there were more, some believe it is better that he does not use them. In any case, most of the time Rabassa's translations can be characterized as fluent. In general, as Venuti remarks, the translations that "supported the canonization of Latin American fiction in English are distinguished by considerable fluency."[36]

The fact that the renditions of Latin American works for North American audiences are fluent is often discussed. In her survey of translations of Brazilian literature, for instance, Heloisa Barbosa finds that Brazilian works in English translation are also rendered fluently most of the time and that this is to a great extent due to the readers themselves, who are willing to "sacrifice the subtleties of the original in order to read what would seem to be authentic English."[37] Barbosa believes that fluent translating "extends as far as accommodating the image of Brazil provided by the translated works to the images of Brazil that readers already have, so that the experience of reading a Brazilian work in English translation does not become too unsettling."[38] She concludes that the desire to read congruent, easy flowing language is a disservice to Brazilian literature, given that — and she gives the example of Guimarães Rosa — it is a tradition that has associated language innovation with establishing its own identity.[39]

The "canon of fluency" has certainly determined the translating methods and strategies that underlie the English versions of the Boom works. It is an important aspect of their coming into existence, and also of their reception. Depending on the perspective from which his translations are viewed, it becomes clear that Rabassa has both conformed to and resisted the canon of fluency. The circumstances surrounding the translation event are complex; thus, it does not seem possible, nor desirable, to establish once and for all whether Rabassa's translations foreignize or domesticate Latin American works, as it is particularly difficult to determine a translation strategy and employ it as a generalizable ideal—this appears particularly true when we face the ambiguity of the traditional ethics of fidelity in translation. As Venuti affirms, "no translation strategy can be linked deterministically to a textual effect, theme, cultural discourse, ideology, or institution."[40] Looking at Rabassa's renditions in terms of the translator's ethics should not be restricted, only, to generalizations concerning the question of fluency. Reflecting on Rabassa's own position as a translator in his particular historical context reveals the many elements that should be taken into consideration in this analysis, some of which go beyond the actual strategies that can be noticed in the translated texts as mere products.

More significant among these elements may be the fact that, in several cases, Rabassa's English translations introduced radically new and experimental Latin American works—e.g., *Hopscotch, Paradiso*—into the Western tradition. These works were foreign and their authors unknown; inasmuch as the selection of the works is part of the translation process, their translation can be seen as an inherently "foreignizing" act—with respect to the tradition. After translation, the original works themselves did not become any less experimental or groundbreaking.

Whether there are moments in Rabassa's translating in which fluency is resisted or not, it is clear that he has translated within a community that privileged this value and set it as a standard. From the beginning, he has had to negotiate the reading community's resistance to "difficult" narratives.[41] The selection of works for translation and publication is affected by translators, publishers, and funding agents; these agents, in turn, have an effect on distribution. They are instrumental in the very existence, profile, and visibility of the works. Looking back at the experience translating García Márquez, Rabassa says: "I never knew back then that García Márquez was going to be this big. But I knew he was good. In Latin America, he was already being talked about, even if the outside world didn't know him."[42]

From a broader historical perspective, the foreignizing impulse of Rabassa's translations in the sixties introduced difference. One has only to see the far-reaching consequences of Rabassa's translations, such as the great influence of magical realism on world literature after García Márquez, to name just one. Whether the reviewers praise the translations or point out their weaknesses, or whether their descriptions are superficial or more substantial and detailed, several commentators have addressed the fact that Rabassa's translations are an "accomplishment" and that the readers are "his debtors" for his bringing the authors and works into existence in the English language. Statements such as, "thanks to the music of Gregory Rabassa's forceful translation the novel manages to sing once again,"[43] are a typical expression of the well-deserved recognition of Rabassa's work.

Among those who have praised Rabassa's translations most highly are translators themselves. As Lowe and Fitz note, Rabassa has been called "the pope of translation"—they themselves call him "the translator's translator."[44] Alastair Reid has stated that "the best of Latin American writing owes about two thirds of its existence to Rabassa.[45] Ronald Christ remarked on how Rabassa's "broad-minded approach as well as his generosity in dealing with texts, translations, and other translators have resulted in his becoming not only the producer of excellent translations but also the incarnation of the model translator." Willis Barnstone has praised Rabassa's "uninterrupted consistency . . . in which the subtlety and poetry of the original comes through magnificently." Because his translations "never call attention to themselves, Rabassa creates the perfect counterfeit."[46] Lowe and Fitz enthusiastically praise Rabassa's commentaries about translation: "His observations on the style and content of the often profoundly different Latin American texts he has re-created in English, on the nature of the act of translation itself, and on the many linguistic differences between Spanish and Portuguese, are a rich resource for both readers and translators of Latin American literature.[47]

Referring to the first translation she saw of Rabassa's, that is, the sample chapters of his translation of *Rayuela* that he sent to the editors, Blackburn said: "Rabassa's sample translation of *Hopscotch* sent us all into paroxysms of sniveling gratitude."[48] Among the United States reading public, this sense of gratitude remains to this day. In a newspaper article by Bach devoted to Rabassa in 2005 the headline was "The veteran translator of the most celebrated Latin American authors continues to open fresh perspectives on contemporary works". Rabassa's translations stand by themselves in the world of literature. Certainly, there still exists what Cortázar called the "Rabassa brand." Both the translator and his works enjoy prestige and visibility.

Translation makes for the very possibility of world literature. It bridges the local to what once was remote and transforms writers and what they write. Jean Franco states that, on one hand, access to world literature through translation "lifts writers out" of their provincialism:

"One symptom of this is that contemporary Latin American novels and short stories take the world as their scenario and are set in Europe, Africa or Asia. Whereas in the old days, culture flowed in one direction only between Paris, London, and New York to Latin America, it is now two-way traffic in a world that has no one cultural center." On the other hand, she acknowledges the tensions to which translation is exposed, given its role as "a road out of provincialism," and the difficulties, when aiming at "opening towards alternative versions of universality," to confronting "the international market that demands easy translatability, which of course constitutes another form of discrimination and selection."[49]

Latin American Literature in English before the Sixties

Historically, the reception of English-language literature in Latin American countries has been much greater than the presence of Latin American writing in North America. Early translations of Latin American novels into English were sporadic, even rare, and never circulated widely. Levine mentions one of the few nineteenth-century Latin American novels, *Aves sin nido*, by the Peruvian Clorinda Matto de Turner, which was first published in England in the early twentieth century as *Birds Without a Nest: a Story of Indian Life and Priestly Oppression in Peru* (1904). Before 1930 only a very small number of translations of Latin American books had been published in the United States. Jorge Isaacs's *María* was first published in 1890, and José Enrique Rodó's *Ariel* in 1922. The attention they received was minimal.

A number of agents were particularly instrumental in the increase in the number of translated works and their insertion into the literary establishment during the second half of the twentieth century. In her overview of the evolution of the reception and diffusion of Latin American literature in the United States, Rostagno identifies North American author Waldo Frank as one of these agents. According to Rostagno, Frank saw in Latin American culture and letters in the thirties a "resurgence" of the novel as an agent of social change and as a way of thinking the whole continent—the ideal of a "new" culture—which only needed adequate promotion. He then "embarked on a long-term project to draw attention to Latin American regional writing in the United States."[50] Rostagno believes that Frank was moved by a romanticized notion of Latin America, in which culture was "an expression of nature." This reading—which he would pass on to critics and reviewers—was one of a mythical culture and geography, and it would influence his writings and the authors he chose to promote.[51] The first translation sponsored by Frank was Mariano Azuela's *The Underdogs*,[52] published in 1929, which, according to Rostagno, mainly attracted the attention of North American intellectuals interested in the Mexican revolution.[53] Frank's choices were based on information he gathered during his trips and through fellow writers—many of whom were from Argentina. Although his choices were somehow arbitrary, they usually matched the preferences of Latin American literary critics with whom he had contact.[54] Frank convinced a number of publishing houses to support him and sponsor some other projects, such as the translation of *Don Segundo Sombra;* however, around 1935, after the publication of the English version of *Martín Fierro,* the initial interest of the publishers in Latin American projects decreased.

Frank and Argentine critic Victoria Ocampo started a literary magazine—which later turned into the influential journal *Sur*—that was intended to be "a bridge between the two Americas."[55] Ocampo was more interested in an experimental, rather than regional, type of writing; she aimed to show that during the 1920s, "Latin America had more to offer than the prevailing taste for regionalism in literature,"[56] that there was an emergent cosmopolitan literature in Latin American letters.[57]

In the forties the interest of some New York publishers in foreign literature increased. According to Rostagno, "wartime conditions had closed off European travel and made necessary the exploration of new authors and markets for the foreign literature lists."[58] Changes in Latin American literature were also taking place at the time—from the realistic novel to more experimental forms of exploration of social questions—and some works attracted the attention of critics. But then, says Rostagno, with the reopening of Europe, "there was more availability of foreign literatures to explore."[59]

Publishers were still reluctant to undertake Latin American projects mostly for financial reasons; however, some of them remained interested in supporting particular types of projects. In the forties some publishers took an interest in Brazilian literature, which resulted in the early publication of the works of Brazilian author Jorge Amado in English translation, for example[60]—Amado's works appeared significantly earlier than those of other authors of his generation. In fact, the English version of his novel entitled *Gabriela, Clove and Cinnamon,* published in

1962, became the first Latin American best seller in the United States. According to Rostagno, in English the novel was received mainly as an exotic romantic novel rather than a novel that is largely about Brazilian reality and change, about "the transformation from a patriarchal plantation society into a modern integrated, urban nation."[61] *Gabriela, Clove and Cinnamon* was read and reviewed as an isolated literary event without much connection with the context and literary tradition in which it was originally inscribed. This type of reading, Rostagno explains, constructed an image of Jorge Amado that undermined the political aspect of his writing. By 1970, Amado was the only South American who had had seven of his works translated and published in English. The translator of most Amado's works at the time was Harriet de Onís, who had been translating major Latin American works—from Spanish and Brazilian Portuguese—into English since the thirties. Other translators, including Rabassa, were also translating Amado.

Among the agents that contributed to bring Latin American literature into the United States, Rostagno identifies an alternative means of diffusion of Latin American writing, the so-called "littles." The "littles" were a type of magazine that proliferated in the sixties and that, beyond the literary establishment, constituted an option for publishing Latin American authors.[62] The most prominent of these magazines was *The Plumed Horn / El Corno Emplumado*, a bilingual magazine edited in Mexico City from 1962 to 1969. According to Rostagno, this magazine channeled both artistic and political enthusiasm—its political agenda revolved mainly around the Cuban Revolution—and created a link among younger generations of writers from North and South America.[63] Writers such as César Vallejo, Ernesto Cardenal, Octavio Paz, and Juan Rulfo began to be published in this and other magazines of the same kind along with North American writers. The large group of English-speaking poets—e.g., Allen Ginsberg—who contributed to *The Plumed Horn / El Corno Emplumado* appreciated the opportunity to be translated into Spanish. They would learn about Latin American literature and be read in Latin American countries. Although when the magazine appeared most major figures of Spanish American poetry had already begun to be translated into English, *The Plumed Horn / El Corno Emplumado* was instrumental in exposing North American poets and intellectuals to Latin American poetry, in particular avant-garde works by young writers. New forms were introduced "without necessarily discouraging romantic visions of Hispanic culture."[64] The editors—both Spanish- and English-speaking—believed that reading the writers of the "other America" would have a liberating effect among the younger generations of writers across the Americas.[65] However, before the sixties there was a relative paucity of translations, as Lowe and Fitz note, as well as a general "disdain" in the United States toward the Spanish language and Spanish-American literature in general.[66]

Translation and Diffusion in Europe in the Sixties

Although in the fifties and sixties Latin American literature already had a long-standing tradition, it was during that time that it began to have international visibility and recognition. There was an intense exchange and rising popularity of modern Latin American fiction in Europe at the time. Spanish publishers—especially Seix Barral—played a major role in the diffusion of the Boom. Associated with this publishing house was the prestigious Premio Biblioteca Breve, which was eventually granted to most of the authors linked to the Boom. As Rostagno notes, at the time Spanish literary agent Carmen Balcells was particularly influential. In the late sixties, Balcells helped bring the works of the Boom authors to European and, subsequently, to North American markets[67]—she still is the representative of some Latin American writers to this day. The Boom authors made significant efforts to be recognized beyond national borders; they resisted the idea of having a reputation only at a national level.[68] It is evident that it was through translation, through the accessibility of the Latin American works to an international readership, that the Boom constituted itself as such and came to occupy a place in the world's literary canon.

Critics and scholars have widely discussed the fact that the Boom novels were not unique exclusively in a literary sense, that their relevance was also valued in terms of their international reception. The importance of the economic aspect in the configuration of the Boom has been emphasized; more specifically, the effects of translation and publishing. Ángel Rama was one of the first critics to discuss this aspect of the Boom; he characterized it as a process of the market, designating a short period of time in which a number of factors coincided to allow for the internationalization of certain literary products and, for the first time in Latin American literature, for the professionalization of a group of novelists.[69] Among the factors Rama identifies are a number of "qualitative changes in the sociological articulation of the literary practice" leading to changes in the Latin American publishing scene, the creation of new and broader audiences, the resurgence of the publishing industry in Spain, and increasingly sophisticated forms of distribution.[70]

The translation of Latin American literature increased significantly during that time. Works were being translated mainly into French and English but also into Swedish, Hungarian, Italian, German, Norwegian, and Russian—by the time Rabassa's English translation came out, the translations of *Cien años de soledad* into French, Italian, Portuguese and Norwegian had already been published.[71] The new interest and recognition of Latin American literature at the time was truly international. The translation activity—into various languages—that surrounded the literary Boom was an important element for its diffusion, as well as a sign of recognition.

Speaking about the international promotion and reception of the Boom literature, Marteen Steenmeijer states that, more than the United States, France played a leading role and was, outside of Spain, the European country that was most receptive to Latin American works—particularly novels.[72] France was the first country to publish translations of works by Asturias, Borges, Cortázar, and García Márquez; this country was often the trendsetter and, when it was not, it would follow the leading country by publishing the translation shortly afterward. Works in translation often appeared first in France, followed by Italy and Germany, and then in the United States.[73] In the early fifties Gallimard created the collection of Latin American fiction called "La Croix du Sud,"[74] and published both experimental writing and works by authors from earlier generations. Several countries were represented in this collection. The role of France was influential in determining the itinerary that led to the international Boom for various reasons: the direct contact with many of the authors at the time, the closeness to the Spanish publishers that had long been publishing Latin American literature—especially in Barcelona—and also an "early familiarity with the literature."[75]

THE LATIN AMERICAN BOOM IN THE UNITED STATES

The term "Boom" has been widely criticized. Associated with Latin American literature, Boom is a multivalent and elusive concept. It is sometimes used in literary history to define the intrinsic qualities of a number of Latin American works, while at other times it is discussed mainly as a phenomenon embedded in the literary marketplace. In his book entitled *The Boom in Spanish American Literature: A Personal History*, José Donoso discusses the common-sense meaning of the English word "boom"—which has come to be used in Spanish and French to designate the same literary phenomenon:

> In English the word "boom" has nothing neutral about it. On the contrary, it is charged with connotations, nearly all of them pejorative or suspicious, except, perhaps, in recognizing expansiveness and superabundance. "Boom" is an onomatopoeia that signifies explosion; but time has added to it a sense of falsity, of an eruption coming from nothing, containing little and leaving less.[76]

It is often because of its economic connotation that the term "Boom" is criticized. In the foreword to Donoso's "personal history," Ronald Christ says that, like the novel itself, a genre that constitutes its principal product, the Boom resists definition and explanation; the term is problematic because it is a label conferring "a unity where there may have been none and a connotation more powerfully economic than esthetic."[77] In general terms, the Boom refers, according to Christ, to a "sudden flowering of writers" in the sixties, who won a greater deal of attention because they began, "almost at once, to be translated into foreign languages and to put Latin America—with some kind of unity—on the international literary map for the first time."[78] The conceptual weakness attributed to the Boom is partly due to the fact that it makes Latin American fiction appear as a new phenomenon—or an event—disconnected from its own tradition and history.

Despite its limitations, critics recognize the validity of the term Boom in literary history. Steenmejier says that at least the evocative power of the very term Boom "makes it suitable to refer to what was indeed a boom: the 'explosively' increasing interest in Spanish American literature in the Spanish speaking world, in Europe, and in the United States of America."[79] This phenomenon led to a literary dialogue across the Americas and created a new reading public.

The Boom marked, indeed, an intense and unanticipated interest in Latin American literature. It should be characterized, at least in part, as the first large incorporation of a group of authors to "mainstream" Western literature. This fact is quite significant in Rabassa's trajectory given that the role of translation, and of Rabassa himself, was key to this internationalization process: Rabassa translated works by the four authors most often associated with Boom, the Mexican Carlos Fuentes, the Colombian Gabriel García Márquez, the Peruvian Mario Vargas Llosa, and the Argentine Julio Cortázar. He also translated works by other authors linked to the Boom, such as José Donoso and Miguel Ángel Asturias.

Particularly in the United States, Latin American literature appeared as a discovery among some audiences in the sixties.[80] *One Hundred Years of Solitude* was the novel that received the greatest attention and was welcomed with the most enthusiasm. It came out at a time when other Latin American works were becoming available in translation and attracting critical attention; this situation increased the sudden proliferation of literature coming from the south. Roberto González Echevarría indicates that, because of its image as a great literary "event," the Boom has left the impression that "Latin American literature is a recent development with no antecedents."[81] As a result, the literature of the sixties has most often been read separately from the Spanish-speaking literary tradition. Johnny Payne describes how *One Hundred Years of Solitude* would "soon and fondly come to be known among English-speaking readers" and quickly "began to forge critical and cultural myths of its own, to such an extent that within a decade it had practically come to stand, by way of synecdoche, for all of Latin American literature."[82]

In the United States in the sixties, Latin American literature attracted critical attention as a phenomenon. It also responded to the critical sentiment of the time. In 1968, right before the time *Cien años de soledad* was published, John Barth published his renowned article "The Literature of Exhaustion" in *Atlantic Monthly*. Other writers and intellectuals—such as Susan Sontag—were also writing at the time about experimental fiction in terms of the crisis of North American letters and of a situation of exhaustion.

In the United States in particular, *One Hundred Years of Solitude* attracted unprecedented attention; to some extent this was due to the fact that it offered a literary alternative to the literature coming out at the time. Moreover, as Payne notes, it signaled the "discovery of a new literary continent" that was independent from "North America's exhausted possibility"; the novel was "a promise that would 'magically' recover the conventions and artifices of the past, while at the same time 'cross-fertilizing' US writing with its organic originality."[83] García Márquez's novel was seen as a source of revitalization of Anglo-American fiction. In 1980 John Barth wrote a follow-up essay entitled "The Literature of Replenishment" in which he celebrates the magical arrival of *One Hundred Years of Solitude* to Anglo-American culture and letters.

Barth calls the author an "exemplary postmodernist" and says the novel is the contemporary successor to *Finnegans Wake*. Along the same lines, in his review of *One Hundred Years of Solitude* in March 1970, the year when the translation was published, Ronald Christ stated: "While we have been worrying about the great American novel, it looks as if García Marquez may well have written the great novel of the Americas." Such critical reactions certainly contributed to the public's attraction toward the literature from the south, which, in turn, led to more translation.

Political and historical circumstances played an important role in the translation and diffusion of Latin American works during the sixties. Overemphasizing the relationship between literary history and the political context of the time is not the most suitable or fair way to approach Latin American literature, especially if the association leads to a reduction of literary works or cultural movements to the mere result of political and institutional manipulation. However, failing to mention this aspect of the Boom's history would be an oversight.

On one hand, changes in the configuration of Latin American reality led to changes in the literary forms of the time. As Gerald Martin asserts, it was during the sixties that Latin American writers began to produce great works of urban fiction consistently. This responded, partly, to the growth of a well-educated middle-class audience and the increasing concentration of the population in large cities.[84] On the other hand, some of the most important developments of the Boom were associated with particular political circumstances. The political changes in Cuba, for example, were very closely linked to the Boom. The Cuban Revolution created a sense of political freedom and opportunity; it attracted the attention and support of many intellectuals, including the authors who would soon be associated with the Boom. These two aspects together, in turn, created an effect that led to greater literary production. As Martin notes, the diverse ideological alternatives offered by Cuba and the various social democratic experiments of the day, combined with the new cosmopolitanism bred by the consumption-oriented capitalist boom and an expansion of the Latin American middle classes—which led to wider potential reading audiences—created a period of intense artistic activity throughout the continent.[85]

Gabriel García Márquez remarks on the cultural importance of Cuba in Latin America, describing it as a bridge to transmit a type of literature that had existed in Latin America for many years:

> In a sense, the Boom in Latin American literature in the United States has been caused by the Cuban Revolution. Every Latin American writer of that

generation had been writing for twenty years but the European and American publishers had very little interest in them. When the Cuban Revolution started there was suddenly a great interest about Cuba and Latin America. The revolution turned into an article of consumption. Latin America came into fashion. It was discovered that Latin American novels existed which were good enough to be translated and considered with all other world literature.[86]

The Cuban revolution had an impact on the quantity and the quality of the artistic production itself. It also had an influence on international audiences, for it brought Latin America to the attention of the United States and the world. Moreover, in the United States the Cuban revolution also intensified fears of the spread of communism in Latin America. As a consequence, the United States began to make greater efforts to have better relations with its southern neighbors. One of the initiatives in this direction was Kennedy's Alliance for Progress, which, as William Luis points out, responded to Castro's cultural policies, for it challenged "Castro's initial emphasis on social, educational, and cultural programs and his attempt to spread revolutions throughout Latin America and the Caribbean."[87] The Alliance for Progress promoted the types of programs that were already in place in Cuba; its emphasis on education, literacy, and culture was accompanied by an increased number of publishing houses and books.[88] Franco also speaks about this issue. She argues that before the Alliance for Progress "was set in motion," Nelson Rockefeller was part of a similar campaign; his vast interests in Latin America "made him one of the few politicians, to propose a project for Latin America designed to reform the infrastructure and avert revolution."[89]

The United States utilized numerous strategies to carry out its friendship program, including art, literature, and film campaigns and funding for artists and scholars to travel across the Americas. Franco explains that the hemispheric policy of the United States in the postwar years was based on the view that "a reformed capitalist system would protect the liberties and enhance the lives of North and South Americans. It was also aimed to keep Latin America open to traders and investors from the United States."[90] There was a need to counter "anti-Americanism and revolutionary ideas in Latin America and, politically, communist or nationalist political movements." Franco characterizes this project, along with the strong campaign for hemispheric cooperation and dependence, as "a propaganda machine and a benevolent form of imperialism."[91] Since "nothing was outside the conflict," neither artistic values nor literary criticism, Franco argues, the interest in preaching universalism, thus reducing heterogeneity, was part of the same impulse.[92]

In the Americas, a number of institutions had a powerful role in the institutionalization of what came to be the Boom. In the Spanish-speaking world, a key center for literature and the arts was the Cuban institution Casa de las Américas. Founded in 1960, it "made the dissemination of new Latin American writing a top priority and succeeded in its mission."[93] Havana became an intellectual center in Latin America and was the meeting place of most well-known Latin American authors. This Cuban institution also supported works by young, lesser-known writers, and its most important contribution was *Revista Casa de las Américas*, a literary and cultural quarterly that has published Latin American literature and criticism since the sixties. Later in the sixties, a journal called *Mundo Nuevo* was founded. It was initially edited from Paris—by Emir Rodríguez Monegal—and, according to some, it was created to challenge the influence of *Revista Casa*. *Mundo Nuevo* offered a great deal of support to Boom novels. The journal had an interesting editorial policy, partly aimed to show Latin American specificity within an international culture. It has been noted—by Franco (2002) and Cohn (2006), among others—that *Mundo Nuevo* received CIA funding indirectly.

In sum, the social, political, and even aesthetic circumstances and changes in the sixties, as well as the political interest and the intellectual and popular curiosity in Latin America contributed to the increasing interest in its literature abroad. Literature was a window to the southern part of the American continent. As Luis puts it, "literature in translation evolved as a way of understanding the cultures of the neighbors to the south, and as an avenue to interpret the complexity of Latin American thought and culture."[94]

Examining the historical and political context of the Boom does not necessarily speak to questions about whether the novels produced at the time were, in some explicit way, attuned with political discourses and agendas. As has been indicated, the authors that were being "discovered" internationally were not very established at the time. Most of the Boom works were in fact experimental, they were cosmopolitan and innovative—some of them were obscure, even to the Latin American reading public. The Latin American canon abroad was just beginning to form. The Boom literature was indeed groundbreaking. Yet the connection between the space that opened up for Latin American projects in the sixties and the political setting at the time remains significant. The literary works translated and promoted were either selected in a context that intended to defend particular cultural values, or read and interpreted according to that particular context as they entered the Western tradition and the Latin American canon began to take shape. Thus, it is important to consider the circumstances under which the international Boom came into existence for it is this context—academic, critical, and politically speaking—in which Rabassa produced his works. His connection to the Boom links Rabassa with a particular moment of global cultural politics.

Rabassa and the Canon: Becoming the Voice of the Masters

As the Boom became established and gained a reputation as a literary phenomenon, translation became a definitive aspect of its development. Since the thirties, it was Harriet de Onís who translated most major Spanish-speaking works and, around 1950, she had become the main translator of Latin American writing. Harriet de Onís played a crucial role in the promotion of Latin American authors among certain publishers, and until the mid-sixties in the United States it was largely she who decided which Latin American novels would be translated into English. Retrospectively, according to some critics, her translations belong to an earlier "era" of Latin American fiction.[95] In the sixties, as the demand for translation increased, more translators began to contribute and get involved, not only with their translations but also as agents, promoters, and commentators of Latin American works. As Lowe and Fitz point out, scholars and writers like Gregory Rabassa, James Irby, Edith Grossman, Helen Caldwell, and Margaret Sayers Peden made crucial decisions about which works from Spanish America and Brazil would be translated. Suzanne Jill Levine has also been a key translator of Latin American literature from the Boom to this day. As Lowe and Fitz point out, these translators "produced English-language versions that would in most cases prove extraordinarily successful, capturing not only the content of the original Spanish and Portuguese texts but their style and tone as well." As they put it, bringing these new perspectives to an English-speaking readership was "largely a function of what some translators were able to achieve."[96]

Rabassa was, without a doubt, the most prominent of these translators. Even though he has translated several authors, among whom there have been lesser-known ones, part of his visibility is due to the key role he played in the translation and popularization of the Boom. As Luis puts it, there is no doubt that Rabassa became the most important translator of Latin American literature; he accepted the challenge of translating the best and most difficult works and is mainly responsible for introducing them to a North American audience.[97] Luis cites Peden's remarks about what many readers felt about *Hopscotch* and Rabassa's translation: "This book, this translation must surely be considered one of the breakthrough publications of Latin American literature in the English-speaking world, setting the stage for many works to follow."[98]

In the United States, Rabassa participated in the activities of institutions that were instrumental in the promotion of the Boom. This is the case, for instance, with the Center for Inter-American Relations. Created in 1967 and funded by private foundations, the Center sponsored painting, music, and other literature from Latin America. Rabassa, as well as other well-known translators and critics—Emir Rodríguez Monegal, Alastair Reid, Suzanne Jill Levine, Ronald Christ, Eliot Weinberger, and others—participated actively in the literature program of the Center, which started a translation subvention program in 1968.[99] The program's committee would select the books, find translators, and offer a subsidy to help publishers by covering half of the translating expenses. Through its magazine *Review* it provided a space to discuss literary topics. According to Rostagno, *Review* was particularly influential because it "reached out to a wider American audience, showing that readers did not need to know Spanish to appreciate Latin American culture; it communicated with the larger US intellectual community and advanced the idea that Latin America was producing genuinely innovative literature."[100]

The Center sponsored and promoted the translations of such "classics" as *Cien años de soledad* and *Paradiso*. As Deborah Cohn notes, the publication of *One Hundred Years of Solitude* marked the program's breakthrough in the United States.[101] Within ten years, the Center had sponsored the translation of more than forty-five books written by Latin American authors, many of whom became known in the United States. Rabassa had a long history with the Center's translation subvention program. In an article recently published in *Review*, reflecting on the role of the Center—which was later blended into the Americas

Society—and on his participation in it, Rabassa says that the forty years of its existence coincide with the number of years he has been translating works from the south.[102] Referring to the many translations he has done that have been subsidized by the Center, he says that it would be apt to "cease talking about 'my' authors and refer instead to 'our' authors."[103] In an earlier article, discussing the Center's collaboration with publishers, he states,

> The publisher is faced with a twofold financial burden in the case of translations: a translation is more costly than a manuscript in English because money must be spent to render it in English, and the American public is notoriously reluctant to buy foreign fiction in the quantity that it does native works. Only rarely does a translated book make the best-seller lists, and then usually quite briefly. The Center for Inter-American Relations has done great work in helping to defray the costs of translation of Latin American works, thus placing the book on the same level financially as an original manuscript in English.[104]

At the time, Rabassa said that translators were in "good company," given the Center's contribution and the fact that some publishers were increasingly believing in the value of foreign authors and support projects on the basis of their prestige, as was the case with poetry. In other articles and interviews Rabassa mentions the role played by publications, such as *Odyssey*—where he published his first short-fiction translations. He recognizes the role of *Odyssey* when he calls the journal—as noted earlier—a "true forerunner" of the Boom.[105] However, he believes that the Center was the organization most responsible for the dissemination in the United States of the works of the Latin American Boom.[106]

Within ten years, the Center had sponsored the translation of books written by "almost every major Latin American author to become known in the United States." During the seventies and eighties, as some of the Boom writers became "commercially viable," as Rostagno puts it, the Center focused its efforts in promoting lesser-known authors, and sponsored some of the so-called post-Boom such as Manuel Puig and Severo Sarduy. In the early eighties there were major changes in the Center's literature program and translation was de-emphasized.[107]

Critics recognize the Center as a powerful institution of literary patronage in the United States and acknowledge the influence it had in creating an international image of Latin American literature, thus shaping the established canon. As María Eugenia Mudrovcic asserts, the Center succeeded in earning a reputation among mainstream critics and publishers, and during more than a decade was almost exclusively dedicated to promoting Latin American writing.[108] Especially during the first decade of its activities it made a considerable impact in bringing Latin American literature into the cycle of consecration.[109] Cohn mentions Michael Bérubé's comment that, in a perverse way, the cold war years were a good time for artistic and intellectual production.[110] She concludes that, despite the mixed interests involved in the cultural programs of some institutions devoted to promoting culture at the time, the Center and its predecessors raised the profile of Latin American literature through political, literary, and marketing channels. She states that the Center was one of the institutions that succeeded in "walking a fine line" by simultaneously taking advantage of the cold war interest in Latin America—which created a favorable climate to receive funds from private foundations—and supporting authors whose politics often ran counter to those of the "Center's political and philanthropic sponsors."[111] As Rostagno also notes, the Center changed the history of Latin American literature in the United States and, thanks to its sponsoring translations of works by a total of almost seventy authors, a half dozen of which have become household names among American intellectuals, more and more publishers feel comfortable with Latin American writing, and Spanish American or Brazilian works are no longer considered curiosities.[112]

Latin American writing became known among the intelligentsia and in the mainstream. As Venuti points out in regard to the Boom, in the United States the success of Latin American writers like Borges and Cortázar was both critical and commercial. It was surrounded by "numerous, mostly favorable reviews, the support of trade publishers like Grove, Pantheon, and New Directions, and publishing subventions."[113] Literary reviews played a major role in this process because they create, feed, and constantly reshape the image of Spanish-American literature in the United States. From the start, as Mudrovcic notes, the works were presented in relation to the Western tradition through what Bourdieu calls "privileged references," that is, references to writers who are already established to give new works and authors legitimacy—e.g., announcing García Márquez as "A Latin Faulkner."[114]

As illustrated in the section about Rabassa's reviews at the beginning of this chapter, the translations were for the most part well received. In addition, as Juliana de Zavalia remarks, the Boom generated "a wide gamut of rewrites and refractions"—in the form of translations, reviews, criticism, anthologies and films—and the position of publishing houses as canon-formers and important means of refractions cannot be overlooked.[115] After their first editions, the Boom novels were quickly reprinted in paperback and some have been followed by several reprints to this day. Mario Vargas Llosa received the Premio Biblioteca Breve from Seix Barral in 1962 and this, as Frederick Nunn notes, helped make his work "required reading" in the Spanish-speaking world.[116] The cumulative effects of his awards and those of others, he says, especially the Nobel Prizes of Miguel Ángel Asturias (1967) and Gabriel García Márquez (1982) established the "new novel" as an international, multilingual phenomenon of historical proportions.[117]

The mere fact that the Boom authors were being translated into hegemonic languages, namely English and French, meant prestige and led to market and critical recognition. As mentioned previously, Rabassa's version of *Hopscotch* won the 1967 National Book Award for Translation; Paul Blackburn's translations of other works by Cortázar were published early in prestigious magazines such as the *New Yorker*. Although from the Boom novels only Rabassa's 1970 version of *Cien años de soledad* was a best seller, reviews and critical articles of Spanish-American writers began to appear in major magazines and newspapers in the United States. To illustrate the extent to which García Márquez—as well as Vargas Llosa and the others—have become "more or less household names" in the English-speaking world, Barbosa gives the example of the opening paragraph of a critical essay entitled "A Pig's Tail":[118] "the text I am considering is a novel in English written by Gregory Rabassa based on a novel in Spanish by Gabriel García Márquez. This is not merely because I do not read Spanish, but also because this text exists as an object in itself that has been received as a novel in English by numerous ordinary readers, critics, and even scholars."[119] The Boom brought critical, commercial, and readership attention to the authors it consecrated. It succeeded in creating an international place and reputation for Latin American writing.

The writers of the Boom period were politically minded; they were publicly critical. Rabassa was not unaware of this fact. Indeed, as Blackburn put it in her 1974 article, Rabassa usually shared the politics of his authors.[120] The Boom authors were politically vocal; they were cultural critics as well. Franco notes that, in the sixties, they substantially redefined the Latin American writer's traditional pedagogical role:

> Poets and novelists influenced the way literature was read, history understood, and language valued. [Gabo and the other Boom writers] introduced

theories of reading and understanding to elucidate not only their own work but also that of their forerunners and contemporaries. They created canons and produced a corpus of criticism that included essays, monographs, speeches, and journalism, that provided a serious evaluation of contemporary culture, and that revamped literary genealogy in a way that transgressed narrow national boundaries.[121]

Franco gives the example of García Márquez's Nobel Prize speech, in which he made an "appeal for an end to Latin America's solitude." This appeal is ironic, she says, if seen in the context of globalization. In regard to the possibilities that opened up to the worldwide recognition of the Boom authors, Franco states, "Such sweeping claims could be advanced because these writers enjoyed a translational status, thanks to the translation of their novels."[122] Cohn remarks that, besides the increasing visibility of a number of Latin American authors, the Boom was also notable for its ideological coherence.[123] Although they held similar political interests at the start, during the seventies, the Boom authors were "divided," largely around their position on the Cuban Revolution and, politically speaking, took separate paths subsequently. Cortázar, for example, became more politically active in the latest part of his life; he also made his political agenda more explicit in his writings. Fuentes and Vargas Llosa became strongly critical of the Cuban Revolution, whereas García Márquez has always supported it and remains close to Castro to this day.

Zavalia believes that the Boom led to movement across borders at various levels: Geographical borders, because it implied crossing national boundaries and moving across Latin America, Europe, and the United States; linguistic borders, because translation was necessary and important for the internationalization process; narrative borders, because the new novel went beyond traditional narrative strategies, having "foster parents" outside the writers' own traditions; to her, these finally coalesced into what Sarah Crichton calls "the hallmark of Latin American literature": magical realism.[124]

The Spanish-American literary Boom implied the internationalization of Latin American writing, which moved across and beyond national boundaries and linguistic and literary territories. This phenomenon would not have been possible without translation, and Rabassa played a key role in its development. The "translational status" of the Latin American works and authors in the sixties shaped the configuration of the world's literary order institutionally, aesthetically, and symbolically.

5

Rabassa's Translations and an Imagined Latin America

> Macondo is Latin America in microcosm.
> —John Leonard

> The Archive is incomplete as evidenced by the many unfinished or mutilated documents that it contains.
> —Roberto González Echevarría

THIS LAST CHAPTER IS AN EXPLORATION OF THE ROLE THAT RABASSA and his translation practice have played in the construction of images of Latin American literature and of collective narratives and representations of Latin America in its literature. I begin by discussing the way in which Rabassa's translations have become inserted in the institution of literature, and the way in which he has operated within the communities—social, literary, and interpretive—in which his work has circulated, particularly after the Boom. I then focus on *One Hundred Years of Solitude* to discuss, in light of critical debates, the extent to which, after its internationalization, the novel has been taken as a document of Latin American reality. I aim to present a general reflection of Rabassa's legacy from the perspective of the socio-historical relevance of translated literature.

THE BOOM AND BEYOND: RABASSA'S TRANSLATIONS AND THEIR "SIDE EFFECTS"

The Boom is the most important turning point in the history of the Latin American literary tradition. The legacy of the Boom has continued evolving through the years and its effects have caused a great deal of controversy. On one hand, for instance, the Boom stimulated the interest of international, and particularly North American, authors in the sixties to various forms of writing coming from Latin America, which were formerly neglected or only studied by specialists. As a genre, poetry also benefited from the literary space opened by the Boom of narrative fiction; a number of authors who had not yet received international attention began to be known and eventually achieved popularity. Octavio Paz was already internationally known in the sixties but he was the exception: generally speaking, Latin American poets received attention and respect only from other poets and were unknown in terms of critical interest and popularity. This was the case, as Rostagno notes, of Pablo Neruda, who became established internationally only after the Boom. "Neruda was accustomed to seeing his work appear in publications by small, avant-garde presses," explains Rostagno, "but in 1972 a major publishing house acquired the exclusive English-language rights to his new work."[1]

The Boom also stimulated Latin Americans—both intellectuals and the mainstream public—to read works by Latin American authors who weren't known to them before. Latin American authors began to read one another more as well, and their novels were allowed access to more powerful distribution networks. One of the most advantageous side effects of the Boom in the context of Latin American writing, according to García Márquez, is that now publishers are "always on the lookout to make sure that they're not going to miss the new Cortázar."[2] With this increasing flow of works and publications, local and international interest in other Latin American literary productions that had been marginalized until then also increased. A larger and more complex literary and institutional system came into existence and the very idea of a Latin American literature, as part of world literature, materialized.

The critical achievements of the Boom were significant. The success of Latin American writing altered the canon of foreign (world) fiction. As Venuti notes, the Boom must be counted as one of the cultural tendencies that altered the canon of British and North American fiction during the sixties, as a "proliferation of diverse narrative experiments inspired by modernism" that undermined the assumptions of classic realism, both theoretical and ideological.[3] In the United States in particular, it not only introduced new texts and writers to Anglo-American culture but, as Venuti points out, it also validated experimentalism, thus introducing cultural difference by "interrogating dominant literary values and influencing the development of new English-language literatures."[4]

In her examination of Brazilian literature in translation, Barbosa explains that, to a certain extent, Brazilian literature also benefited from the Boom. She argues that during the sixties Brazilian literature ceased to be seen as an "offshoot of Portuguese literature" and came to be seen as an entity on its own. Although the numbers of translated works from Brazil have never reached the magnitude of those of translations of Spanish-American works after the sixties, she says, the number of translations of Brazilian works did increase significantly after the Boom.[5]

Although certain questions remain regarding what exactly made the Boom so decisive in the literary history of its time, critics agree that among the major effects produced by the dissemination of Latin American fiction in translation in the sixties was "a reasonable amount of discriminating appreciation to Latin American literature."[6]

At the same time, as is the case with most processes of canon formation, the Latin American Boom participated in the exclusion and silencing of certain authors and certain literary forms and tendencies. Examining the relationship of translation and canon formation in the history of Latin American literature in particular, it may be possible to imagine radically different outcomes had things been different in the sixties. This aspect relates, partly, to the extent to which works have been "made to fit" the local readerships as they travel and need to be promoted, as well as the extent to which the choices made in their translation have overemphasized or obscured symbolic and representational elements in the novels. This is the case about translation at large. As Venuti states, the selection of foreign texts and the development of translating strategies can establish "peculiarly domestic canons for foreign literatures, which will conform to domestic aesthetic values and therefore reveal exclusions and admissions, centers and peripheries that deviate from those current in the foreign language."[7] As part of the translation process, as Venuti illustrates, the imposition of the domestic canon entails rewriting the foreign texts to conform to prevalent styles and themes, as well as a process of dehistorization of foreign literatures that results from removing them from the literary tradition where they draw a particular significance.[8]

As it traveled north, what became known as "Latin American literature" came to shape and be part of particular configurations and arrangements; it even appeared, as Christ noted, to have a unity where there may have been none. If we were to follow Itamar Even-Zohar and view literary traditions as systems,[9] we could study Latin American works as being dislodged from their local systems to move to others—

either to other reading communities or as part of (new) international arrangements. Moreover, the literary works were (re)presented in intelligible and recognizable forms, according to the norms of the new or newly formed readerships. This phenomenon is common when works travel from the periphery to the center. As Zavalia explains, the stronger the tradition of the literature into which the translated works are introduced—the host literary polysystem—the more fluent translations are often produced.[10] For a translator of a cultural other within a strong monolingual polysystem, explains Venuti, it is difficult to try to practice translation as a "locus of difference."[11]

The exclusions and misconceptions surrounding the Boom have been widely debated and documented. Lowe and Fitz, among others, discuss the "misreading" of Latin American literature in the States:

> What we can now see as a classic problem of influence and reception, this ardent response to Borges and Márquez was both encouraging and dismaying for Latin American writers and scholars, who were only too aware that their literature involved much more than "magical realism," a notoriously imprecise critical term that has led astray as many readers as it has helped.[12]

They also note that, writers and scholars of Latin American—including Brazilian—literature, see this reception as misguided, in part because of the lack of knowledge of the audience about Latin American history and culture: "[they] read the Boom novels, naively, as texts that not only represented but defined Latin American letters and in ways that distorted the more complex nature of Brazilian and Spanish American literature."[13]

Among the most frequently discussed exclusions of the Boom is its emphasis on male writers. A glance at the history of Latin American literature in translation will easily confirm this observation. Rabassa's list of authors can be used as an example: from the more than thirty authors he has translated, the great majority are male writers. Besides Clarice Lispector and Luisa Valenzuela, the only women he has translated are Ana Teresa Torres and Irene Vilar—this pattern does not relate to Rabassa's translations alone; it is a function of a male-dominated literary system. Another exclusion of the Boom literature that has been discussed is the neglect of Brazilian developments at the time. Even though the Boom itself contributed, in an indirect way, to a perception of Brazilian literature as an "entity of its own" in the Americas, during the Boom it received less attention than Spanish-language works—which were considered to be representative of all Latin American writing—and was thus not as visible to mainstream audiences.

In this regard, it is significant to note that Rabassa turned to Brazilian literature very early in his career. His translation of Clarice Lispector's *A maçã no escuro* came out in 1967. Although the first works Rabassa translated were the Spanish-language novels that later formed the Boom, and despite the fact that it is the Spanish-speaking writers he translates who have become most famous, out of the totality of the authors from all over Latin America and the Iberian Peninsula whose works he has translated—around thirty—more than ten authors are from Brazil. Rabassa has been translating Brazilian writers ever since the publication of *An Apple in the Dark*.

Nevertheless, Barbosa states that between 1960 and 1979, British and American publishers brought out 330 translations from Spanish, but only sixty-four translations from Brazilian Portuguese. According to her, this situation continues, and "Portuguese is still largely seen as a dialect of Spanish." She believes that, even though Brazilian literature is no longer associated, to such a large extent, "to Portuguese literature or even to a Portuguese-language system, it is translated in the wake of Spanish-American literatures."[14]

As they became accessible through translation, several Latin American novels, but mostly *One Hundred Years of Solitude*, attracted widespread public interest in the literature. They also called attention to Latin American people and culture. But it was precisely this novel, in Gregory Rabassa's excellent translation, as Zavalia puts it, that "set the mould" for what was expected from Latin American writing. It did so to such an extent that "writers who did not fit into the mould were excluded from commercial success."[15] It is a common critical view that magical realism became the "ready-made formula" used to label works produced by America's "southern backyard," be they Latin American or works from Latino communities in the United States.[16] Whether this is a misunderstanding or a real and concrete imposition, critics complain that what publishers and readers look for in Latin American literature is magical realism. As Zavalia explains, writings that stray from the model are marginalized to smaller, more academic publishing presses, and branded as not Latin American enough.[17]

In literature there are market exclusions and institutional exclusions at play. As Franco points out, the literary market exercises its own exclusions and produces a kind of "repressive selectivity" because certain kinds of literature are judged "too marginal to reach the mass public, and there are not enough independent publishers and galleries to serve as a counterbalance."[18] However, internationally, expectations and exclusions sometimes differ. Steenmeijer identifies a difference between the European reception and expectations of contemporary Latin American literature and that of the United States:

> Critics have often lamented the US publishing expectations of Latin American writers to solely produce novels in the magic realist mode. The reception of the new Latin American novel in Europe and the United States is not a single unified story, but a series of microhistories that reflect the reading public, cultural institutions, and the initiative of individual translators, promoters, and agents.[19]

Whether there was indeed a sense of imposed homogeneity, or whether it was a question of rather random preference on the part of the public, magical realism is recognized as the most salient characteristic of Latin American literature in the West. Mudrovcic speculates that if the literature of the Boom had followed a different pattern of diffusion and consecration, the Latin American canon would likely be a more heterogenous, diverse, and a more open body of texts (and authors): "it would also be a more unstable, and perhaps even more flexible canon."[20] The somewhat rigid standard was partly created by the Boom's critical reception. As Payne notes, as much as they were eager to give the Boom coverage and promote its diffusion, mass-media critics and reviewers played a role in homogenizing and synchronizing the innovations and subtleties of Boom writing, and in representing it "in its mythic-realist dimension."[21] Instead of presenting the Boom as "nothing more than a calculated instance of economic opportunism," these comments illustrate how "a body of literature, selectively produced and disseminated in conjunction with certain cultural crises and the economic demands of consumer culture, becomes subject to extremely limited possibilities of interpretation within that culture."[22]

If translation inscribes, reshapes, and at times domesticates works and traditions, it follows that it participates in the exclusions resulting from canon-formation processes. The exclusion process has to do not only with the selection of the works translated, but also with their legitimation through interpretation. In this respect, translation not only has to negotiate social and cultural contradictions: it embodies them. Thus, it may reveal them. If exclusion is inherent in translation, it becomes increasingly important to unveil this aspect of the mediation in order to understand the mechanisms through which certain authors and particular types of works are considered "legitimate" or "valuable." The promoters of the Boom opened possibilities for works to be known, and they also restricted access to other works and authors, according to a certain rationale created for and by the canon. It is problematic to see Latin America, in its literary representations, as a conceptual whole. Payne finds it puzzling that "the upsurge in translation that began in the sixties has not, by and large, provided the readership of Latin American literature in the United States with a substantively more complex view of Latin American history and politics. He goes as far as saying that, if translation, in this historical instance, were to provide a solution to cultural misapprehension, "it would have to be described on the whole a failed solution" because the Boom as a phenomenon, he says, appears to have reinforced long-standing exotic and essentializing stereotypes about Latin America.[23]

The position of viewing the Boom solely as a "failed solution" is debatable. As a phenomenon, and as an epoch, the Boom was a creative and productive space. Fredric Jameson—along the lines of several enthusiastic critics—remarks that "Latin American literature since the boom has today become perhaps the principal player on the scene of world literature."[24] However, during and after the Boom, Anglo-American audiences, in particular, related to a specific image of Latin American fiction, which was "premised on a diagnosis of the North American literary scene."[25] This image, conveyed in and through translation, was fragmented and decontextualizing. Mudrovcic discusses how, for example, in the case of the translation of the Boom, some of the selecting criteria—e.g., a modernist aesthetics—often worked as a politics of exclusion more than as a category of inclusion; recognized authors in the Spanish-speaking literary scene were left out of the "international Boom";[26] as this happened, an English-language canon was formed.

One of the "classic" examples of this situation is Ernesto Sábato's *Sobre Héroes y Tumbas*, first published in Buenos Aires in 1961. In the sixties, Sábato was an author as prestigious as Borges or Cortázar and had been translated into several languages. However, twenty years passed between the Argentine publication of the novel and its appearance in English—the translation, by Helen Lane, came out in 1981. Mudrovcic states that, "far from being exceptional, *Of Heroes and Tombs*'s long trek into English is, in the broader context, a more common event than it initially appears to be."²⁷ A different situation, but one that also results from the re-shaping of canon structure as literature travels, is that of Borges's works. Borges was translated into English late, in the sixties, and as a result of his "belated" wide-spread recognition, became a contemporary of the Boom writers; thus, his important role as one of the forerunners of the Latin American fiction of the sixties is often overlooked. There is also the more extreme case of Machado de Assis who, having written in the nineteenth century, is at times read as a contemporary of late twentieth century Brazilian writers.

More recent generations of writers, despite recognizing the significance of the Boom as a literary moment, have shown their desire to distinguish themselves from it. Often, their thematic and aesthetic interests and questions are different from those of their predecessors—witness the aesthetics of the so-called post-Boom and of Latin American writing of today. Comparing post-Boom works with novels from the Boom, one can observe how a form of universalizing impulse has been de-emphasized. Garrels states that she sees in the post-Boom less of an anxiety to define "Latin-Americanness," the "essence" of the continent. She also finds that there is a new, though equally complex, relationship with language, as well as a reflection on contemporary crises of political hegemony that has resulted in a new realism that reflects political changes as well as changes in values.²⁸ There is also an emphasis on local specificity and a stronger presence of an urban ideology, at times articulated around velocity, violence, and death. Some critics argue that the tendencies of the post-Boom writers are partly a reaction against the neo-conventionalism of the Boom.²⁹ This perception is a function of the time and of the institutionalization of avant-garde forms. What was experimental in the sixties lost its newness, its transgressive quality, and became more conventionalized.

Works in translation undergo a process that occurs in complex networks of selection, publishing and distribution.³⁰ The relationship between Latin American literature and the United States publishing industry in the aftermath of the Boom is ambiguous. Today, almost as much as before the sixties, publishers do not want to take great risks with Latin American projects. In general, the translations of foreign fiction constitute a minimum percentage of annual publications in North America. According to the international PEN report on translation and globalization that came out in 2007,³¹ in the U.S. only 3 percent of the books on the market are translations—2 percent in the UK. United States publishers still wait for authors to be translated into other languages before they decide to embark on introducing them to the Anglo-

American audience. Publishers rely on authors whose works have sold well in the past, and on those whose work has similarities to already popular ones. Moreover, they rely on the academic market and on the preferences of other institutional agents. Levine believes that given "the shrinking of the globe and a heightened awareness of the relations among different cultures which began to take foreground in the 1960s," publishers no longer cultivate total isolationism. However, she says, following cultural-political as well as market pressures, they continue to exclude worthy writers.[32]

Susan Sontag noted the relationship between the lack of interest in foreign translations and the hegemony of "colonial" contemporary English. For her, the notion of English as a world language, a language that is, also, the one spoken by the richest and most powerful nation, has a great deal of power when it comes to making decisions about what is translated and what—i.e., large infusions of foreign literature—is simply not allowed to enter.[33] The choices made by Anglo-American translators have an effect on translation worldwide. Esther Allen finds the difficulty that many foreign authors face in having their works translated into English very problematic given the hegemonic position of English: "translating a book into English puts it in a position to be translated into many different languages."[34] This phenomenon underscores the power (and censorship) of the Anglo-American marketplace.

Discussing this situation from the perspective of the reading public, Barbosa has used the metaphor of the "virtual image" to present the foreign reader as an observer who "chooses texts, fictional or otherwise, to perceive reality outside her or his field of vision"; the text thereby becomes "an apparatus that allows the reader to perceive the inner workings" of individuals from different backgrounds, classes, races, and religions, as well as the workings of their environment. Whether it be a traveler's account, a sociological, historical, or geographical account, a film, a radio program, or a translation of a literary work from the other culture, the reader of the translated text has chosen that text as a mediating element to make use of another, intermediary observer. As a result, according to Barbosa, translation may be the most complex of such mediating apparatuses, given that the mechanisms of the production and consumption of texts, which help to shape the image of the object, are duplicated. In the case of the canon of Brazilian literature, as Barbosa remarks, the combined result of the interaction of the forces at play in the publishing of translations (political, economic, marketplace, the randomness of translator choice) is that the virtual image obtained of Brazil by the Anglo-American reading public through literary translation, where some points are magnified while others are reduced, is at best fragmented.[35]

Following the metaphor of the "virtual image," the Latin American novels translated in the sixties, and those that have come in the aftermath of the Boom, constitute the mediating element chosen by Anglo-Americans to construct an image of Latin America. Moreover, as English becomes, increasingly, the world's hegemonic language—i.e., the most widely accepted means of symbolic exchange, to use Cronin's analogy[36]—translation into English becomes a "universal" means of symbolic exchange. Latin American literature in translation is thus, the global "virtual image" of Latin America, to the extent that this image gets realized in and through literature.

Translated Literature as Archive: Macondo and Rabassa's Legacy

> The very act of reading and sharing that knowledge assumes the form of ritual, of celebrating the common knowledge, the transpersonal history. Archives keep the secrets of the state; novels keep the secrets of culture, and the secret of those secrets.
> —Myth and Archive

Literary conventions have a social dimension; they condition works, traditions, and symbolic orderings. As noted in chapter 2 in relation to Rabassa's translations as uncontested literary products, literary conventions "enlist support for a *particular* system of values";[37] literary discourse has an evaluative and persuasive character in that "the more a rhetorical formulation is turned into a commonplace, the more persuasive it will be."[38] Some forms are privileged while others are obscured in the context in which the translator operates. Why do certain works travel? Why certain writers? Why does what gets translated get translated? What does it represent? How does it circulate? When? What gets incorporated into the canon?

Critics and translators play a key role in processes of canon formation. Mudrovcic suggests that, in the formation of the Latin American canon, critics and translators improved the perception and appreciation of Latin American literature but also "produced" it: "its meaning and its value."[39] To understand the social dimension of literary conventions, it is necessary to look at the recombinations generated by diffusion and encounter among works, genres, and traditions. Thus, examining the interpretive value given to the works that Rabassa has translated is another way to discuss the effects of his legacy and, through it, to reflect on the legacy of translators within particular communities and institutions.

Regarding the relationship between prevalent readings of the Boom works and the exclusions deriving from the canon, Mudrovcic suggests that, during the insertion of Latin American literature into the mainstream, there was a preference for works that allowed for "apoliticized" readings, in which national/local specificities could be effaced for more universalized readings, at least those that would help define or understand the "continent."[40] Other critics agree with this view and stress the importance of rethinking the canon to examine its social implications. Payne finds it necessary to discourage attempts to "reduce" the "vast array of history and culture" of a continent to one cultural event, which as a result of the selection and dissemination of a body of literature, "in conjunction with certain cultural crises and the economic demands of consumer culture, becomes subject to extremely limited possibilities of interpretation within that culture."[41] He criticizes readings that turn *One Hundred Years of Solitude* into a novel "large as a continent," and says that this kind of "cultural mythologizing, however enthusiastic," restricts the variety and historical complexity of the literature being embraced, and is problematic, especially inasmuch as the myth relies on "an appeal to exoticism."[42]

Such critical perspective of this aspect of the literary experience does not seek to question the greatness or the importance of the works themselves (i.e., the originals and the translations); rather, it emphasizes the fact that a selection of texts cannot be fully representative of the writing of a designated time or place; it also stresses the importance of contextualizing the works to comprehend their historical relevance, recognizing that literature has a social status as a document that contains particular historical realities.

González Echevarría examines certain myths and misconceptions resulting from the widespread image of Latin American literature created until the seventies, many of which, he says, are due to readings of the canon that became established abroad. As he rightly explains, "the novel, having no fixed form of its own, often assumes that of a given kind of document endowed with truth-bearing power by society." The novel is part of the textual economy, of the discursive totality of a given epoch.[43] He finds a connection between literature and anthropology in that "anthropology is the mediating element in the modern Latin American narrative because of the place this discipline occupies in the articulation of the founding myths by Latin American states."[44] He believes that Latin Americans, as well as other "inhabitants of the postcolonial world" provide a model for a reduction to myths of origin, whereby literary works are read as "timeless stories" about "changeless societies."[45]

One Hundred Years of Solitude, the prototypical novel of Latin American magical realism, has been read as a document. The reality of *One Hundred Years of Solitude*, particularly after translation, has been read as a magical, alien, timeless reality—in the definition of the significance of magical realism the "magical" is often stressed. In his exploration of the possible uses of magical realism in literary history, Franco Moretti explains that after a long history of Western literature, when *One Hundred Years of Solitude* was published, magical realism transported the Western readership to the one continent not mentioned at all in *The Waste Land*. "For the first time in modern history," says Moretti, "the center of gravity of formal creation leaves Europe, and a truly worldwide literary system replaces the narrower European circuit."[46]

This, he remarks, is the reason why no postwar work has been greeted with more enthusiasm in the West than *One Hundred Years of Solitude*. "Does this mean," asks Moretti, "that García Márquez's novel really belongs, like it or not, to the Western tradition?" He believes that it does not, but that it "appeared to be sufficiently at home there to make itself understood, and sufficiently alien to say different things."[47] The West, in particular Europe, "went crazy over *One Hundred Years of Solitude*," says Moretti, because the novel—with gypsies, Arabs, Italians, Jews, French, Spaniards, etc.—was open to the world: "It is a reality that surfaces from the very first words of the novel, with ice and wars." Macondo, says Moretti, is a "m(ac)ondo" (i.e., a world).[48] The novel has a mixed geography, such as the one that, according to Moretti, characterizes world literature: broad, heterogeneous, complex. We may see the world in it but we see it from the periphery.[49]

Cien años de soledad is deeply rooted in history. Yet it is often read as an ahistorical narrative. Although the historical and political aspect of the novel has not been the most explored, it is crucial, as is the fact that the novel is self-reflective and aware of the historical dimension of its narrative significance. Moretti associates the reception of the novel in the West with Europe's coming to terms with its own colonial history.

He notes that, in the sixties, with the withdrawal of colonial powers from Africa, the phase of open colonial conquest had come to an end—the phase of "gunboats" and military violence. "And a novel reaches Europe which recounts those hundred years of history as an adventure filled with wonder." Moretti wonders whether this is, perhaps, the secret of *One Hundred Years of Solitude*.[50] He finds that, in any event, the novel signaled an "incorporation" of an isolated community being caught up in the modern world-system, subject to rapid changes and to an "extremely violent acceleration," leading to "uneven and combined development."[51] In light of readings such as Moretti's, the novel is, importantly, about the unfolding of the neo-colonial world and the contemporary global order.

One Hundred Years of Solitude as a magical narrative of wonder is, thus, a result of a process of reception and commentary. Nevertheless, such a representation is still in effect, and its implications are rather problematic within and beyond the world of literature. Describing Colombia in particular as "an effect of Gabo's writings," the Colombian scholar Armando Silva calls for a rethinking of the images and symbols most often associated with the country:

> In his voluptuous writing, García Márquez has constructed and exported us as a happy, irresponsible world. This world needs to find direction in order to prevent death in the Hegelian diatribe of ahistorical subjects. Colombian reality has gone astray; it's lost and it's fed up with war. We Colombians are dominated by the repeated accounts of abuses, kidnappings and deaths in our daily news, and there's a delirious sense of death's inevitability. Colombian reality remains an unredeemable fantasy, closer to a false paradise.[52]

In translation, the Colombian novel *One Hundred Years of Solitude* stands as a document about Latin America. The novel—as I previously indicated—is not ahistorical. Clearly, as González Echevarría asserts, *One Hundred Years of Solitude* is self-reflexive, and it is so "not merely to provoke laughter or to declare itself literary and thus disconnected from reality or history." The formal aspects of García Marquez's writing and of other experimental writing from Latin America, and their self-reflexivity, are ways of "disassembling the mediation through which Latin America is narrated, a mediation that constitutes a pre-text of the novel itself."[53] This narrative language provides a counterpoint to other forms of historical discourse.

Cien años de soledad is Melquiades's manuscript. As González Echevarría puts it, novels are not content with fiction; "they must pretend to deal with the truth, a truth that lies behind the discourse of the ideology that gives them form."[54] The novel functions both as a myth and as a document. In the archive, says González Echevarría, the presence of Melquiades—the manuscript's writer—and that of Aureliano—who has the task of deciphering it—is "an insurance that the individual consciousness of a historian/writer will filter the ahistorical pretense of myth by subjecting events to the temporality of writing."[55] At the end of the novel, these oracular figures, which, according to González Echevarría, are links with the past and living archives, i.e., repositories of knowledge, die. The manuscript, which stands for a fragmented, unfinished historical narrative, in the end is not deciphered.

Framed within a historicizing reading, *One Hundred Years of Solitude* is not a story of magic, charm and wonder, detached from history. The novel is opaque and deceptive, it defies literal readings. Among other questions, it points to the absence of an existing language to capture experience. One of the first lines in the novel, "The world was so *recent* that many things still *lacked names*, and in order to indicate them one had to point,"[56] establishes that lack of language and positions the enunciation temporally—"recent"—thereby marking its historicity.

Critics and reviewers remark on the centrality of the story of the United Fruit Company to the novel, partly as a marker of its historical-political dimension. However, as Martin remarks, few critics have realized just how profoundly the episode of the banana company is the heart of it. The arrival of the company is announced in the novel with the arrival of "The innocent yellow train that was to bring so many insecurities and uncertainties, so many joys and misfortunes, so many changes, calamities and nostalgias to Macondo."[57]

As Martin points out, García Márquez was born in 1928, the very year in which the historic massacre took place in Colombia.[58] The "innocent" train brings "the multinational banana company, United States imperialism, and eventual disaster" a logical sequence of events explained by the author himself, and that has "little to do with pigs' tails," as Martin puts it;[59] the event narrated is real, not a fiction, it is connected to Colombian history and with the country's peripheral position with the advent of modernization, and constitutes a metaphor for its condition of modernity. There is nothing "magical" about it.[60] The novel, like an omen, signals the economic decline of the southern part of the Americas. Rather than a novel disconnected from reality and history, Moretti also argues, the United Fruit Company episode proves that *Cien años de soledad* depicts a history of "black magic," of "the enormity of the crimes committed, the trains loaded with corpses, which vanish from the collective memory as though it had never been."[61] In the narrative act, language and history are superimposed in the literary work. Moretti views the narrative form as marked by inevitability and failure: "A thousand and one possibilities," says Moretti, "then really do become a thousand and one dead ends," and the multiplicity of possible developments, "a set route."[62] *Cien años de soledad* is, thus, a narrative of confusion and desperation—perhaps even madness—rooted in the economic, political, and social realities of its moment. Franco has also remarked that, in *One Hundred Years of Solitude*, the change that comes from the outside is a degeneration. Many writers of the Boom generation, says Franco, experienced history as a cycle of failed experiments; in their novels, they re-enact the inevitable foundering of those other booms—of rubber or coffee, or bananas or mining—that left the landscape marked by the "monuments of failure."[63] At the end, the state wins, says Moretti, the war ends, and Macondo comes back into contact with the outside world—more precisely the United States—and what "suddenly becomes clear is Macondo's role in the international division of labour." The United Fruit Company episode, Moretti concludes, signals "the turning-point from which Macondo will never manage to recover."[64]

What, then, to make of the novel's "myth" form? Martin explains that the myth is in essence about the relation of the New World to the Old as it tells the story of discovery and conquest, which is "endlessly reproduced and repeated, and of desperate struggles, usually fruitless, to resist, rebel and liberate, to overcome solitude and attain some kind of unity and identity;" it shows how art can sometimes "make itself the written record of that memory, and thus unite past, present and future at the level of representation."[65]

Cien años de soledad is structured using a conventional mythical form. Archival fictions are mythic inasmuch as they deal with origin, i.e., the beginning of history, or a commonly accepted source of culture, in a thematic or in a semiotic way.[66] They have a "dispersive quality," says González Echevarría, and the power to negate previous narrative forms and to question received knowledge and its "ideological coagulations as identity, culture, educational institutions, even language."[67] The dispersive quality of *Cien años de soledad* is one of the reasons that it has become the quintessential novel of Latin America. As an archive, says González Echevarría, this novel has an accumulation function and appears "made up of a series of high points common to the whole continent and reducible to a single, shared story."[68]

Comparing these—historicized, politically-aware—readings of *Cien años de soledad* with more prevalent readings, which overemphasize the "magical" and underestimate the value of the "real" in magical realism, underscores the fact that turning *One Hundred Years of Solitude* into a narrative of magic and wonder has effects within and beyond the literary. To the extent that such narrative of magic is, in turn, an effect of the novel's reception, it is an effect of translation. In the realm of representation, as much as it is "an effect of Gabo's writing"—to follow Silva's claim—the narrative of *One Hundred Years of Solitude* is also an effect of Rabassa's translation. In the most canonized and privileged reading of the novel—i.e., as a narrative of magic and wonder—magic is complicit with empire.

The political reality of Latin America is very present, not only in García Márquez's writings, but also in those of many others from the Latin American tradition. Martin notes an ever-growing self-consciousness of narrative fiction in Latin America since the sixties, which he finds to be part of a continuing tradition of responsibility and commitment to those "external others whose existence and predicament pose particularly pressing questions of self-definition and conscience for the Latin American intellectual."[69] The writers of the Boom had come to see—largely thanks to the Cuban Revolution—"that no writer could produce the Great Latin American novel without a consciousness of colonialism as the determining structural fact of Latin American history, and without integrating this consciousness into the very structure of his or her fiction."[70] What happens to the "effects" of their writings after translation? What aspects of the interpretation travel? Which ones are rejected, obscured, or simply left behind? When does an interpretation become "global?" Magical realism has been institutionalized through privileged readings as a result, at least in part, of the internationalization of the Spanish-speaking novel. Moretti believes that it has played a particular role in the West, for, in an effort to satisfy the desire of contemporary societies for "meaning, imagination, re-enchantment . . . we are ready to believe almost anything about what is far away from us. It was true for the crónicas of the Conquista, and it has been true again for magical realism."[71] This desire informs the canonical readings and interpretations of the novel.

Investigating the social dimension of literary conventions sheds light on how processes of canon formation relate to questions of culture contact, negotiation of difference, and understandings of the world and of the other. As the metaphor of the "virtual image" also suggests, literary works in translation are perceived not only as a possibility of access to a foreign imagination, but as documents to explain alien realities *through images*. The Boom novels were seen as archival sources, having a documenting value. There may even have been an expectation set in place about the function of *One Hundred Years of Solitude* from the start. As a 1970 review of the novel remarked, "Macondo is Latin America in microcosm."

This statement seems to have marked the path of reception the novel was to follow in translation. If such statements are taken at face value, then it is all the more necessary to follow the itinerary of the novel—i.e., of literature—as it moves across time, across borders, and outside of the world of literature itself, to understand their interplay with other forms of discourse. How far does translation go? How far has Rabassa gone? As he says, he did not foresee that *One Hundred Years of Solitude* would become so "big." Works that travel enter, in one way or another, into contact and form a relationship with dominant ideology and hegemonic discourse.[72] *One Hundred Years of Solitude*, other novels, and even Rabassa's translations as a body of work, may have served as political instruments at certain points in time. Addressing this aspect of literature and of translation is by no means a simplistic attempt to render works, authors, or translators individually accountable. It is a way of examining the paths followed by translated narratives, which, as narratives, are never merely a "self-contained discourse nor a raw reflection of sociopolitical conditions; but in productive and determining relationships with non-literary forms of discourse."[73] Through this mode of reflection we can also see the extent to which literary works and their translations participate in shaping—and have the potential to shape—the collective imagination.

One Hundred Years of Solitude was the first Latin American novel ever to achieve international best-seller status. It is said to have been the most widely read novel in the twentieth century—Martin states that only Shakespeare and his works can claim such widespread and instant recognition.[74] Critics discuss the potential risks of decontextualization, particularly as they note the truth-bearing value of literary works taken as documents. In the case of *One Hundred Years of Solitude*, Martin goes as far as stating that no misreading has been more serious for Latin American literary history than the "mythreading" of its most celebrated work.[75] Payne also warns against overusing a representation of "the power of imagination," as conceived by García Márquez, in the United States cultural debate about the literature of replenishment. If linked with its more patently economic dimension, he says, one can see how such a myth might conform uncritically to the expansionist narrative of unlimited Western progress and to the contours of United States capitalist consumer culture; imagination would be, in this version, a "utilitarian concept with little potential for representing otherness in its manifold nuance and historical fullness."[76]

But it is not Macondo nor the novel in translation per se, that generates the image of replenishment; it is a foreign gaze, perhaps the appropriation of the symbol. *One Hundred Years of Solitude,* the "Great American novel," combines magic and history. This leads to the question of what foreign—especially Anglo-American—readers saw in the book, and whether what they saw was in fact in the novel, as a text and as part of a particular textual economy. The privileged reading of the novel was shaped partly on the basis of the circulation and perpetuation of preconceived representations, which are reinforced through the tension between magnified and reduced images. Translation is potentially "misleading," as Rabassa tells us, speaking of the ambiguities inherent to translation if it is understood as a form of writing.[77] Translators are not the only agents that participate in the "translating event." As subjects that exist in history, translators expose the negotiations and disparate interests that may be at stake in the translating exchange, whereby individual texts are part of universes of discourse.

It is worth asking, at this point, what do we learn from *Cien años de soledad?* And can it be learned from *One Hundred Years of Solitude?* However circular the interpretation may be, and to whatever extent the international reception of *One Hundred Years of Solitude* may have influenced the interpretation in the context of the Spanish-language literary scene and readership, the sound of *One Hundred Years of Solitude* is an English-language sound. This is the "recontextualizing" aspect of translation, in which the difference of the text lies in its materiality. It takes up a different body. In *One Hundred Years of Solitude* some see magic and unbelievable wonders, some see anguish and pain. In both cases, the novel is perceived as a repository of the history of Latin America.

According to González Echevarría, from the novel we learn that while its writing may be "mired" in myth, it cannot be turned into myth. The novel is about a "new" world—"new," that is, historical and subject to change. This newness "makes it impervious to timelessness, circularity, or any such delusion." In a sense, he says, García Márquez has substituted the anthropologist for the historian, and turned "the object of attention away from myth as an expression of so-called primitive cultures to the myths of modern society: the book, writing, reading, instruments of a quest for self-knowledge that lie beyond the solace mythic interpretations of the world usually afford."[78] For González Echevarría, using *Cien años de soledad* to escape temporality is a willful misreading, for the novel does precisely the opposite: it warns us against that.[79]

The novels of the Boom were so attractive, at least in part, because they connected life and history, i.e., they documented a reality. As Franco explains, in the sixties and seventies the prestige of literature derived, in part, from the alternative realities it represented.[80] But, as García Márquez reminds us, "those who read stories read the story of their own lives, and the consciousness of author, character and reader slide into overlap again."[81] Certainly, that which can be learned in *Cien años de soledad* is there to be learned in *One Hundred Years of Solitude* as well.

Narratives in translation exist in a continuum that is connected to that of the contact between languages. As Cronin puts it, "the power nexus between languages is constantly shifting so that our translation relationships have to be endlessly calibrated."[82] If we believe that the relationships between languages are reenacted in translation, narratives in translation ought to be revisited in light of this continuous relation. Examining the archival value of the novels, as says Nunn, is critical to an understanding of the intellectual and cultural response to domestic and international developments of a social, economic, environmental, and political nature in the twentieth century.[83] This circumstance is currently relevant to translation of Latin American literature in various respects, for we must ask, as he notes, what will generate translation? Quality, author-identification, place in canon, or the market place? Will canonization and the image of Latin America conveyed through translation influence history as much as the "new novel" has been influenced by history? Will foreign views of Latin America continue to be shaped by what is read in translation?"[84] The answers to these questions are different now, after the Boom and in its aftermath, and require engaging its critique. Levine, for instance, posits that the novel as a genre and medium has to come into question in general, and then in the Latin American case. She notes that, even though it is difficult to foresee the future of the Latin American novel translated into English, one question to ask is, "in the global marketplace, will the novel (and not only the

Latin American novel) as innovation and not mere commodity survive technology's vertiginous spin into the future?"[85]

Rabassa's material, symbolic, intellectual, and institutional contribution is undeniable. As for the question of the actual scale of his legacy, it may be "too soon to tell"—to use Gayatri Spivak's words as she addressed the question of Derrida's legacy. As Spivak points out, the idea of legacy is, on the one hand, "tied to reproductive heteronormativity, and even the most literal notion of heir is metaphoric, insofar as a legacy is what promises an imaginary continuity for an individual: succession, immortality, transcendence."[86] Levine, for example, will have her own thoughts about the significance of her translations—of Puig and Cabrera Infante, for instance—or about a male translator's legacy vis-à-vis that of a woman translator. It is an ambiguous task to speak of a translator's legacy, to do justice to her or his work and put it in perspective. Spivak believes that Derrida's legacy, performed in his writings, speaks of a "difference to come," which could be interpreted as an invitation "to face forward."[87] Perhaps understanding someone's legacy is, importantly, a matter of looking forward.

Rabassa's translations are foundational. As a translating subject, and given the complexity of cultural contact in the Americas, his work goes far beyond the idea of translation as a harmonious and transparent "bridging of cultures"; Rabassa has participated in the translation negotiations among communities between the south and the north. As a writer of narratives in translation, Rabassa not only inscribed his translations as texts; he participated in creating their "meaning and their value." The direction that Latin American letters have taken and will continue to take after the Boom will occur as a result of the spaces opened up and the images created by his practice, and within the institutional space that now exists among the reading communities that have granted Latin American literature a place of recognition.

Rabassa has been a careful, enthusiastic, and respectful reader. He has also created a mode in which literature travels and disseminates. The questions posed by Nunn and Levine will undoubtedly be answered by the literary and reading community he has helped create and those that will follow. Inasmuch as this is the case, the answers will relate to Rabassa and his practice. They will also relate to structures and forces analogous to those that have played a role in it through the years. As an ethical subject, Rabassa faces the tensions of his position as the agent of a cultural practice. As a translator, Rabassa embodies a particular experience of cultural and linguistic contact in the Americas. Significantly, he has embraced ambiguity and uncertainty. His ethical position can inform our thinking about translation, for, within that indeterminate space, translation remains possible, and the translator's task, legitimate. After Rabassa, and following his lead, translators will face questions regarding the specificity of translating Latin American literature into English. Who will translate?

Afterword

Translation is a practice of negotiation that occurs in dynamic social spaces. This book was a study of the legacy of Gregory Rabassa as a translator in the configuration of Latin American literature as it is known today, as well as the complex interplay of forces within which he operates and the extent to which his practice is bound to communities and institutions. It emphasizes the plural and relational nature of the translator's space, in an effort to characterize translation as a form of writing that unfolds within complex interactions and negotiations. In recent years, there has been an increasing interest in translation studies to conceptualize the translator as a historicized agent in the production of culture. This book was conceived from that perspective and taking as a point of departure theoretical questions and assumptions that originate in it. It is premised on a view of the translator as a subject in history who participates in the construction of narratives that are associated with cultures and with communities. It understands translation as a continuum that involves selecting the texts and engaging them intellectually and politically, as well as influencing the status the texts will have in and across literary traditions after translation.

As a translator for several decades, Rabassa has been an active agent in the traveling of Latin American narratives to English-speaking readerships; he embodies the value and power of the translator. Thus, by placing Rabassa at the center of inquiry I was able to look at his life and works. Also, since he is a recognizable individual, as a translating subject, Rabassa served as a common referent to speak about translators at large. To me, studying Rabassa's legacy was also a form of recognition of the translator's participation in literature.

I used translators' documents (drafts, manuscripts, correspondence, etc.) because I was interested in exploring their scholarly value as archival material—an area that has barely been explored in translation studies. I believe that these documents are important elements in tracing the relations inherent in translation. I incorporated Rabassa's documents (his articles and reviews, his memoir, as well as drafts and interviews—including my own) as research materials that, besides being part of the totality of the translator's body of work, are also symptomatic, or rather, reflexive, of the translator's practice. Moreover, they are a way to render the translator's voice. It was important for me to find a way to engage the texts without taking them strictly at face value. In this case, by integrating Rabassa's reflections on his practice I was able to reflect on his conceptions about language, textuality, and translation. I was also able to explore the translator's ethics—particularly the question of embracing uncertainty, what I called Rabassa's "ethics of doubt"—to a point that might not have been possible without his documents.

Another goal of this study was to investigate the translator-author relationship. Particularly in light of theoretical issues in contemporary translation studies—such as those addressed by Cronin, Venuti, Arrojo, or Robinson, for example—that problematize the role of the author in relation to questions of discourse and textuality, it becomes relevant to examine the relationships between authors and translators—the actual interaction, as well as their status and their expectations. I conceptualized the figure of the translator alongside that of the author, independent but in conversation with the author. My exploration of Rabassa's experiences with his authors and the reflection on the nature of the translator-author relationships in Rabassa's translating practice were partly aimed to illustrate this aspect of the plurivocity of translation.

A number of Rabassa's translations have become "classics"; as a translator—which is not usual—he has become a household name among the Anglo-American reading communities who are interested in Latin American—and world—literature. I was able to foreground the important role of translation, and of Rabassa, in the very configuration of what is known as Latin American literature today—particularly in the formation of the Boom. During the research, the question of Rabassa's institutional status in the Anglo-American literary milieu became increasingly central. Through the examination of his translation processes, it became evident that the formation of the international canon of Latin American literature, particularly in the sixties, and the selection, production, diffusion, and reception of the works, were intricately intertwined with translation.

I explored the translation of Latin American literature as a process bound to individual subjects and performed in social contexts with institutional, artistic, and symbolic dimensions. Studying Rabassa, I found it crucial to reflect on translation in terms of cultural capital—to use Bourdieu's term—to view it in terms of social processes, production, and value. I have shown the connection between the status of translated literature and the political situation of the sixties and seventies, particularly with the material conditions of possibility of the Boom—also of magical realism—a connection that Franco, among others, has documented, in terms of the relationship between literary and aesthetic values and cold war politics. Looking at the translator's role from the perspective of the relationship between culture and politics offers numerous possibilities of analysis. It would be worth exploring, for example, the consequences of this connection—politically and aesthetically—for the translation and the production and circulation of Latin American literature today.

The final section in this book emphasized the extent to which Rabassa's translations—i.e., texts in the English language, a number of which have become canonical, such as *One Hundred Years of Solitude*—have been taken as documents. These texts are part of the Latin American archive—in Foucault's sense—in that they count as memory and are treated in their truth-bearing value. Documents have the potential of representing a community. Rabassa's translations of Latin American literature have, indeed, participated in constructing collective narratives and representations of Latin American peoples. Thus, given the cultural complexities of the Americas—the north-south divide, the neocolonial reality—it may not be enough to hear the voices of the "other" America but to understand how these voices are created, reconstructed, and recontextualized. Rabassa's practice and his legacy are but one example of the potential of translation to enable, as well as enact, hemispheric exchange.

Even though there already exists a body of works about the experience of translation in the Americas, particularly from recent years, there is still a lot of work to be done in translation studies in this area. It is worth exploring the question that critics such as Pérez Firmat pose, of whether the Americas have a common literature, or rather, a *literatura americana*, in light of translation. Translation is vital to understanding the literature of the Americas, both because of its concrete role at the intersection between the literatures of the south and of the north, and for its potential, as an image, for a conceptualization of the transcultural experience.

It is my wish that this study will engender other—maybe similar—studies of translator's "sociographies" as well as projects that examine, in one way or another, the experience of translation in the Americas. It may be worth exploring the contribution and legacy of other translators, for example, as well as revisiting Latin American canonical texts through the experience of translation. My project exposed some aspects of the materiality of the process of production inherent in translation, of the ruptures and exclusions inherent in it—particularly in the process of selection of the texts. I hope that, as a result, it will also draw attention to lesser-known narratives.

As a practice of negotiation, translation is also one of power, conflict, and consent. Questions of translation remain increasingly relevant if we want to look at the material and symbolic realities of language contact in our contemporary, fluid, and complex geographies and temporalities. Understood as a global practice, translation is an experience shared by communities throughout the world. Because these fragmented, fluid geographies generate the very possibility of translation, it is precisely in such spaces that translation, and the role of the translator, should be studied. I am certain that important questions of difference and identity, of transcultural negotiations, and of the complexity of cultural contact, can be addressed in and through translation.

Appendix I

Interview with Gregory Rabassa
(New York City, August 1, 2005)

Question: Translators are multifaceted. They possess various identifiable public and professional personae. You are a literary translator and an intellectual, associated with famous writers such as Gabriel García Márquez and Julio Cortázar. Recently you also published the book *If This Be Treason: Translation and Its Dyscontents*. How did these various personae come to life and how do they relate to one another?

Answer: I don't separate these personae, and any difference between them would be accidental or dependent on circumstance. In the book I quote Ortega y Gassett, "yo soy yo y mi circunstancia"; the *yo* is there all the time, under different *circunstancias*. It is more importantly my self, *yo soy yo en mi circunstancia*. The *yo* is always there and you change it to fit. I remember the American actor who was playing Othello and got so involved in the character that he killed his own wife. When an actor takes a role, who is he? That is a danger, to get too deep into one role.

Q: Your writing is playful, it is sincere and ironic at the same time. For *If This Be Treason: Translation and Its Dyscontents* you changed the title of an article you had published in 1984, "Translation and Its Possibilities," to the one you used in the book. Your book is a statement before a jury. It starts with an accusation, "treason," and ends with a verdict. How did you come up with the title and with the structure of the book? Why did you submit the act of translating to judicial inquiry? Are you defending translation? Are you pleading guilty or innocent?

A: I always liked the title because of the Italian comment, *traduttore traditore*. Then I thought of Patrick Henry's line "if this be treason, make the most of it." The challenge is the second part. For the title I was fooling around with words; the "dys" prefix has almost become a cliché today, everything is "dys" this and "dys" that. So I took *Civiliza-*

tion and its Discontents[1] for translation and made it "dys," which changes it to "*dys*-contents." You get a double meaning, which signals the mixed up things you come across in translation. Sometimes they are off, that would be the dys-contents. I used the judicial structure because of the common association of translation with the word "treason," which is a crime. The idea came strictly from the word. Since *traduttore traditore* implies an accusation of translation as being a criminal activity, I put it in the courtroom. That is why I ended up with what they call the Scots verdict. In Scottish jurisprudence the jury can come up with a third verdict, which is very handy, it isn't guilty, it isn't innocent, it is "not proven." So it can go either way. The treason has not been proven, but it may be there.

Q: You have translated mostly living authors. About half of your book is about your authors. You said at Instituto Cervantes in May of 2005 that you want to rely on the authors only when necessary. In any case, you seem to have an exceptionally good relationship with your authors. In fact, collaboration seems to be an important part of your translating practice. What is the nature of the collaboration you have with the authors? What do you expect from the author-translator relationship? What are the mutual expectations?

A: I haven't really had that much collaboration. Cortázar was the exception. A big exception, probably because it was my first translation, I wanted to see what he thought about the translation as it progressed. He read everything and commented on it, we commented back and forth. Most of the time when I was working on his translations he was in Paris, so we discussed them mostly by mail—when he was in New York we wouldn't work. Another author I got to know pretty well was Aguilera Malta. I would consult with him, it was a good relationship. He lived in Mexico so I would see him down there sometimes. And the other one was Luis Rafael Sánchez; we spent some time with him in Puerto Rico, where he is from. In fact we were at the beach in Luquillo with him when I was finishing the translation of *La guaracha*. I'm trying to think about others. I think I sent Vargas Llosa some stuff and he gave me some comments, but not much. In the case of Lezama Lima, our exchange was really through Julio Cortázar, a triangulation, and he was helpful in some ways. Gabo was always off somewhere or other, so for the translations of his works I consulted with a friend, a Colombian doctor—from either Cartagena or Barranquilla—who is also a writer and lives in Long Island. If there was a difficult word I couldn't make out I would call him immediately and he usually knew what it was. But in general I didn't need Gabo that much. There were other writers I could meet easily; Luisa Valenzuela was living in New York. But apart from Cortázar I don't think there was really close collaboration. There are some historical cases, mostly poets, I think, who would sit down together and work through the piece. Not in my case.

Q: The three-volume collection of Cortázar's letters includes several letters that he wrote to you. You were friends. Did you ever talk to him about his own translations, of Yourcenar, for example, or Gide, or Poe?
A: Not really, it's strange. We would talk about the authors but not about the translations. I don't really know what he thought about translation in that sense.

Q: How were other authors helpful? What kinds of questions did you ask Lezama Lima when you were translating *Paradiso?* And Luis Rafael Sánchez? Did you approach them partly because you had the chance to do so or was it because of the nature of their work?
A: I would ask Lezama Lima often questions about words. He would use a word in his own way or he would make up a combination of words and meanings in different ways. In his replies he would partly explain. Mostly, he would push me in the right direction, he'd say, "I was thinking about maybe something like . . . ," or he would give me a reference to some classical work or other that he had in mind. Once I got that, I knew the answer. In the case of Luis Rafael Sánchez, I knew him before I started doing the translation. We had met in Puerto Rico and had hit it off. He is a fun person. He is similar to Julio in the sense that Julio had serious ideas but was never serious about them; he spoke ironically in many ways. Uico too, Luis Rafael—everybody calls him Uico because his nephew couldn't pronounce tío Luis so he would call him Uico.

Q: Did you meet Jorge Franco when you were translating *Rosario Tijeras?*
A: I didn't meet him until the book was finished and he came up to New York for the reading. I didn't have much trouble figuring out what he was saying because the environment of that world was so close to one I know in this country, the druggies, and so I could spot what the slang in the novel would be in English. The only word that I had trouble with was that word for companion . . .

Q: *"Parcero"*?
A: Yes, *"parcero."* Buddy? I had trouble translating that word into English. But I can translate it from Spanish to Spanish, in Cuba it would be *"compinche."*

Q: At the moment you are translating António Lobo Antunes. You have translated his work before. What is this experience like?
A: Among the works by him I have translated this is the "worst" one. This is so good. It is called *Que Farei Quando Tudo Arde?* or "what can I do when everything is on fire?"[2] It is a story based on the life of a famous drag queen in Lisbon. Antunes throws you off because he'll change subjects in the middle of a paragraph, and he changes gender, one person goes from male to female, you have to keep an eye on it. It's like *Finnegans Wake,* that is the closest I can think of in terms of the style, free. There's a touch of Cortázar too.

Q: Have you translated any unpublished manuscripts?
A: Master of the Sea by José Sarney was one. Sarney is a former president of Brazil, but he really was a writer who got into politics. He got to be governor of the state of Maranhão, then vice president, and the president died so he had to take over. Now he's the president of the senate in Brazil. But he is a better novelist. I translated the novel a few years ago at his request and it's just coming out.[3] A second novel may come out, like this one, which finally got published. And I did a Portuguese one, an Azorean book. One of my students gave it to me and I liked it, it is very much like *Cien años*. I did it but couldn't find a publisher at first. A small press run by a former student of mine brought it out. We're having a *lançamento,* a book party, in October in New York. I think the backing of the whole Brazilian establishment will be good for this press.

Q: You mentioned New Directions earlier. Your memoir is one of the few nonfiction books they have published.
A: Yes, they generally publish mostly fiction and poetry. I had always thought of writing a book on translation. They said they'd like to do something when I had it, I signed the contract and started writing a book on translation. When I sent it to them they said, "this sounds like a memoir." They called it a memoir because the editor wanted to give it some kind of literary function. They sprinkled holy water on it and baptized it a memoir. It's the age of the memoir. But I didn't write it

as my memoir; for that I would have put a whole lot of things there — I can write a better memoir than that. I just tied the personal aspects of it with what I was doing in translation.

Q: There has been an increasing interest recently in turning to translator's documents as scholarly materials. Often the relationship an author establishes with a translator is different from that with scholars and critics; authors may be willing to open up to translators more than to critics and scholars. What do you think is unique about the translator-author relationship and about the documents resulting from it? What kind of documents do you have in your archive at Boston University?
A: At first there was some correspondence that I didn't want to send so I sent mostly translation manuscripts and proofs, I wanted to get rid of them. Afterwards I did send letters. Now when I finish something, as soon as it comes out, I pack up the manuscripts and ship them off. In terms of the relationship between authors and translators, I think the important word is "sharing." The translator and the writer "share" something that the critic and scholar don't; the scholar takes its object and works on it, same with the critic. The translator and the writer are putting it together themselves, so even if they don't know each other it's a closer relationship than with the critic because as a translator you are redoing what the author did. Even with a dead author, Machado de Assis for example, I was redoing his work. It's not a question of taking it apart, it's not deconstruction. If it were so it would be like with the Quixote, when the priest and the barber are chasing him and what they do finally is deconstruct him back into Alonso Quijano, who is nobody.

Q: So, would you say that the different nature of the relationship may be due to the materiality of the act, to the fact that the translator deals with the text and the words directly?
A: I think so, yes. The translator has to deal with words like "the," "in," "on," which the reader doesn't always . . . the critic doesn't always . . . All the dust and dirt that's in the book, we have to cover that too.

Q: What do you think of the fact that you are sometimes called the translator of the Boom? Do you think that the works you translated in the sixties and seventies constituted a "replenishment" at a time when North American writing was at a point of "exhaustion?" At this point of your career, how does it feel to have participated in shaping such a crucial moment in Latin American literature?

A: It feels fine [laughs]. I think that the Boom did do that. From the authors that I grew up with in this country, very few—not to reproach this or that—were good writers. They stopped with Faulkner. There is Saul Bellow, for instance, but he is not at the height of the generation of Fitzgerald and Hemingway. One author that needs more attention is Dos Passos, some people are beginning to pick him up. He has much in common with some of the Boom writers in his techniques. I met him in Brazil, he was already in his late years and hadn't been writing much. When I was a teenager, fifteen or sixteen, I read a lot of him, and many others. So I think that there was a gap, indeed. Now going from Faulkner to García Márquez is not difficult at all, or from Dos Passos to Cortázar.

Q: Did you see this as it was happening or is it a perception you have now?

A: I definitely didn't think of it then. I was waiting for the great American novel, which wasn't coming along, but I didn't put two and two together that it was down there. But then it sort of blended in. It happened with French literature also, Camus was about the only writer at the time—I think Sartre's novels didn't think much. The Spaniards sort of picked up from the Latin Americans—plus Spain is a small country. Take the case of Goytisolo, for example. Ah, there is one Spaniard that stands out in my mind, one of "my" authors, Juan Benet. He is one of the difficult ones in a way but I think he's the best. And then you have the Portuguese, of course, Antunes, Saramago, and some others.

Q: How do you see books like those, and even Nobel Prize works, coming into the mainstream U.S. public? Does the U.S. still "yawn at foreign fiction," as the *New York Times* article put it? Is Saramago (to take one example) more widely read now?

A: No. He's read by good readers. Even Bellow is more read; I think that is because he's an American (I was trying to think of Bellow's novels and the one I like best is *Henderson the Rain King*, which doesn't take place in the U.S.). Philip Roth is more read. I think it may have to do with our environment; the American public wants to read what's in its own backyard. But I don't think it's chauvinism, provincialism is a better word. The French are very chauvinistic but they read a lot of foreign literature.

Q: They translate things quicker.
A: António Lobo Antunes had three translations already out that I used to help me with the rough spots: the Spanish, the French, and the German. I don't know about the Italians, they probably had translated him too. So yes, the French had published the novel before the U.S. publisher even got started. For this novel I've been following the other translations—when I don't know what's going on I look at the others. The Spanish and Portuguese mostly just substituted words. The French one dumbed it down; he made it much clearer. What Antunes suggests the translator nailed down. The German is very good. German, like English, is so different from Portuguese, maybe that gives the translator more liberty to do what he's doing rather than follow the language, while the Spanish goes right along with it and the French corrects it.

Q: Speaking of dumbing down translations and of provincialism, how do you negotiate market demands, translation demands, in the English in which you render the works? How do you deal with questions of readability and smoothness? What is the most common reaction from editors to your translations, and has it changed through the years?
A: I don't think of those demands. If you start thinking about that too much you're going to lose it. When I tell somebody what I'm doing when I'm reading García Márquez I say I love reading the Spanish. I read the Spanish, but I'm reading it in English. Then, somewhere in the process, the two come together and the description, what he's telling, can go either way. I just put the English right there. Editors like my translations, and for the most part critics like them too. The only marks I have got are from "Professors Horrendo," who are not really critics. Often critics don't even catch the translation, you just rewrite the thing and as long as it sounds nice to them ... I appreciate critics' comments because I don't do what they do, I rewrite and translate, that's what I do.

Q: It has been suggested that there is a connection between the sixties and contemporary Latin American narrative. At the reading of *Rosario Tijeras* you spoke about Jorge Franco's book as one of the representatives of a new generation of Latin American writers. In your view, is this some kind of Boom? What similarities do you see between this moment and the Boom of the sixties and seventies? Do you think this generation would have international presence as a unity, like the Boom did? Would it be offering any sort of "replenishment?"

A: There is a big difference, I think, between the Boom and this generation, and it is that the Boom writers were not the children of the writers before them. This new generation is the children of the Boom, without the Boom they wouldn't be possible. The Boom writers internationalized Latin American literature. What you had before that was at the level of regional literatures, the Mexicans could only be Mexican, and the gaucho could only mind his own business. It was like that before in the continent, Argentineans didn't know about Mexicans. With the Boom writers, with Carlos Fuentes, and even Rulfo, who is the most Mexican of all, what happens in the novels could happen anywhere. *Pedro Páramo* could have lived in Siberia and you would have the same book. The only difference would probably be the language. This new generation is not fighting against anybody, they are not really antagonistic against their forebearers, whereas the Boom didn't have too high an opinion of the generation before them. For the most part they respected the poets, but not the novelists. The first really good prose to come out of Latin America was that of Machado de Assis, but that is Brazil, there's no Machado de Assis in the Spanish Americas. Brazil has a different literary history, although I think that Guimarães Rosa, for example, could be seen as part of the Spanish American literature. He is like Rulfo, you can't take Guimarães Rosa out of the *sertão*, and yet he could be in Siberia and it would work out. Before the Boom there were some good novels in Spanish America but there was no Flaubert; then these Latin Americans got together almost as if they were one country. You can't compare that phenomenon to any other, there is no other community of nations like that, there is no word for twenty-one French- or English-speaking countries—Africa is a different story. These Latin American authors came together as one country, one literature. And I think the new generation bore on them, in that sense there is continuity.

Q: How are they marking the difference from their forebearers?
A: I think that they may be a little bit more adventurous. I would say that the established writer they seem to follow most, formally, would be Cortázar, or even such writers as Luisa Valenzuela, although she is of a slightly different generation. In general they seem to follow that generation. I don't know where the next generation will go.

Q: Do you think women are more present in Latin American literature now or does it seem, like the Boom, to be characterized predominantly by male writers?
A: I haven't really kept up, but I think there have been a lot of very good women writers, you have Clarice Lispector, Lygia Fagundes, Nélida Piñon, Luisa Valenzuela, they're not exactly of the same generation, maybe a half generation later than Gabo, but they were part of the Boom. It seems to me that women used to be relegated to poetry but now there are more male poets.

Q: Speaking as someone who has spent much of his career as a translator and who has also trained translators, in your opinion what should scholarly work in translation look like? What kind of conversation do you think it would be fruitful for translators to have?
A: I don't know whether they still talk about this, the new critics, but there is a branch called stylistics and I guess that's where translation would fit. A French professor at Columbia had a course called *Le Style*, and that course was about the style of writers. I think you could have analogous translation courses, where you could try to find out about style. On the other hand if you find out that a translator has a style that's probably not good, because as a result García Márquez would sound like Cortázar, for example, and that shouldn't be the case. When I was young I became interested in the Russian novel, and I couldn't figure out why Tolstoy and Dostoyevsky, who were two completely different people, sounded alike. Then I realized that it was because of the translation, both of them sounded like the translator. I think Constance Garnett just used her own style and fit them in it. But for the English reader, they shouldn't sound alike. That's something to watch out.

Q: At Instituto Cervantes you spoke about the dominance of the English language in today's world. You are located in the United States; this is your country and comprises most of your audience. In this context, how does the translator's role look different to you now from what it was thirty years ago? What were the ethical questions then and what are they now?
A: In my case I don't know that it looks very different. For me it feels the same because I follow the text, I just keep doing that. You have to stay on the side of the author, otherwise you are doing a different book, not only in terms of meaning but also of style. And in terms of ethics,

I would say that you should not stick your own attitudes, whatever they are, into the book. Just follow the text, you are García Márquez writing in English. That is the ideal.

Q: As a translator into English, how do you compare yourself to other translators, colleagues of yours in other countries and translating into other languages? What do you think is their experience in terms of the institution of literature, of editorial demands, and so on?
A: I haven't had that much contact. This time with Antunes is the first time I've really worked with the other translations so I can make more of a judgment. But I don't know what they do. I haven't read that many translations, and the only translations I hear people talk about lately, saying they are excellent, are translations into German. I do know a little about the situation in Brazil. Recently I wrote a book review of a translation of *Ulysses* into Portuguese, a very good translation, by Antonio Houaiss. He is a linguist—he compiled a very good dictionary. I think he was paid a little more than what translators are used to getting, but still it isn't that much. Even though the situation is getting a little better, I don't think translation is lucrative here in the States either.

Q: You usually say that your career has been a question of chance all the way. In an interview with Harry Morales you also said that even though you became a translator by chance, you did have your own ideas about language. Do you see translation as a form of writing? Can you identify notions about translation or writing that are foundational to your own translation "theory" and practice?
A: Well, I think translation is the easiest form of writing because you don't have to worry about plot, character, background, all you have to think about is words, and if you come right down to it writing is really about words. When you translate you are writing. To tell a story about the clouds you think of the story. The difference is that in translation somebody has already told the story about the clouds, but you still have to write it. Translation is a rewrite.

Q: You have often translated works by authors whose narrative form is inventive and self-reflective—Lezama, Cortázar, Antunes, to mention a few. You seem to get right at the heart of the problem of untranslatability: you translate the untranslatable. Would you say that your works prove that translation *is* possible?

A: I would and I wouldn't. I do think that translation is impossible if you think you can reproduce, that is, clone; you can't clone from one language to the other because of the sound. Take *"Les sanglots longs des violons de l'automne."* You can't do it because French is French and Spanish is Spanish. That's where the impossibility lies, if we see translation as "cloning." However, you can get pretty close, and that's when we get into the territory of the reader, because nobody can read the same book. When you read a book you are translating it, even if you read it in the same language. Thus translation is possible.

Q: How do you pick your projects now?
A: I don't, they pick me. When something comes along I think about it and if the time is right and I can and want to do it, I do it. Recently I promised to do a 700-page project that will keep me busy for some years. And I was just asked to do a retranslation of *Os sertões* by Euclides da Cunha, which I said I'd do if they wait until I finish this long project. And at New Directions, my publisher, they are trying to get the rights to do a new translation of João Guimarães Rosa's *Grande Sertão: Veredas*, a Brazilian novel which Rodríguez Monegal thought was the best novel written in Latin America in the twentieth century. That one is difficult as well.

Q: Is Machado de Assis one of "your" authors?
A: Definitely, he is the best because he's a classic, you put him next to Flaubert, Tolstoy, Dickens, and he matches them. He's better than Henry James. He is wiser. And he had to be a genius, a poor mulatto boy with no education, who educated himself and got to write such great novels and to found the Brazilian Academy of Letters. And he's so cosmopolitan.

Q: Is there an unfulfilled dream, a book you would like to translate or to have translated?
A: I guess there are a lot of them. Mostly classics, older books. When I did Machado de Assis, that took care of one. In the sixties or seventies I was trying to get someone to publish a book by Lucio Cardoso. The title had caught me first—this is before García Márquez—*Crônica da Casa Assassinada*, It's a family chronicle of a very mixed up family. Someone wanted to get in touch with him for the publication but Lucio had a stroke at the height of his forties. He couldn't speak, you could see the frustration because he wanted to say something but he couldn't.

He took up painting and then he died. I was very upset. There are other authors whose works I wish I had translated or would like to translate. Lima Barreto, for example, a Brazilian who lies between Machado de Assis and contemporary writers—I mention him in my book. I did one of his stories for the Oxford anthology that Echeverría brought out. That's good stuff.

Appendix II: List of translations by Gregory Rabassa

- Aguilera Malta, Demetrio (Ecuador)

Seven Serpents and Seven Moons. Austin: University of Texas Press, 1979.

- Amado, Jorge (Brazil)

Show Down. New York: Bantam Books, 1988.
The War of the Saints. New York: Bantam Books, 1993.
Sea of Death. New York: Avon Books, 1984.
Captains of the Sands. New York: Avon, 1988.

- Andrade, Carlos Drummond de (Brazil)

Travelling in the Family: Selected Poems. New York: Random House, 1986.

- Antunes, António Lobo (Portugal)

What Can I Do When Everything is on Fire? New York: W. W. Norton, 2008.
The Return of the Caravels: A Novel. New York: Grove Press, 1988.
Fado Alexandrino. New York: Grove/Weidenfeld, 1990.

- Asturias, Miguel Ángel (Guatemala)

Strong Wind. New York: Delacorte Press, 1968.
The Eyes of the Interred. New York; Delacorte Press, 1973.
The Green Pope. New York: Delacorte Press, 1971.
Mulata. New York: Delacorte Press, 1967. Published in England as *The Mulatta and Mr. Fly: A Novel.* London: Owen, 1963.

- Benet, Juan (Spain)

Return to Región. New York: Columbia University Press, 1985.
A Meditation: A Novel. New York: Persea Books, 1982.

- Carvalho, Mário de (Portugal)

A God Strolling in the Cool of the Evening: A Novel. Baton Rouge: Louisiana State University Press, 1997. Reprinted by Grove Press (New York: 1997).

- Cortázar, Julio (Argentina)

Bestiary: Selected Stories. London: Harvill Press, 1998.

Hopscotch. New York, Pantheon Books, 1966.
We Love Glenda So Much and Other Tales. New York: Knopf, 1983.
A Change of Light and Other Stories. New York: Knopf, 1980.
A Certain Lucas. New York: Knopf, 1984.
Sixty-Two: A Model Kit. New York, Pantheon Books, 1972.
A Manual for Manuel. New York: Pantheon Books, 1978.
Paris: Essence of an Image. Geneva: RotoVision, 1981.
- Coutinho, Afrânio (Brazil)

An Introduction to Literature in Brazil. New York, Columbia University Press, 1969.
- Donoso, José (Chile)

Taratuta and Still Life with Pipe: Two Novellas. New York: W. W. Norton, 1993.
- França Júnior, Oswaldo (Brazil)

The Man in the Monkey Suit. New York: Ballantine Books, 1986.
- Franco, Jorge (Colombia)

Rosario Tijeras: A Novel. New York: Seven Stories Press, 2003.
- García Aguilar, Eduardo (Colombia)

Boulevard of Heroes. Pittsburgh, PA: Latin American Literary Review Press, 1993.
- García Márquez, Gabriel (Colombia)

The Autumn of the Patriarch. New York: Harper & Row, 1975.
One Hundred Years of Solitude. New York: Harper & Row, 1970.
Chronicle of a Death Foretold. New York: Knopf, 1983. Also published in England by J. Cape (London, 1982).
Innocent Eréndira, and Other Stories. New York: Harper & Row, 1978.
Leaf Storm, and Other Stories. New York: Harper & Row, 1972.
In Evil Hour. New York: Harper & Row, 1979.
Collected Novellas. New York: HarperPerennial, 1990.
Collected Stories. New York: Harper & Row Publishers, 1978.
Cuba, Mi Amor. Castro, Fidel, García Márquez, Gabriel, Gorgoni, Gianfranco, and others. Verona, Italy: Adriano Parise Stampatore, 1990.
- Goytisolo, Juan (Spain)

Marks of Identity. New York: Grove Press, 1969.
———. Trans. Gregory Rabassa. Champaign, IL: Dalkey Archive Press, 2007.
- Lezama Lima, José (Cuba)

Paradiso. New York: Farrar, Straus and Giroux, 1974.
- Lins, Osman (Brazil)

Avalovara. New York: Knopf, 1980.

- Lispector, Clarice (Brazil)

The Apple in the Dark. Austin: University of Texas Press, 1967. Also published by Knopf (New York, 1967).

- Machado de Assis, Joachim Maria (Brazil)

The Posthumous Memoirs of Brás Cubas: A Novel. New York: Oxford University Press, 1997.

Quincas Borba. New York: Oxford University Press, 1998.

- Melo, João de (Portugal)

My World is Not of this Kingdom. Minneapolis: Aliform Publishing, 2003.

- Moraes, Vinicius de (Brazil)

The Girl from Ipanêma. Merrick, NY: Cross-Cultural Communications, 1982.

- Mujica Lainez, Manuel (Argentina)

Bomarzo: A Novel. New York: Simon and Schuster, 1969.

- Oliver Labra, Carilda (Cuba)

Dust Disappears. Merrick, NY: Cross-Cultural Communications, 1995.

- Pires, Fernando (Brazil)

Fazendas: The Great Houses and Plantations of Brazil. New York: Abbeville Press, 1995.

- Ribeiro, Darcy (Brazil)

The Brazilian People: The Formation and Meaning of Brazil. Gainesville: University Press of Florida, 2000.

- Sánchez, Luis Rafael (Puerto Rico)

Macho Camacho's Beat. New York: Pantheon Books, 1980.

- Sarney, José

Master of the Sea. Minneapolis: Aliform Publishing, 2005.

Saraminda: Black Desire in a Field of Gold. Minneapolis: Aliform Publishing, 2007.

- Torres, Ana Teresa (Venezuela)

Doña Inés vs. Oblivion: A Novel. Baton Rouge: Louisiana State University Press, 1999. Also published by Grove Press (New York, 1999).

- Trevisan, Dalton (Brazil)

The Vampire of Curitiba and Other Stories. New York: Knopf, 1972.

- Valenzuela, Luisa (Argentina)

The Lizard's Tail: A Novel. New York: Farrar, Straus, and Giroux, 1983.

- Vargas Llosa, Mario (Peru)

Conversation in the Cathedral. New York: Harper & Row, 1975.

The Green House. New York: Avon Books, 1965.

- Vilar, Irene (Puerto Rico)

A Message from God in the Atomic Age. New York: Pantheon Books, 1996.
The Ladies' Gallery: A Memoir of Family Secrets. New York: Other Press, 2009.
- Zárate Moreno, Jesús (Colombia)

Jail. Minneapolis: Aliform Publishing, 2003.

Appendix III

LIST OF CONTENTS

1. Annotated draft of the opening page of *One Hundred Years of Solitude* (1 page).
2. Copy of *Rayuela* sent by Cortázar to Rabassa with annotations (2 pages).
3. Annotated manuscript of *Hopscotch* (1 page).
4. Draft of *Paradiso*'s translation with Lezama and Rabassa's annotations (1 page).
5. Annotated draft of *Macho Camacho's Beat* with Sánchez and Rabassa's annotations (1 page).
6. Annotated draft of *Rosario Tijeras* (1 page).

(Years 1)

Many years later, ~~facing~~ as he faced the firing-squad, Col. Aureliano Buendía would remember that distant afternoon when his father ~~took~~ had taken him to ~~see what~~ discover ice ~~was~~. Macondo was at that time a village of twenty adobe huts built on the bank of a river ~~with~~ of clear water~~s~~ that ran along a bed of polished stones, that were white and enormous, like prehistoric ~~bones~~ eggs. The world was so recent that many things lacked names, and in order to indicate them it was necessary to point ~~at them~~. Every year, ~~in~~ during the month of March, a family of ragged gypsies would set up their tent near the village, and with a great uproar of pipes and kettledrums they would show off ~~the~~ new inventions. First they brought the magnet. A heavy gypsy, with an untamed beard and ~~the~~ hands ~~of a sparrow~~ sparrow, who introduced himself ~~with the name of~~ as Melquíades, put on a truculent, public demonstration of what he himself called the eighth wonder of the learned alchemists of Macedonia. He went from house to house dragging two metal ingots, and everybody was ~~startled~~ amazed to see pots, pans, tongs, and braziers ~~tumbling~~ tumble down from their places~~, and the~~ as beams creaked ~~from~~ with the desperation of ~~the~~ nails and screws ~~as they tried to get out~~ trying to emerge, and even ~~lost~~ objects that had been lost for a long time appeared from where they had been ~~looked for the most~~ most searched for, and went dragging along in turbulent ~~the~~ confusion behind ~~the~~ magical irons ~~of~~ Melquíades. "Things have a life of their own," the gypsy proclaimed with a harsh accent, "it's ~~only~~ simply a matter of waking up their souls." José Arcadio Buendía, whose unbridled imagination always went beyond the genius

HOPSCOTCH

A Gregory Rabassa

Querido amigo:

A veces subrayo simplemente una palabra o frase. Just a 'red light' for you to be on your guard.

A veces pongo un equivalente en inglés, pero eso no quiere decir que lo considere la traducción exacta, puesto que sé muy poco inglés. Lo hago para darle una idea de lo que quise decir.

Le pido perdón si a veces "aclaro" cosa que Vs. ha de conocer muy bién. Pero trato de ayudarlo más posible. Muchas veces me siento muy culpable al aclarar palabras que usted no ignora.

Siempre que viene el tiempo fresco, o sea al medio del otonio, a mí me da la loca de pensar ideas de tipo eséntrico y esótico, como ser por egenplo que me gustaría venirme golondrina para agarrar y volar a los país adonde haiga calor, o de ser hormiga para meterme bien adentro de una cueva y comer los productos guardados en el verano o de ser una bívora como las del solójicO, que las tienen bien guardadas en una jaula de vidrio con calefación para que no se queden duras de frío, que es lo que les pasa a los pobres seres humanos que no pueden comprarse ropa con lo cara questá, ni pueden calentarse por la falta del querosén, la falta del carbón, la falta de lenia, la falta de petrolio y tamién la falta de plata, porque cuando uno anda con biyuya ensima puede entrar a cualquier boliche y mandarse una buena grapa que hay que ver lo que calienta, aunque no conbiene abusar, porque del abuso entra el visio y del visio la dejeneradés tanto del cuerpo como de las taras moral de cada cual, y cuando se viene abajo por la pendiente fatal de la falta de buena condupta en todo sentido, ya nadie ni nadies lo salva de acabar en el más espantoso tacho de basura del desprastijio humano, y nunca le van a dar una mano para sacarlo de adentro del fango enmundo entre el cual se rebuelca, ni más ni meno que si fuera un cóndoR que cuando joven supo correr y volar por la punta de las altas montanias, pero que al ser viejo cayó parabajo como bombardero en picada que le falia el motor moral. ¡Y ojalá que lo que estoy escribiendo le sirbalguno para que mire bien su comportamiento y que no searrepienta cuando es tarde y ya todo se haiga ido al corno por culpa suya!

CÉSAR BRUTO, *Lo que me gustaría ser a mí si no fuera lo que soy* (capítulo: Perro de San Bernaldo).

COPIES OF ANNOTATED DRAFTS AND MANUSCRIPTS 155

Everytime it starts to get cool, I mean in the middle of autim, I start
gettin nutty ideas like I was thinkin about what was forein and diffrent,
like for exsample how I'd like to turn into a swallow and get away and fly
to countrys where it gets hot, or be an ant so's I could get deep into a cave
and eat the stuff I stored away durin the summer or be a snake like what they
got in the zoO, the ones they keep lockt up in glass cages thats heated so's
they dont get stiff from the cold, which is what happens to poor human beans
who cant buy no close cause the price is to high, and cant keep warm cause theys
no keroseen, no coal, no wood, no fule oil and besides theys no loot, cause
when you go around with bocoo bread you can go into any bar and get some sneaky
pete that can be real warmin, even tho it aint good to overdo it cause if you
overdoes it it gets to be a bad habbit and bad habbits is bad for your body just
like they is for youre selfrespeck, and when you start goin downhill cause your
actin bad in everythin, they aint nobody or nothin can stop you from endin up a
stinkin piece of human garbidge and they never gone give you a hand to haul you
up outen the dirty muck you rollin around in, not even if you was a eaglE when
you was young and could fly up and over the highest hills, but when you get old
you like a highflyin bomber thats lost its moral engines and fall down outen the
sky. I jes hope what I been writin down hear do somebody some good so he take a
good look at how he livin and he dont be sorry when it too late and everythin is
gone down the drain cause it his own fault.

CÉSAR BRUTO, What I Would Like to Be If I
Wasn't What I Am (Chapter: "A St. Bernard Dog").

sunsún: (orn) humming bird, pájaro mosca, colibrí.
filipina: casaca que usaban los criados, de tela blanca, abotonada, con cuello alto. Se supone que deba su nombre al hecho de haberse comenzado su uso en las islas Filipinas, cuando España dominaba allí.[16]

or I'll give you a pinch
and you won't be the same.

The metallic sound of reveille seemed to be pushing him toward the center of the parlor. At that moment the dust in the light filtering in through a sepia-blue louver began to slip across his hair.

Señora Rialta and her mother were whispering about the secret of double-yolk sweets. Señora Augusta -- Grandmother -- a woman from Matanzas most faithful to her creamy home-made sweet nothings: I would call the yolks a double *hummingbird*. Her blue dress was lost in a search for lace that would go with something blue. Finally she decided in favor of what she thought was simplicity, lace that was also blue, giving the sensation of those expensive dolls wrapped in *Filipina jackets* worthy of an equerry, or the elegance shown simply in the ceramic rose of the cheeks or fingernails. At that moment Juan Izquierdo, the cook, passed in front of them. It was the third day of the week, which meant that his white suit and white vest were showing a part of the ominous total of some residue from his gastronomical art. "Pooh," he said. "What do they know about sweet yolks today. They're

¿no no a qué si you?

You
IF ~~THEY~~ TURN around now, a cautious turn, a cautious look,
you
~~they~~'ll see her sitting and waiting, calmness or the shadow of
calmness passing through her. She's got a dreamer's face, a wake
                                                          you
me up and touch me face, her legs crossed in a cross. ~~they~~'ll see
her sitting and waiting on a sofa: her arms open, bracelets on her
arms, a small watch on one wrist, rings on her fingers, over her
left heel an anklet with a trinket on it, on each leg a knee, on
each foot a striking big shoe. A restless body, she has a body of
                                 you
oh x cut it out, can (~~nosy~~ see?), a body that she sits down, lays
down out, and plops onto a sofa upholstered with a woolen material
that's useful for overcoming polar chills but most unreal for any
use in these tristes tropiques: the sun carries out an ungodly
vendetta here, it stains the skin, prostitutes the blood, roils
the senses: here (in) Puerto Rico, the successive colony of two empires
and an island in the Archipelago of the Antilles. Sweaty too,
you
~~they~~'ll see her waiting sweaty, sweaty and plopped onto a sweaty *¿qué*
ploppy sofa, a sweaty ploppy sofa that changes into a bed ~~that~~   *quiere*
                                                                     decir
changes into a sofa, an elegant member of a transvestite domestic   *esto?*
                           you
cast that can do everything. /The way her can can./ If ~~they~~ turn
                                              you
around now, a cautious turn, a cautious look, ~~they~~'ll see her
waiting, sweaty, in spite of the shower of a little while ago. Did
they hear her showering? Impossible: she was guarachaing. Under
the shower, guaracha and woman in a mating of superb agitation:
voice unleashed, body bumping bathroom walls, the shower curtain's

→ en español yo escribí que ½ ¿no
sería mejor ~~here is~~?

Franco - 2

PRAYER TO THE HOLY JUDGE

"If ~~you~~ they have eyes that do not see me,
if they have hands that do not grasp me,
if they have feet that do not catch me,
do not let them ~~surprise~~ take me from the rear,
do not ~~don't~~ let my death be violent,
do not ~~don't~~ let my blood ~~pour~~ gush out,
You who ~~know everything~~ are all-knowing,
know of my sins,
but you also know of my faith,
do not ~~don't~~ abandon me,
Amen."

Notes

Introduction

1. Hoaksema, "The Translator's Voice," 8.
2. There are a number of articles about Rabassa, by Blackburn (1974), Peden (1980), Calleja (1992), and Bast (2004), and a number of interviews such as Hoaksema's (1978), McDowell's (1986), and Morales's (2001). Lowe and Fitz included a chapter entitled "Gregory Rabassa: The Translator's Translator and the Foundations of Inter-American Literary Study" in their recently published book *Translation and the Rise of Inter-American Literature* (2007)—which they dedicated to Rabassa. Munday also included a chapter on Rabassa, "One Translator, Many Authors: The 'Controlled Schizophrenia of Gregory Rabassa'" in his 2009 book *Style and Ideology in Translation: Latin American Writing in English*.
3. E.g., *The Translator's Dialogue: Giovanni Pontiero* (1997), *El traductor Martí* (2000), and the collection of essays *Translators Through History* (1995).
4. Such is the case of the books *Le traducteur, l'Église et le Roi* (1998) and *Writing Between the Lines* (2006).
5. Term coined by Mary Snell-Hornby in the collection of essays *Translation, History and Culture*, edited by Lefevere and Bassnett (1990), in which the need to address "the larger issues of context, history, and convention" (11) in translation studies was stressed and presented as a collective initiative for the first time.
6. See Venuti 1995, 1998; Robinson 2001.
7. See Lefevere 1992; Eco 2003.
8. See Cronin 2003; Arrojo 2005.
9. See Rafael 1988; Niranjana 1992.
10. See Levine 1991; Vieira 1998.
11. In discussing projects for future research, translation scholar Daniel Simeoni argued for the need to carry out modern "sociographies of single translators' professional trajectories" that he felt were lacking. He proposed carrying out this type of project through interviews or biographical research ("The Pivotal Status of the Translator's Habitus," 31).

Chapter 1. Why Rabassa?

1. In terms of U.S. copyright, a translation is derivative, but that is a separate issue.
2. See Georges Mounin (*Les problèmes théoriques de la traduction,* 1963) or Vinay and Dalbernet (*Stylistique comparée de l'anglais et du français,* 1958).

3. Rosemary Arrojo has discussed the fact that, by being rooted in the belief of absolute equivalence, linguistics-oriented theories continue to promise "a body of allegedly objective data" that could be applied "regardless of the peculiarities, the interests and the circumstances of those involved" so as to fulfill the scientific ideal of a "totalizing metadiscourse" ("The Ethics of Translation," 4).

4. Venuti, *The Translation Studies Reader*, 69.

5. This essay was first published in the volume *On Translation* edited by Reuben Brower (Cambridge: Harvard University Press, 1959).

6. Nida, 196.

7. Jakobson, "On Linguistic Aspects," 146.

8. Originally published as a preface to his own translations of Baudelaire's *Tableaux Parisiens* in 1923.

9. Benjamin, "The Task," 146.

10. Derrida, "Des Tours de Babel," 179.

11. Ibid., 176.

12. Ibid., 183.

13. Ibid., 203.

14. Ibid., 191.

15. Ibid., 74.

16. Venuti, *The Translator's Invisibility*, 290.

17. Arrojo, "Death of the Author," 21. According to this author, in any culture in which authorship and property are equated, and which perceives writing as a site for the conscious presence of the producer, the translator's activity is always related not only with secondariness and failure but also with "indecency" and "transgression."

18. This is precisely the issue in contemporary translation studies that is at stake at the core of this study, for one of my major aims in theorizing Rabassa's legacy in the first place is to look for ways to reveal the implications of this concealment.

19. Arrojo, "Death of the Author," 30–31.

20. Derrida, *The Ear of the Other*, 20.

21. Robinson, *Who Translates?* 3–4.

22. Ibid., 7.

23. Given that the translator cannot channel the author's spirit, Robinson asks: "Who does the translator channel? What 'spirits' or 'ghosts' or 'demons'? . . . Just what sorts of channel is the translator allowed to be, encouraged to be, expected to be, required to be?" (ibid., 7).

24. Ibid., 36.

25. Ibid., 7.

26. These views are largely grounded on post-structuralist thought that, as Venuti has remarked, is critical for a translation strategy that acknowledges complex and unavoidable notions in translation such as "the concept of meaning as differential plurality" (*Rethinking Translation*, 12).

27. Eco, *Mouse or Rat: Translation as Negotiation*, 4.

28. Venuti, "Translation, Community, Utopia," 469.

29. Ibid., 485.

30. As Stanley Fish understands it, an interpretive community is a meaning-making entity in which texts are realized as a function of interpretation. The community "authorizes" a finite number of interpretive strategies and there are agreements (whether or

not they are subject to change) that determine how a text is produced (343). The community has the authority of determining the core meanings that will constitute the normative or public way of construing and the shared basis of agreement—what he calls the "institutional way of making sense" (320).

31. Venuti "Translation, Community, Utopia," 484.
32. Ibid., 485.
33. Arrojo, "The Ethics of Translation," 3.
34. Cronin, *Translation and Globalization*, 3.
35. Ibid., 8–41.
36. Ibid., 6.
37. Cronin, "Altered States," 86.
38. Rose, *Translation and Literary Criticism*, 4.
39. Cronin, *Translation and Globalization*, 6
40. Levine, *The Subversive Scribe*, xii–xiv.
41. Ibid., 10.

Chapter 2. Translation and Language

1. Epigraph to Rabassa's *If This Be Treason: Translation and its Dyscontents*. New York: New Directions, 2005.
2. This book was published in April of 2005, as I was writing the first version of this chapter. The interview I conducted with the translator—in appendix I—is from August of the same year.
3. Rabassa, *If this be Treason*, 4. Prince and protagonist of Calderón de la Barca's *La vida es sueño*. Transl. as *Life is a Dream* by Edward Fitzgerald.
4. Rabasssa qtd. in Venuti, *Rethinking Translation*, 3.
5. Venuti, *Rethinking Translation*, 3.
6. Venuti, *Scandals of Translation*, 31.
7. Venuti, *Rethinking Translation*, 4.
8. Rabassa qtd. in Calleja, "Rabassa, el traductor del boom," 39.
9. Venuti, *Rethinking Translation*, 4.
10. Blackburn, "Translator Supreme," 495.
11. Hoaksema, "The Translator's Voice," 8.
12. Rabassa, "No Two Snowflakes are Alike," 1.
13. Ibid., and *If This Be Treason*, 5.
14. Nietzsche, "Of Truth and Lies," 83.
15. Ibid., 81.
16. Ibid., 86; emphasis added.
17. Ibid., 82.
18. Rabassa, "No Two Snowflakes are Alike," 1.
19. Rabassa, "The Ear in Translation," 83.
20. Ibid., 85.
21. Personal interview (see appendix I at the end for a complete transcript of the interview).
22. Rabassa, "If This Be Treason: Translation and its Possibilities," 21.
23. Rabassa, *If This Be Treason: Translation and its Dyscontents*, 13.

24. Suzanne Jill Levine explains her characterization of translators and of herself as a "subversive scribe" along these lines for, as she puts it, "originals and translations, acts of communication, both fail and succeed, both fulfill and subvert the drive to communicate" (167).
25. Personal interview.
26. Personal interview.
27. Morales, "You Can't Say 'Ain't,'" 120.
28. Rabassa, "The Ear in Translation," 84.
29. Ronald Christ, qtd. by Rabassa.
30. Rabassa, "If This Be Treason: Translation and Its Possibilities," 22.
31. Rabassa, "Translation: The Recreative Art," 1.
32. Rabassa, "The Silk-Purse Business," 36.
33. Talking about his "untranslatables," Rabassa mentions one of the works he was translating in 2005 (when the interview was conducted), by António Lobo Antunes, saying, ironically, that it was the "worst" one: "This is good. It is called *Que farei quando tudo arde?*, or *what can I do when everything is on fire?*, and it is a story based on the life of a famous drag queen in Lisbon. And he throws you off because he'll change subjects in the middle of a paragraph, you have to keep an eye on it, and he changes gender, one person goes from male to female. It's good. It's like *Finnegans Wake*; that is the closest I can think of, in terms of the style, free" (personal interview).
34. Rabassa, "If This Be Treason: Translation and its Possibilities," 22.
35. Robinson, *Who Translates?* 3.
36. With the exception of Machado de Assis, Rabassa has always translated works written by living authors. A discussion about his relationship with the authors follows in the next chapter.
37. Robinson, *Who Translates?* 7.
38. Rabassa, *If This Be Treason*, 3.
39. Rabassa, "If This Be Treason: Translation and Its Possibilities," 21; emphasis added.
40. Ibid., 21.
41. Rabassa explains that the book ended up being called a memoir but that he started out writing a book about translation. He says that it was the editor's decision to "baptize" his book as a memoir in order to give it some literary function and make it more marketable: "I didn't write it as a memoir, for a memoir I would have put a whole lot of things there, I didn't do much that didn't have to do with translation in the memoir part of it, I tied everything in so it would have to do with what I was doing in translation" (personal interview). The book, however, as is often the case with Rabassa's writings, is largely anecdotal; it may well be labeled "a translator's memoir."
42. Rabassa, *If This Be Treason*, 3.
43. Rabassa, "If This Be Treason: Translation and Its Possibilities," 21.
44. Rabassa, "Slouching Back Toward Babel," 30.
45. Personal interview.
46. Rabassa, *If This Be Treason*, 4.
47. Ibid.
48. Ibid.
49. Ibid.
50. Ibid.

51. Ibid., 6.
52. Ibid., 7.
53. Ibid., 8.
54. Ibid., 9.
55. Rabassa, *If This Be Treason*, 4.
56. Ibid., 7.
57. Ibid., 13.
58. Ibid., 5.
59. Rabassa, "Words Cannot Express," 42.
60. Personal interview.
61. Venuti, *The Translator's Invisibility*, 8.
62. Kihss, "Higher Pay Urged for Translators," 25.
63. Personal interview.
64. Lowe and Fitz, *Translation and the Rise of Inter-American Literature*, 159.
65. Venuti, *Rethinking Translation*, 6.
66. Venuti, "The Difference That Translation Makes," 215.
67. Rabassa, "Words Cannot Express," 39.
68. Morales, "You Can't Say 'Ain't,'" 121.
69. Venuti critiques Weaver's writings using a psychoanalytical framework to explain how Weaver's argument that he cannot explain his choices because they are "unconscious" is not justifiable. He argues that a psychoanalytical approach helps to differentiate aspects of the translator's unconscious, between the "translatorly" and "the personal, the cultural and the political" (Venuti, 2002, 215). Several other translation theorists insist on the importance of contesting statements about "instinctive" or "unconscious" decision-making as they find that some so-called instinctive choices, that some of the translator's "unconscious" (or "instinctive") decisions, and also some effects and connections (or errors), may in fact be conscious. Others, as Venuti puts it, may exceed even the experienced translator's conscious intention, taking the form of misconstructions or misreadings that are symptomatic of an unconscious motivation. Others may be caused by the foreign text, its formal and thematic features, and yet others may be triggered by something that lies outside of the immediate context of the error but is nonetheless connected to it, the larger cultural and social situation in which the translation is produced (2002, 238).
70. Venuti, "The Difference That Translation Makes," 216.
71. Ibid.
72. Hoaksema, "The Translator's Voice," 17.
73. Ibid.
74. Ibid.
75. Morales, "You Can't Say 'Ain't,'" 119–121. Interestingly, Lowe and Fitz, citing this same statement of Rabassa, find his view to be "both succinct and instructive, the product of a lifetime of professional experience and critical thought" (Lowe and Fitz, 161).
76. Venuti, *Rethinking Translation*, 11.
77. Venuti, "The Difference that Translation Makes," 238.
78. Rabassa, "The Ear in Translation," 82.
79. Rabassa, *If This Be Treason*, 43.
80. Rabassa, "If This Be Treason: Translation and its Possibilities," 27.

81. Morales, "You can't say 'Ain't,'" 122.
82. Levine, *The Subversive Scribe*, xiii.
83. Sara Blackburn comments that Rabassa's attitude toward his own accomplishments is so modest as to appear self-effacing (1974, 495).
84. Rabassa, "No Two Snowflakes," 12.
85. Rabassa, "Words Cannot Express," 39.
86. Rabassa, *If this be Treason*, 189.
87. Rabassa, "You Can't Say 'Ain't'" 120; emphasis added.
88. Rabassa, "If This Be Treason: Translation and Its Possibilities," 21.
89. Susan Sontag articulates the relationship between the lack of interest in foreign translations and the hegemony of English—which she calls a contemporary "colonial" language. She believes that the notion of English as a world language, which is, also, the one spoken by the richest and most powerful nation, has a great deal of power in deciding what is translated and what—i.e., large infusions of foreign literature—is simply not allowed to enter (139). The choices made by Anglo-American translators have an effect on translation worldwide.
90. Venuti, "The Difference that Translation Makes," 217.
91. Ibid.
92. Ibid.
93. Ibid.
94. Ibid., 216.
95. Opening lines of Gabriel García Márquez's *Cien años de soledad*. Buenos Aires: Sudamericana, 1967.
96. Opening lines of Rabassa's English translation of García Márquez's novel, entitled *One Hundred Years of Solitude*. New York: Harper & Row, 1970.
97. Rabassa, "Words Cannot Express," 35.
98. As R. Barsky remarked on a paper entitled "Translating into Fifteen Years of Prison or When Not to Say 'You May, Officer'" presented during the *Translation and Social Activism Conference* at Glendon College, York University (October 20, 2005).

Chapter 3. Dialogue with Authors

1. Letter of Cortázar to Rabassa, in 1970, commenting on the translation of Lezama Lima's *Paradiso* (*Cartas III*, 1375). Cortázar's letters have been published only in Spanish; the translations from the excerpts cited in this chapter are my own. This is the case also for other Spanish texts not available in English translation cited from this chapter on.
2. In an interview he conducted with Luis Rafael Sánchez ("De la guaracha al beat," 194).
3. Rabassa, *If this be Treason*, 22.
4. Ibid., 29.
5. Whitfield, introduction, 2.
6. Ibid., 3.
7. Levine qtd. in Lowe and Fitz, *Translation and the Rise of Inter-American Literature*, 80.
8. Rabassa qtd. in *Translation and the Rise of Inter-American Literature*, 158.

9. Rabassa, *If This Be Treason*, 30.
10. Ibid., 31.
11. Ibid., 32.
12. Ibid., 33.
13. Ibid., 34.
14. Ibid., 46.
15. Ibid., 35.
16. Ibid., 37.
17. Ibid.
18. Ibid., 38.
19. Rabassa, *If This Be Treason*, 24.
20. Ibid.
21. Ibid., 51.
22. See appendix II for complete list of translations.
23. Ibid., 82.
24. Ibid., 84.
25. Ibid.
26. Ibid., 185.
27. Ibid., 130.
28. Rabassa, *If This be Treason*, 143.
29. Personal interview.
30. Rabassa, *If This Be Treason*, 25.
31. Rabassa, "Words Cannot Express," 37.
32. Ibid., 42.
33. Bach, 22.
34. Rabassa, *If This Be Treason*, 62.
35. Ibid., 43.
36. Personal interview.
37. Hoaksema, "The Translators Voice," 8.
38. Suzanne Jill Levine and Paul Blackburn also translated Cortázar's works, mainly his short stories.
39. Cortázar, *Cartas II*, 708–9.
40. See appendix III (annotated manuscript).
41. Cortázar, *Cartas II*, 764
42. Fragment of chapter 69 of *Rayuela*: "Ingrata sorpresa fue leer en 'Ortográfico' la notisia de aber fayesido en San Luis de Potosí el 1 de marso último . . ." (534).

Rabassa's translation: "It waz a sad surprize to rede in the 'Orthografik' the newz ov the demise in San Luis Potosí on march furst . . ., (384).

43. Fragment of chapter 68 of *Rayuela*: "Apenas él le amalaba el noema, a ella se le agolpaba el clémiso y caían en hidromurias, en salvajes ambonios, en sústalos exasperantes . . ." (533).

Rabassa's translation: "As soon as he began to amalate the noeme, the clemise began to smother her and they fell into hydromuries, into savage ambonies, into exasperating sustales . . ." (383).

44. Rabassa, "Words Cannot Express," 37.
45. Cortázar, *Cartas II*, 856.
46. Ibid.

47. See appendix III (annotated manuscript).
48. Cortázar, *Cartas II*, 834.
49. Ibid., 881.
50. Cortázar, *Cartas III*, 1361.
51. Rabassa, *If This Be Treason*, 54.
52. Cortázar, *Cartas II*, 891.
53. Cortázar, *Cartas II*, 906.
54. Cortázar, *Cartas III*, 1054.
55. Personal interview.
56. Cortázar, *Cartas III*, 1353.
57. Ibid., 1545.
58. Ibid., 1572.
59. Rabassa, *If This Be Treason*, 58.
60. Cortázar, *Cartas III*, 1564.
61. Ibid., 1735.
62. Rabassa, *If This Be Treason*, 59.
63. Cortázar, *Cartas III*, 1784.
64. Rabassa, *If This Be Treason*, 61.
65. Ibid., 60.
66. Personal interview.
67. Cortázar, "Translate, Traduire, Tradurre: Traducir," 21.
68. Cortázar, interview, 115. Cortázar also translated into Spanish works by Daniel Defoe, G. K. Chesterton, Luisa May Alcott, Auguste de Villiers de L'isle Adam, and Alfred Stern, among others.
69. Hoaksema, "The Translator's Voice," 8.
70. Cortázar, *Cartas III*, 1572.
71. Rabassa, *If This Be Treason*, 54. This refers to the inclusion of official documents from UNESCO in the novels.
72. Cortázar, "Translate, Traduire, Tradurre: Traducir," 21.
73. Examples of Cortázar's writings that deal with translation are the novel *A Manual for Manuel* and the short stories "Letter to a Young Lady in Paris" and "Blow-up." I have discussed Cortázar's fictional accounts of translation in the article "The Spectrum of Translation in 'Letter to a Young Lady in Paris.'"
74. Personal interview.
75. Cortázar, "Translate, Traduire, Tradurre: Traducir," 22.
76. Rostagno, *Searching for Recognition*, 134.
77. Ibid., 133.
78. Lezama, *Como las cartas no llegan*, 182.
79. Ibid., 183
80. Rabassa, *If This Be Treason*, 108.
81. Rostagno, *Searching for Recognition*, 134.
82. Lezama, *Como las cartas no llegan*, 190.
83. Ibid., 195.
84. Cortázar, *Cartas III*, 1411.
85. Cortázar, *Cartas III*, 1387.
86. Other ways he used to refer to the "triangulation" are "el Triángulo Jodedor de Pentágonos" and "El inconcebible triángulo no-euclideano en que estamos metidos

tú, *Paradiso*, Rabassa, yo, el correo, la buena suerte, el fatum, Cubana de Aviación y las nueve Musas" (Cortázar, *Cartas III*, 1401).
    87. Cortázar, *Cartas III*, 1442.
    88. Rabassa, *If This Be Treason*, 109.
    89. Ibid., 108.
    90. Ibid.
    91. Rostagno, *Searching for Recognition*, 134.
    92. Ibid.
    93. Lowe and Fitz, *Translation and the Rise*, 149.
    94. García Márquez, interview, 128.
    95. Ibid., 129.
    96. Rostagno, *Searching for Recognition*, 124.
    97. Ibid., 125.
    98. Rabassa, *If This be Treason*, 100. "Gabo" is a popular nickname for García Márquez.
    99. García Márquez, interview, 137.
    100. Ibid., 133.
    101. Rabassa, *If This Be Treason*, 94.
    102. Personal interview.
    103. McDowell, "A Wizard of Words," 39.
    104. Hoaksema, "The Translator's Voice," 9.
    105. Rabassa, *If This Be Treason*, 97–98.
    106. Ibid., 98. See also appendix III (annotated manuscript).
    107. Ibid., 96.
    108. Ibid., 99.
    109. Ibid., 100.
    110. Ibid.
    111. Ibid., 102.
    112. García Márquez, interview, 148.
    113. Ibid.
    114. Ibid., 147.
    115. Ibid., 148.
    116. García Márquez, "The Desire to Translate," 23.
    117. Ibid., 25.
    118. Rabassa often quotes García Márquez on this remark. He says it is generous and, as noted earlier, he calls it "outlandish."
    119. García Márquez, "The Desire to Translate," 25.
    120. Lowe and Fitz, *Translation and the Rise*, 146.
    121. García Márquez, "The Desire to Translate," 25.
    122. Ibid.
    123. Ibid.
    124. Ibid.
    125. Ibid., 23.
    126. Rabassa, *If This Be Treason*, 83.
    127. Ibid., 71.
    128. Ibid., 74.
    129. Ibid., 119.

168   NOTES

130. See appendix III (annotated manuscript).
131. Rabassa, *If This Be Treason*, 119.
132. Ibid., 120.
133. Rabassa, *"De la guaracha al beat,"* 177.
134. Ibid., 176.
135. Rabassa, *If This Be Treason*, 121.
136. Rabassa, "De la guaracha al beat," 181.
137. Ibid., 193.
138. Ibid.
139. Ibid., 194.
140. Rabassa, *If This Be Treason*, 122.
141. Ibid., 112.
142. Hoaksema, "The Translator's Voice," 8.
143. Rabassa, *If this Be Treason*, 113.
144. In the following chapter I expand on the role of the Center for Inter-American Relations in the publication of Rabassa's translations as well as in the translation of other Latin American works, in the sixties and seventies in particular.
145. Rostagno, *Searching for Recognition*, 112.
146. Rabassa, *If This Be Treason*, 107.
147. Ibid.
148. Ibid.
149. Ibid., 160.
150. Hoaksema, "The Translator's Voice," 9.
151. McDowell, "A Wizard of Words," 39.
152. Rabassa, *If This Be Treason*, 175.
153. See appendix III (annotated manuscript).
154. Personal interview.
155. Rabassa, *If This Be Treason*, 157.
156. Rabassa, personal interview.
157. Rabassa, *If This Be Treason*, 150.
158. Hoaksema, "The Translator's Voice," 8.
159. Rabassa, "If This Be Treason: Translation and Its Possibilities," 23.
160. Rabassa, *If This Be Treason*, 115.
161. Rabassa, *If This Be Treason*, 60.
162. Venuti, "Translation, Community, Utopia," 484.
163. From a practical standpoint, Rabassa acknowledges that a translation also belongs to the editors; this shows that he sees it as a collective enterprise.
164. Rabassa, *If This Be Treason*, 61.

Chapter 4. Canon and Reception

1. These comments are made on the basis of numerous reviews of different translations of Rabassa's—from *One Hundred Years of Solitude* and *Hopscotch* to *Rosario Tijeras* and *Jail*—which appeared in newspapers and literary journals in the United States between 1966 and 2005 (see for example Lask, 3; Leonard, 39; Coleman, 340).

2. Lowe and Fitz, *Translation and the Rise of Inter-American Literature*, 140.

3. See for example Keates, 20; West, 3; Bannon, 19.
4. Mac Adam, 95.
5. White, "Four Ways to Read a Masterpiece," 515.
6. Rodríguez Monegal, 7.
7. Pye, 13.
8. Jackson, 381.
9. Amdahl 64; emphasis added.
10. Mujica, 62.
11. Charyn, 3.
12. Peden, 38.
13. Ibid.
14. Ibid.
15. Blackburn, 494.
16. Ibid.
17. Levine, "The Latin American Novel in English Translation," 306.
18. Munday, "One Translator, Many Authors," 145–48.
19. Ibid., 149–50.
20. The connections that Rabassa makes are partly due to his being a scholar; they often reveal literary moments and tendencies across national literatures and across traditions. They are also part of his translation practice. An example of this is his remark, in *If This Be Treason*, that it was strange, maybe even "magical," that after he stopped working on García Márquez he did a number of works by Jorge Amado. He says: "Suddenly I got the feeling that Macondo was located somewhere in the State of Bahia, down in the southern cacao country or perhaps more likely on the Reconcavo, as the bayshore is called." He believes this was "a nice transference" (*If This Be Treason*, 104).
21. Rabassa, "A Minor Novel by a Major Writer," 287.
22. Rabassa, "In Bahia, It's Living Theater," 52.
23. Rabassa, "Catalan Magic," 68.
24. Rabassa, "If This Be Treason: Translation and Its Possibilities," 26.
25. Rabassa, *If This Be Treason*, 40.
26. Rabassa, "The Ear in Translation," 83.
27. Rabassa, "The Silk-Purse Business," 35–40. Blackburn explains that Rabassa wrote the article "The Silk-Purse Business: A Translator's Conflicting Responsibilities" as a response to having been taken to task for the "excesses" of an Asturias novel he had translated (495).
28. Hoaksema, "The Translator's Voice," 14.
29. Rabassa, "Words Cannot Express," 39.
30. Rabassa, *If This Be Treason*, 42.
31. Venuti, *The Translator's Invisibility*, 2.
32. Ibid., 81
33. West, 3.
34. Venuti, *The Translator's Invisibility*, 67.
35. Ibid., 268.
36. Venuti, *The Translator's Invisibility*, 267.
37. Barbosa, "The Virtual Image," 352.
38. Ibid.

39. Ibid., 353.
40. Venuti, introduction, "What is a 'Relevant' Translation," 172.
41. In the next chapter I elaborate on this point referring to the 2007 PEN report on literary translation.
42. Rivera, 66.
43. Vernon, 30.
44. Besides devoting a chapter to Rabassa, Lowe and Fitz dedicated *Translation and the Rise of Inter-American Literature* to him and "to the important work that all translators do."
45. Lowe and Fitz, *Translation and the Rise of Inter-American Literature*, 136–37.
46. Ibid., 138.
47. Ibid., 135.
48. Blackburn, "Translator Supreme," 495.
49. Franco, "Decline and Fall," 261.
50. Rostagno, *Searching for Recognition*, 13.
51. Ibid., 11.
52. A retranslation of *The Underdogs* by Sergio Waisman was published in 2008 (Penguin Classics).
53. Rostagno, *Searching for Recognition*, 13.
54. Ibid., 21.
55. Ibid., 20.
56. Ibid.
57. Patricia Willson's book *La Constelación del Sur* documents the contribution of the translations of *Sur* to Latin American literature. In another work dealing with this topic, Beatriz Sarlo comments on the fact that Victoria Ocampo was an important social agent, despite the fact that, according to Sarlo, she was not able to recognize the asymmetries of the "cultural machine" whereby Argentina was positioned in a peripheral location with respect to European culture, and through which Argentinean cultural institutions were also conditioned by the state.
58. Rostagno, *Searching for Recognition*, 31.
59. Ibid., 32.
60. By 1955 he had been translated into twenty-four different languages, including French, Spanish, and German; this made him appear as a "low-risk author" to U.S. publishers.
61. Rostagno, *Searching for Recognition*, 36–38.
62. Ibid., 59.
63. Ibid.
64. Ibid., 67.
65. Ibid., 68.
66. Lowe and Fitz, *Translation and the Rise of Inter-American Literature*, 29. The authors cite Rodríguez Monegal's 1968 complaint that in a country where influential critics "like Edmund Wilson and Lionel Trilling could routinely disparage the literature and culture of Latin America, it was small wonder that the general population had so little regard of the cultures of Spanish America and Brazil."
67. Rostagno, *Searching for Recognition*, 99.
68. Ibid., 90.
69. Garrels, 295.

70. Ibid.
71. Joset, 58.
72. Steenmeijer, "How the West," 146.
73. Ibid., 150–52.
74. In 1968, Gallimard transferred the authors of the Latin American collection to its collection of world literature, Du Monde Entier (Steenmejier, 146).
75. Ibid.
76. Donoso, *The Boom*, 4.
77. Christ, foreword, 8.
78. Ibid.
79. Donoso, *The Boom*, 145.
80. As translator Esther Allen notes, in the 1950s even the idea of Latin American literature barely existed in the United States (133).
81. Echeverría, introduction, 3.
82. Payne, *Conquest of the New Word*, 15.
83. Ibid., 17.
84. Martin, *Journeys through the Labyrinth*, 205.
85. Ibid.
86. García Márquez, interview, 150.
87. Luis, "Culture as Text," 8.
88. Ibid.
89. Franco, *Decline and Fall*, 23.
90. Ibid.
91. Ibid.
92. Ibid., 37.
93. Rostagno, *Searching for Recognition*, 94.
94. Luis, "Culture as Text," 9.
95. Rostagno, *Searching for Recognition*, 34.
96. Lowe and Fitz, *Translation and the Rise of Inter-American Literature*, 1.
97. Luis, "Culture as Text," 10.
98. Ibid.
99. As Cohn points out, as part of the Center's activities experienced translators such as Rabassa and Reid assisted with the development of younger ones. This was the case, for instance, of Suzanne Jill Levine and Eliot Weinberger (154).
100. Rostagno, *Searching for Recognition*, 109.
101. Cohn, "A Tale of Two Translation Programs," 153.
102. Rabassa, "Parallel Lines that Meet," 130.
103. Ibid., 128.
104. Rabassa, "If This Be Treason: Translation and Its Possibilities," 29.
105. Rabassa, *If This Be Treason*, 24.
106. Cohn discusses the case of the Center as well as that of a translation subsidy program, also funded by the Rockefeller Foundation, which was administered by the Association of American University Presses (AAUP) from 1960 to 1966. She also notes that, during the 1950s and 1960s there were a number of government initiatives for cultural and educational projects, such as the Congress for Cultural Freedom—clandestinely funded by the CIA—which were "inspired by the liberal belief that greater understanding and mutual respect for the cultural production of other countries would directly benefit national security" (141).

107. Rostagno, *Searching for Recognition*, 137–38.
108. Mudrovcic, "Reading Latin American Literature Abroad," 138.
109. Ibid.
110. Cohn, "A Tale of Two Translation Programs," 141.
111. Ibid., 162.
112. Rostagno, *Searching for Recognition*, 138.
113. Venuti, *The Translator's Invisibility*, 265.
114. Mudrovcic, "Reading Latin American Literature Abroad," 137.
115. Zavalia, "The Impact of Spanish-American Literature in Translation," 191.
116. Nunn, "The Latin American 'New Novel' in Translation," 68.
117. Ibid.
118. Watson, 89
119. Barbosa, 49.
120. Blackburn, 494.
121. Franco, *Decline and Fall*, 4.
122. Ibid., 6–7.
123. Cohn, "A Tale of Two Translation Programs," 140.
124. Zavalia, "The Impact of Spanish-American Literature in Translation," 190.

Chapter 5. Latin America

1. Rostagno, *Searching for Recognition*, 137.
2. García Márquez, interview, 150.
3. Venuti, *The Translator's Invisibility*, 266.
4. Ibid., 267.
5. Barbosa, "The Virtual Image," 345.
6. Payne, *Conquest of the New Word*, 34.
7. Venuti, *Scandals of Translation*, 67.
8. Ibid.
9. Even-Zohar refers to literary systems as structures that do not necessarily denote homogeneity; he finds that, for literature, it is more appropriate to speak of "semiotic systems" that can be conceived of as heterogeneous, open structures. He uses the term "poly-system" to better describe the intersections and interdependencies of literary traditions (11).
10. Zavalia, "The Impact of Spanish-American Literature in Translation," 193.
11. Venuti, *The Translator's Invisibility*, 13.
12. Lowe and Fitz, *Translation and the Rise of Inter-American Literature*, 11.
13. Ibid.
14. Barbosa, "The Virtual Image," 344.
15. Zavalia, "The Impact of Spanish-American Literature in Translation," 191.
16. Ibid., 192.
17. Ibid., 192.
18. Franco, *The Decline and Fall*, 164.
19. Steenmeijer, "How the West was Won," 153.
20. Mudrovcic, "Reading Latin American Literature Abroad," 139.
21. Payne, *Conquest of the New Word*, 24.

22. Ibid., 34.
23. Payne, *Conquest of the New Word*, 2.
24. Jameson qtd. in Lowe and Fitz, *Translation and the Rise of Inter-American Literature*, 135.
25. Payne, *Conquest of the New Word*, 20.
26. Mudrovcic, "Reading Latin American Literature Abroad," 139
27. Ibid., 130.
28. Ibid., 309.
29. The post-Boom as a category is controversial. Loosely, it can be said to refer to literature after the Boom, outside, and often critical, of the Boom canon. This includes authors that are conventionally known as post-Boom ones, such as Manuel Puig and Severo Sarduy, as well as more recent literature such as the new urban Latin American novel (see for example Levine 2005). This group includes authors such as Mario Mendoza, Jorge Franco, as well as Jorge Volpi and Ignacio Padilla—the latter are the co-founders of the "Crack" generation—as well as the McOndo movement.
30. Barbosa believes that in order to become available to the reading public, literary works undergo the same selection, publishing and distribution processes as original texts, and that they undergo them twice: once in the culture that originates them, a second time in the culture that receives or imports them (2).
31. Allen, *To Be Translated or Not To Be*, 20. This report, entitled *To Be Translated or Not To Be: PEN/IRL Report on the International Situation of Literary Translation*, which was edited by Esther Allen, contains detailed data about translation into English from specific countries between 2000 and 2006. Earlier data, based on the 1999 *Bowker Annual*, show that all the hard and trade paper titles published in the United States in 1997 and 1998 amounted to less than 3 percent (White, "Translation and Teaching," 235). Stephen Kinzer's article, "America Yawns at Foreign Fiction" (2003), confirms this situation.
32. Levine, "The Latin American Novel in English Translation," 315.
33. Sontag, 139.
34. Eller qtd. in Kinzer, "America Yawns at Foreign Fiction," 7.
35. Barbosa, "The Virtual Image," 247.
36. Cronin, "The Cracked Looking Glass of Servants," 152.
37. Moretti, *Modern Epic*, 3.
38. Ibid., 5.
39. Mudrovcic, "Reading Latin American Literature Abroad," 136.
40. Ibid.
41. Payne, *Conquest of the New Word*, 34.
42. Ibid., 17.
43. González E., *Myth and Archive*, 8.
44. Ibid., 13.
45. Ibid.
46. Moretti, *Modern Epic*, 233.
47. Ibid.
48. Ibid., 238.
49. Ibid., 243.
50. Ibid., 250.
51. Ibid., 243.

52. Silva, 7.
53. González, E., *Myth and Archive*, 29.
54. Ibid., 18.
55. Ibid., 183.
56. García Márquez, *One Hundred Years*, 1; emphasis added.
57. Martin, *Journeys*, 228.
58. Colombian workers of the branch of the United Fruit Company—U.S. banana company—in a town near Aracataca, where García Márquez was born, were on strike for better working conditions. One night, during a demonstration, the government sent the troops that fired on the unarmed people. Hundreds of workers were killed, and some disappeared during the months that followed. This event remains unrecorded in Colombian official history. Joset reports that García Márquez has confirmed this episode to refer to this historical event (48).
59. Martin, *Journeys*, 230.
60. Lowe and Fitz remark that Latin Americans have long understood that "this landmark novel demands to be read as an interlocking parable about Colombia's tragic political history—in particular the *violencia* that has long plagued it—and about Latin and inter-American political and economic history generally." They note that a similar situation could be said about other "politically charged Latin American novels and poems, that were being introduced into and misconstrued by the American cultural consciousness during the Boom period," such as Jorge Amado's novels and others (*Translation and the Rise of Inter-American Literature*, 17, 18).
61. Moretti, *Modern Epic*, 250.
62. Ibid.
63. Franco, *Decline and Fall*, 8.
64. Moretti, *Modern Epic*, 244.
65. Martin, *Journeys*, 9.
66. González, E., *Myth and Archive*, 174.
67. Ibid., 34.
68. Ibid., 175.
69. Martin, *Journeys through the Labyrinth*, 361.
70. Ibid.
71. Moretti, *Modern Epic*, 247.
72. González Echevarría defines hegemonic discourse—one that has prestige and socio-political power—as one backed by a discipline, or embodying a system, that offers the most commonly accepted description of humanity and accounts for the most widely held beliefs of the intelligentsia. "Within such a discourse, the individual finds stories about himself and the world that he or she finds acceptable, and in some ways obeys" (*Myth and Archive*, 41).
73. González E., introduction, xvi.
74. Martin, "Translating García Márquez," 156.
75. Martin, *Journeys*, 235.
76. Payne, *Conquest of the New Word*, 29.
77. Rabassa, "If This Be Treason: Translation and Its Possibilities," 21.
78. González E., *Myth and Archive*, 29.
79. Ibid.
80. Franco, *Decline and Fall*, 7.

81. Martin, *Journeys*, 222.
82. Cronin, "The Cracked Looking Glass," 161.
83. Nunn, "The Latin American 'New Novel' in Translation," 73.
84. These questions go beyond literature; they apply to humanistic and social scientific thought in general. However, especially in a tradition such as the Latin American one, where there are more avenues for translating literature than there are for other forms of intellectual production, translated novels occupy an even more prominent position as repositories of history and knowledge.
85. Levine, "The Latin American Novel," 315.
86. Spivak, "Forum: The Legacy of Jacques Derrida," 492.
87. Ibid., 493.

Bibliography

Aguilera Malta, Demetrio. *Siete lunas y siete serpientes*. México: Fondo de Cultura Económica, 1970.

———. *Seven Serpents and Seven Moons*. Translated by Gregory Rabassa. Austin: University of Texas Press, 1979.

Allen, Esther, ed. *To Be Translated or Not To Be: PEN/IRL Report on the International Situation of Literary Translation*. Barcelona: Institut Ramon Llull Spain, 2007.

———, Ammiel Alcalay, Michael Hofmann, Susan Sontag, and Steve Wasserman. "The Politics of Translation." *PEN America: A Journal for Writers and Readers: 6 Metamorphoses*. New York: PEN American Center, 2005. 133–41.

Amado, Jorge. *Gabriela, Clove and Cinnamon*. Translated by James L. Taylor and William L. Grossman. New York: Knopf, 1962.

Amdahl, Gary. "Still Dead." Review of *Posthumous Memoirs of Brás Cubas*, by J. M. Machado de Assis. Translated by Gregory Rabassa. *The Nation*, November 3, 1997, 64.

Antunes, António Lobo. *The Return of the Caravels: a Novel*. Translated by Gregory Rabassa. New York: Grove Press, 1988.

———. *Que farei quando tudo arde?* Lisbon: Publicações Dom Quixote, 2001.

Arencibia, Lourdes. *El traductor Martí*. Pinar del Río, Cuba: Ediciones Hermanos Loynaz, 2000.

Arrojo, Rosemary. "The 'Death' of the Author and the Limits of the Translator's Visibility," in *Translation as Intercultural Communication*, edited by Mary Snell-Hornby, Zuzana Jettmarová, and Klaus Kaindl, 21–32. Philadelphia: John Benjamins, 1997.

———. "The Ethics of Translation in Contemporary Approaches to Translator Training," in *Training for a New Millenium: Pedagogies for Translation and Interpreting*, 225–45. Philadelphia: John Benjamins, 2005.

Asturias, Miguel Ángel. *Mulata*. Translated by Gregory Rabassa. New York: Delacorte Press, 1967.

Bach, Caleb. "Gregory Rabassa: Words of Instinct." *Americas* 57, no. 5 (2005): 22.

Balderston, Daniel and Marcy E. Schuwartz, eds. *Voice-Overs: Translation and Latin American Literature*. Albany: SUNY Press, 2002.

Barnstone, Willis. *The Poetics of Translation: History, Theory, Practice*. New Haven: Connecticut, 1995.

Bannon, Barbara. Review of *One Hundred Years of Solitude*. Translated by Gregory Rabassa. *New York Times*, Feb. 22, 1970, BR19.

Barbosa, Heloisa. *The Virtual Image: Brazilian Literature in English Translation*. PhD diss., University of Warwick (UK), 1994.

Barsky, Robert. "Translating into Fifteen Years of Prison or When Not to Say 'You May, Officer'." Translation and Social Activism Conference. Glendon College, York University, Oct. 20, 2005.

Barth, John. "The Literature of Exhaustion." *Atlantic Monthly* 220, no. 2 (1967): 29–34.

———. "The Literature of Replenishment." *Atlantic Monthly* 245 (1980): 65–71.

Bassnett, Susan and André Lefevere, eds. *Translation, History and Culture*. New York: Pinter Publishers, 1990.

Bast, Andrew. "A Translator's Long Journey Page by Page." *New York Times*, May 25, 2004.

Benet, Juan. *A Meditation: A Novel*. Translated by Gregory Rabassa. New York: Persea Books, 1982.

Benjamin, Walter. "The Task of the Translator." Translated by Harry Zohn. In *Theories of Translation*, edited by Rainer Schulte and John Biguenet, 71–82. Chicago: University of Chicago, 1992.

Berman, Antoine. *The Experience of the Foreign: Culture and Translation in Romantic Germany*. Translated by Stefan Heyvaert. Albany: SUNY Press, 1992.

Bérubé, Michael. "American Studies Without Exceptions." *PMLA* 118, no. 1 (2003): 103–13.

Blackburn, Sara. "Translator Supreme." *New York Times*, Sep. 15, 1974, 494.

Bonnell, Victoria and Lynn Hunt. *Beyond the Cultural Turn: New Directions in the Study of Society and Culture*. Berkeley, University of California Press, 1999.

Bourdieu, Pierre. *The Field of Cultural Production*. New York: Columbia University Press, 1993.

Brower, Reuben, ed. *On Translation*. Cambridge: Harvard University Press, 1959.

Calderón de la Barca, Pedro. *Life is a Dream*. Translated by Edwin Honig. New York: Hill & Wang, 1970.

Calleja, Gilda. "Gregory Rabassa, el traductor del boom." *Livius: revista de estudios de traducción* 1 (1992): 35–42.

Charyn, Jerome. "Swinging Through San Juan." Review of *Macho Camacho's Beat*, by Luis Rafael Sánchez. Translated by Gregory Rabassa. *New York Times Book Review*, Jan. 18, 1981, 3.

Christ, Ronald. Foreword. In *The Boom in Spanish American Literature: A Personal History*. New York: Columbia University Press, 1977.

———. Review of *One Hundred Years of Solitude*. Translated by Gregory Rabassa. *New York Times*, Mar. 4, 1970.

———, and David Jackson. "Madness in a Tropical Manner." Review of *Posthumous Memoirs of Brás Cubas*, by J. M. Machado de Assis. Translated by Gregory Rabassa. *New York Times*, Feb. 22, 1998, 381.

Cohn, Deborah. "A Tale of Two Translation Programs: Politics, the Market, and Rockefeller Funding for Latin American Literature in the United States during the 1960s and 1970s." *Latin American Research Review* 41, no. 2 (2006): 139–64.

Coleman, Alexander. "Why Asturias?" Review of *Mulata*, by Miguel A. Asturias. Translated by Gregory Rabassa. *New York Times*, Nov. 19, 1967, 340.

Cortázar, Julio. *A Certain Lucas*. Translated by Gregory Rabassa. New York: Knopf, 1984.

———. *A Change of Light and Other Stories*. Translated by Gregory Rabassa. New York: Knopf, 1980.

———. *A Manual for Manuel*. Translated by Gregory Rabassa. New York: Pantheon Books, 1978.

———. *Cartas 1964–1968*. Vol. 2. Buenos Aires: Alfaguara, 2000.

———. *Cartas 1969–1983*. Vol. 3. Buenos Aires: Alfaguara, 2000.

———. *El libro de Manuel*. Buenos Aires: Editorial Sudamericana, 1973.

———. *Hopscotch*. Translated by Gregory Rabassa. New York: Pantheon Books, 1966.

———. *Hopscotch*. Rev. ed. Translated by Gregory Rabassa. New York: Pantheon Books, 1987.

———. Interview. In *Latin American Writers at Work: The Paris Review Interviews*, edited by George Plimpton and Derek Walcott, 109–26. New York: Modern Library, 2003.

———. *Rayuela*. Buenos Aires: Editorial Sudamericana, 1963.

———. *Rayuela*. Edited by Andrés Amoros. Madrid: Cátedra, 1991.

———. *Sixty-Two: A Model Kit*. Translated by Gregory Rabassa. New York, Pantheon Books, 1972.

———. "Translate, Traduire, Tradurre: Traducir." In *Voice-Overs: Translation and Latin American Literature*, edited by Daniel Balderston and Marcy E. Schuwartz, 21–23. Albany: SUNY Press, 2002.

———. *We Love Glenda So Much and Other Tales*. Translated by Gregory Rabassa. New York: Knopf, 1983.

Coutinho, Afrânio. *An Introduction to Literature in Brazil*. Translated by Gregory Rabassa. New York: Columbia University Press, 1969.

Cronin, Michael. "Altered States: Translation and Minority Languages." *TTR* VIII, no. 1 (1995): 85–103.

———. "The Cracked Looking Glass of Servants." *The Translator* 4 (1998): 145–62.

———. *Translation and Globalization*. New York: Routledge, 2003.

Delisle, Jean, and Judith Woodsworth. *Translators Through History*. Amsterdam; Philadelphia: John Benjamins, 1995.

Derrida, Jacques. "Des Tours De Babel." In *Difference in Translation*, edited by Joseph Graham, 165–208. Ithaca: Cornell University Press, 1985.

———. *The Ear of the Other: Otobiography, Transference, Translation: Texts and Discussions with Jacques Derrida*. Edited by Christie V. McDonald. New York: Schocken Books, 1985.

———. "What is a 'Relevant' Translation?" Translated by and introduction by Lawrence Venuti. *Critical Inquiry* 27 (2001): 169–200.

———. *Writing and Difference*. Translated by Alan Bass. Chicago: University of Chicago Press, 1978.

Donoso, José. *The Boom in Spanish American Literature: a Personal History*. New York: Columbia University Press, 1977.

Eco, Umberto. *Mouse or Rat: Translation as Negotiation*. London: Weidenfeld & Nicolson, 2003.

Even-Zohar, Itamar. "Polysystem Studies." *Poetics Today* 11, no. 1 (1990): 253–68.
Fish, Stanley. *Is There a Text in This Class? The Authority of Interpretive Communities.* Cambridge: Harvard University Press, 1980.
Foucault, Michel. "What is an Author?" In *Textual Strategies: Perspectives in Post-Structuralist Criticism,* edited by Josué V. Harari, 141–60. Ithaca: Cornell University Press, 1989.
Franco, Jean. *Decline and Fall of the Lettered City: Latin America in the Cold War.* Cambridge: Harvard University Press, 2002.
Franco, Jorge. *Rosario Tijeras: A Novel.* Translated by Gregory Rabassa. New York: Seven Stories Press, 2003.
Foz, Clara. *Le traducteur, l'Église et le Roi: Espagne, XIIe et XIIIe siècle.* Ottawa: University of Ottawa Press, 1998.
García Márquez, Gabriel. *Chronicle of a Death Foretold.* Translated by Gregory Rabassa. New York: Knopf, 1983.
———. *Cien años de soledad.* Buenos Aires: Editorial Sudamericana, 1967.
———. *In Evil Hour.* Translated by Gregory Rabassa. New York: Harper & Row, 1979.
———. Interview. In *Latin American Writers at Work: The Paris Review Interviews,* by Silvana Paternostro. Edited by George Plimpton and Derek Walcott, 127–54. New York: Modern Library, 2003.
———. *Leaf Storm, and Other Stories.* Translated by Gregory Rabassa. New York: Harper & Row, 1972.
———. *The Autumn of the Patriarch.* Translated by Gregory Rabassa. New York: Harper & Row, 1975.
———. *One Hundred Years of Solitude.* Translated by Gregory Rabassa. New York: Harper & Row, 1970.
———. *One Hundred Years of Solitude.* Rev. ed. New York: Harper Collins, 1991.
———. "The Desire to Translate." In *Voice-Overs: Translation and Latin American Literature,* edited by Daniel Balderston and Marcy E. Schwartz, 23–25. Albany: SUNY Press, 2002.
Garrels, Elizabeth. "Resumen de la discusión." In *Más allá del boom: literatura y mercado.* 287–326. México: Marcha, 1981.
Gide, André. *El inmoralista.* Translated by Julio Cortázar. Buenos Aires: Argos, 1947.
González Echevarría, Roberto. *Myth and Archive: A Theory of Latin American Narrative.* New York: Cambridge University Press, 1990.
———. Introduction. In *The Oxford Book of Latin American Short Stories,* edited by Roberto González Echevarría. New York: Oxford University Press, 1997.
Guzmán, María Constanza. "The Spectrum of Translation in Cortázar's 'Letter to a Young Lady in Paris'." *Ikala: revista de lenguaje y cultura* 11, no. 17 (2006): 75–86.
———. "Rabassa and the 'Narrow Act': Between Possibility and an Ethics of Doubt." *TTR* 21, no. 1 (2008): 211–39.
———. "Gregory Rabassa: el rastro de un traductor visible." *Traducción/Género/Poscolonialismo.* Ed. P. Calefato and P. Godayol. *Designis* 12 (2008). 167–174.
Halka, Chester S. "*One Hundred Years of Solitude:* Two Additional Translation Corrections." *Journal of Modern Literature* 24, no. 1 (2000): 173–75.

Hoaksema Thomas "The Translator's Voice: An Interview with Gregory Rabassa." *Review* 1 (1978): 5–18.

Isaacs, Jorge. *Maria, a South American Romance*. Translated by Rollo Ogden. New York: Harper & Brothers, 1890.

Jackson, K. David. "Madness in a Tropical Manner." Review of *The Posthumous Memoirs of Brás Cubas*, by J. M. Machado de Assis. *New York Times*, Feb. 22, 1998, 381.

Jakobson, Roman. "On Linguistic Aspects of Translation." In *Theories of Translation*, edited by Rainer Schulte and John Biguenet, 144–51. Chicago: University of Chicago, 1992.

Joset, Jacques. Introduction. In *Cien años de soledad*, by Gabriel G. Márquez. Madrid: Cátedra, 2003.

Joyce, James. *Finnegans Wake*. New York: Viking Press, 1939.

Keates, Jonathan "The Emperor's New Dog." Review of *Quincas Borba*, by Machado de Assis. *New York Times*, Dec. 20, 1998, BR 20.

Kihss, Peter. "Higher Pay Urged for Translators: PEN at Latin Conference Asks for Recognition through credits, cash, royalties." *New York Times*, Feb. 13, 1971, 25.

Kinzer, Stephen. "America Yawns at Foreign Fiction." *New York Times*, Jul. 26, 2003, 7.

Lask, Thomas. "The Soil and Some of its Fruits." Review of *The Vampire of Curituba*, by Dalton Trevisan. Translated by Gregory Rabassa. *New York Times*, Dec. 1, 1972, BR3.

Lefevere, André. *Translation, Rewriting, and the Manipulation of Literary Fame*. London; New York: Routledge, 1992.

Leonard, John. "Myth is Alive in Latin America." Review of *One Hundred Years of Solitude*, by Gabriel García Márquez. Translated by Gregory Rabassa. *New York Times*, March 3, 1970, 39.

Leopardi, Giacomo. *Cantos*. Roma: Scuola tipografica salesiana, 1929.

Levine, Suzanne Jill. "The Latin American Novel in English Translation." In *The Cambridge Companion to the Latin American Novel*, edited by Efraín Kristal, 297–371. Cambridge: Cambridge University Press, 2005.

———. *The Subversive Scribe: Translating Latin American Fiction*. Saint Paul, MN: Graywolf Press, 1991.

Lezama Lima, José. *Como las cartas no llegan*. Edited by Ciro Bianchi Ross. La Habana: Ediciones Unión, 2000.

———. *Paradiso*. Translated by Gregory Rabassa. New York: Farrar, Straus and Giroux, 1974.

Lins, Osman. *Avalovara*. Translated by Gregory Rabassa. New York: Knopf, 1980.

Lispector, Clarice. *The Apple in the Dark*. Translated by Gregory Rabassa. Austin: University of Texas Press, 1967.

———. *A maçã no escuro*. Rio de Janeiro: Francisco Alves, 1961.

Lowe, Elizabeth and E. Fitz. "Gregory Rabassa: The Translator's Translator and the Foundations of Inter-American Literary Study." In *Translation and the Rise of Inter-American Literature*, by Elizabeth Lowe and Earl Fitz. Gainesville: University Press of Florida, 2007.

Luis, William. "Culture as Text: The Cuban/Caribbean Connection." In *Translation Perspectives VI: Translating Latin America: Culture as Text*, edited by William Luis and Julio Rodríguez-Luis, 7–20. Binghamton: State University of New York, 1991.

Mac Adam, Alfred. Review of *The Posthumous Memoirs of Bras Cubas/Dom Casmurro*, by J. M. Machado de Assis. Translated by Gregory Rabassa. *Hispanic Review* 68, no. 1 (2000): 95.

Machado de Assis, Joachim Maria. *The Hand and the Glove*. Translated by Albert Bagby, Jr. Lexington: University of Kentucky Press, 1970.

———. *The Posthumous Memoirs of Brás Cubas*. Translated by Gregory Rabassa. New York: Oxford University Press, 1997.

Martin, Gerald. *Journeys through the Labyrinth: Latin American Fiction in the Twentieth Century*. London: Verso Press, 1989.

———. "Translating García Márquez, or, the Impossible Dream." In *Voice-Overs: Translation and Latin American Literature*, edited by Daniel Balderston and Marcy E. Schuwartz, 156–69. Albany: SUNY Press, 2002.

Matto de Turner, Clorinda. *Birds Without a Nest: A Story of Indian Life and Priestly Oppression in Peru*. Translated by J. G. H. London: Thynne, 1904.

McDowell, Edwin. "A Wizard of Words." *Americas* 38, no. 4 (1986): 36–39.

Morales, Harry. "You Can't Say 'Ain't' in Spanish—Or Can You?: A Conversation with Gregory Rabassa." *Hopscotch: A Cultural Review* 2, no. 4 (2001): 116–27.

Moretti, Franco. *The Modern Epic: The World-System from Goethe to García Márquez*. New York: Verso, 1996.

Mounin, Georges. *Les problèmes théoriques de la traduction*. Paris: Gallimard, 1963.

Mudrovic, María Eugenia. "Reading Latin American Literature Abroad: Agency and Canon Formation in the Sixties and Seventies." In *Voice-Overs: Translation and Latin American Literature*, edited by Daniel Balderston and Marcy E. Schuwartz, 129–43. Albany: SUNY Press, 2002.

Mujica, Barbara. "Intriguing Family Histories" Review of *Taratuta and Still Life with Pipe: Two Novellas*, by José Donoso. Translated by Gregory Rabassa. *Americas* 45, no. 4 (1993): 62.

Munday, Jeremy. "One Translator, Many Authors: The 'Controlled Schizophrenia' of Gregory Rabassa." In *Style and Ideology in Translation: Latin American Writing in English*, 125–50. New York: Routledge, 2009.

———. "The Translation of Spanish American Literature: An Inevitable Cultural Distortion?" *Livius* 8 (1996) 155–64.

Nida, Eugene. *Language Structure and Translation*. Stanford: Stanford University Press, 1975.

———. "Principles of Correspondence." In *The Translation Studies Reader*, edited by Lawrence Venuti, 126–40. New York: Routledge, 2000.

———. *Toward a Science of Translating, with Special Reference to Principles and Procedures Involved in Bible Translating*. Holland: E. J. Brill, 1964.

Nietzsche, Friedrich. "Of Truth and Lies in a Nonmoral Sense." In *Philosophy and Truth: Selections from Nietzsche's Notebooks of the Early 1870's*, 79–91. Amhest: Humanity Books: 1999.

Niranjana, Tejaswini. *Siting Translation: History, Post-structuralism, and the Colonial Context*. Berkeley: University of California, 1992.

Nunn, Frederick. "The Latin American 'New Novel' in Translation: Archival Source for the Dialogue Between Literature and History." In *Translation Perspectives VI: Translating Latin America: Culture as Text*, edited by William Luis and Julio Rodríguez-Luis, 67–73. Binghamton: State University of New York, 1991.

Orero, Pilar, and Juan C. Sager, eds. *The Translator's Dialogue: Giovanni Pontiero*. Philadelphia: John Benjamins, 1997.

Payne, Johnny. *Conquest of the New Word: Experimental Fiction and Translation in the Americas*. Austin: University of Texas Press, 1993.

Peden, Margaret Sayers. "Aguilera Malta's *Seven Serpents and Seven Moons*." *Translation Review* 5 (1980): 37–41.

Poe, Edgar Allan. *Cuentos*. Translated by Julio Cortázar. La Habana: Instituto del Libro, 1965.

———. *Ensayos y críticas*. Translated by Julio Cortázar. La Habana: Editorial Nacional de Cuba, 1963.

———. *Eureka*. Translated by Julio Cortázar. Madrid: Alianza, 1972.

———. *Obras en prosa*. Translated by and introduction by Julio Cortázar. Puerto Rico: Río de Piedras, 1956.

Pye, Michael. "Afloat in the Seas of the Past." Review of *The Return of the Caravels*, by António Lobo Antunes. Translated by Gregory Rabassa. *New York Times*, Apr. 7, 2002, F13.

Rabassa, Gregory. "A Minor Novel by a Major Writer." Review of *The Hand and the Glove*, by J. M. Machado de Assis. Translated by Albert Bagby, Jr. *New York Times*, Nov. 22, 1970, 287.

———. "A Wizard of Words." Interview by Edwin McDowell. *Americas* 38, no. 4 (1986): 36–39.

———. "Catalan Magic." Review of *My Christina*, by Mercè Rodoreda. Translated by David Rosenthal. *New York Times Book Review*, Dec. 2, 1984, 68.

———. "If This Be Treason: Translation and its Possibilities," In *Translation: Literary, Linguistic, and Philosophical Perspectives*, edited by William Frawley, 21–29. Newark: University of Delaware Press, 1984.

———. *If This Be Treason: Translation and Its Dyscontents*. New York: New Directions, 2005.

———. "In Bahia, it's living theater." Review of *Tent of Miracles*, by Jorge Amado. Translated by Barbara Shelby. *New York Times*, Oct. 24, 1971, 52.

———. "Luis Rafael Sánchez: De la guaracha al beat." Interview by Gregory Rabassa. In *Espejo de escritores: Entrevistas con: Borges, Cortázar, Fuentes, Goytisolo, Onetti, Puig, Rama, Rulfo, Sánchez, Vargas Llosa*, edited by Reina Roffé 174–94. Hanover, NH: Ediciones del Norte, 1985.

———. "No Two Snowflakes are Alike: Translation as Metaphor." In *The Craft of Translation*, edited by John Biguenet and Rainer Schulte, 1–12. Chicago: University of Chicago Press, 1989.

———. "Slouching Back Toward Babel: Some Views on Translation in the Groves." In

Translation: Literary, Linguistic, and Philosophical Perspectives, edited by William Frawley, 30–34. Newark: University of Delaware Press, 1984.

———. "Parallel Lines that Meet: Translation in the Americas Society." *Review: Literature and Arts of the Americas* 38:2 no. 71 (2005): 128–31.

———. Personal interview. By María C. Guzmán. Aug. 1, 2005.

———. "The Ear in Translation." In *The World of Translation,* 81–86. New York: PEN American Center, 1971.

———. "The Silk-Purse Business: A Translator's Conflicting Responsibilities." In *Translation: Literary, Linguistic, and Philosophical Perspectives,* edited by William Frawley, 35–40. Newark: University of Delaware Press, 1984.

———. "The Translator's Voice: An Interview with Gregory Rabassa." Interview by Thomas Hoaksema. *Translation Review* 1 (1978): 5–18.

———. "Translating, a Conversation on the Craft: Albert Bermel, Mary Ann Caws, Gregory Rabassa, Alex Szogyi, Virginia Teller, Renee Waldinger." Interview. *Thesis. The Magazine of the Graduate School and the University Center* 1, no. 2 (1987): 4–9.

———. "Translation: The Recreative Art." *Humanities* 3, no. 6 (1982): 1–2.

———. "Words Cannot Express . . .: The Translation of Cultures." In *Translation Perspectives VI: Translating Latin America: Culture as Text,* edited by William Luis and Julio Rodríguez-Luis, 36–44. Binghamton: University Center at Binghamton (SUNY), 1991.

———. "You Can't Say 'Ain't' in Spanish—Or Can You?: A Conversation with Gregory Rabassa." Interview by Harry Morales. *Hopscotch: A Cultural Review* 2, no. 4 (2001): 116–27.

Rafael, Vicente. *Contracting Colonialism.* New York: Routledge, 1988.

Rama, Ángel. *La transculturación narrativa en América Latina.* México: Siglo XXI, 1982.

Ribeiro, Darcy. *The Brazilian People: The Formation and Meaning of Brazil.* Translated by Gregory Rabassa. Gainesville: University Press of Florida, 2000.

Rivera, Lucas. "A Translator's Life." *Hispanic* 12, no. 6 (1999): 66.

Robinson, Douglas. *Who Translates? Translator Subjectivities Beyond Reason.* Albany: SUNY University of New York, 2001.

Rodó, José Enrique. *Ariel.* Translated by Frederic Jesup Stimson. Boston and New York: Houghton Mifflin Company, 1922.

Rodoreda, Mercè. *My Christina and Other Stories.* Translated by David Rosenthal. Port Townsend, WA: Graywolf Press, 1984.

Rodríguez Monegal, Emir. Review of *The Green Pope,* by Miguel Ángel Asturias. Translated by Gregory Rabassa. *New York Times Book Review,* Feb. 28, 1971, 7.

Rose, Marilyn Gaddis. "Speculative Approaches." In *Routledge Encyclopedia of Translation Studies,* edited by Mona Baker, 238. New York: Routledge, 2001.

———. *Translation and Literary Criticism: Translation as Analysis.* Manchester: St. Jerome, 1997.

Rostagno, Irene. *Searching for Recognition: the Promotion of Latin American Literature in English.* Westport, CT: Greenwood Press, 1997.

Sánchez, Luis Rafael. "De la guaracha al beat." Interview by Gregory Rabassa. In *Espejo de escritores: Entrevistas con: Borges, Cortázar, Fuentes, Goytisolo, Onetti, Puig, Rama,*

Rulfo, Sánchez, Vargas Llosa, edited by Reina Roffé, 174–94. Hanover, NH: Ediciones del Norte, 1985.

———. *La guaracha del macho Camacho*. Buenos Aires: Ediciones de la Flor, 1976.

———. *Macho Camacho's Beat*. Translated by Gregory Rabassa. New York: Pantheon Books, 1980.

Sarlo, Beatriz. *La máquina cultural: maestras, traductoras, vanguardistas*. Buenos Aires: Ariel, 1998.

Silva, Armando. "Colombia: The Effect of Gabo's Writing." Translated by María C. Guzmán. "The Imagined City: a Critical Reading of Colombia's Daily Events." M.A. Thesis. Kent State University, 2001.

———. "Gabo: el efecto de su escritura." *Polvos de ciudad*. Bogotá: La Balsa, 2005. 109.

Simeoni, D. "The Pivotal Status of the Translator's Habitus." *Target* 10, no. 1 (1998.): 1–39.

Simon, Sherry. "William Hume Blake, or the Translator as Amateur Ethnologist." In *Writing Between the Lines: Portraits of Canadian Anglophone Translators*, edited by Agnes Whitfield. Canada: Wilfrid Laurier University Press, 2006.

Spivak, Gayatri Chakravorty. Response. "Forum: The Legacy of Jacques Derrida." *PMLA* 120, no. 2 (2005): 492–93.

Steenmeijer, Maarten. "How the West Was Won: Translations of Spanish American Fiction in Europe and the United States." In *Voice-Overs: Translation and Latin American Literature*. Edited by Daniel Balderston and Marcy E. Schuwartz, 144–55. Albany: SUNY Press, 2002.

Steiner, George. *After Babel: Aspects of Language and Translation*. New York: Oxford University Press, 1975.

Sturrock, John. "Fiction Roundup." Review of *A Manual for Manuel*, by Julio Cortázar. *New York Times*, Nov. 19, 1978.

Tannenbaum, Jeffrey A. "The Translator's Role is Crucial and Delicate, and Widely Unnoticed." *Wall Street Journal*, Sept. 15, 1977.

Trevisan, Dalton. *The Vampire of Curitiba and Other Stories*. Translated by Gregory Rabassa. New York: Knopf, 1972.

Vázquez Ayora, Gerardo. "La traducción de la nueva novela latinoamericana al inglés." *Babel* 34, no. 1 (1978) 4–18.

Venuti, Lawrence, ed. *Rethinking Translation: Discourse, Subjectivity, Ideology*. London: Routledge, 1992.

———. "The Difference That Translation Makes." In *Translation Studies: Perspectives on an Emerging Discipline*, edited by Alessandra Riccardi, 214–41. UK: Cambridge University Press, 2002.

———. *The Scandals of Translation: Towards and Ethics of Difference*. New York: Routledge, 1998.

———. *The Translation Studies Reader*. New York: Routledge, 2000.

———. *The Translator's Invisibility*. New York: Routledge, 1995.

———. "Translation, Community, Utopia." In *The Translation Studies Reader*, edited by Lawrence Venuti. New York: Routledge, 2000.

Vernon, John. "Ghosts." Review of *Doña Inés vs. Oblivion*, by Ana Teresa Torres. Translated by Gregory Rabassa. *New York Times*, Nov. 7, 1999, 30.

Vieira, Else R. P. "New Registers for Translation in Latin America." In *Rimbaud's Rainbow: Literary Translation in Higher Education*, edited by Malmkjaer, Bush. Amsterdam; Philadelphia: John Benjamins, 1998.

Vinay, J. P, and J. Dalbernet. *Stylistique comparée de l'anglais et du français*. Paris: Didier, 1958.

Waisman, Sergio. *Borges and Translation: The Irreverence of the Periphery*. Lewisburg: Bucknell University Press, 2005.

Watson, Richard. "A Pig's Tail." In *Latin American Literary Review* 15, no. 29 (1987): 89–92.

Weaver, William. "The Process of Translation." In *The Craft of Translation*, edited by John Biguenet and Rainer Schulte, 117–24. Chicago: University of Chicago Press, 1989.

Weissbort, Daniel. "Recent and Contemporary Writings: Gregory Rabassa." In *Translation: Theory and Practice: A Historical Reader*, edited by Daniel Weissbort and Astradur Teysteinsson. Oxford: Oxford University Press, 2006.

West, Paul. "Ambushed in the Cacao Groves." Review of *Tocaia Grande*, by Jorge Amado. *New York Times*, Feb. 7, 1988, BR3.

———. Review of *One Hundred Years of Solitude*, by G. G. Márquez. Translated by Gregory Rabassa. *Book World* 22, Feb. 4, 1970.

White, Edmund. "Four Ways to Read a Masterpiece." Review of *Paradiso*, by José Lezama Lima. Translated by Gregory Rabassa. *New York Times*, Apr. 21, 1974, 515.

White, Stephen. "Translation and Teaching: The Dangers of Representing Latin America for Students in the United States." In *Voice Overs: Translation and Latin American Literature*, edited by Daniel Balderston and Marcy E. Schuwartz, 235–44. Albany: SUNY Press, 2002.

Whitfield, Agnes, ed. *Writing Between the Lines: Portraits of Canadian Anglophone Translators*. Canada: Wilfrid Laurier University Press, 2006.

Willson, Patricia. *La constelación del sur: Traductores y traducciones en la literatura argentina del siglo XX*. Buenos Aires: Siglo Veintiuno, 2004.

Yourcenar, Marguerite. *Memorias de Adriano*. Translated by Julio Cortázar. Buenos Aires: Editorial Sudamericana, 1951.

Zárate Moreno, Jesús. *Jail*. Translated by Gregory Rabassa. Minneapolis: Aliform, 2003.

Zavalia de, Juliana. "The Impact of Spanish-American Literature in Translation on U.S. Latino Literature." In *Changing the Terms: Translating in the Postcolonial Era*, edited by Sherry Simon, 187–206. Ottawa: University of Ottawa Press, 2000.

Index

Africa, 94, 121, 142
Aguilera Malta, Demetrio, 14, 59, 77, 85, 90, 136; Rabassa's translations of works by, 147
Alice in Wonderland, 71
Allen, Esther (translator), 118, 171 n. 80
alterity, 29, 56, 57, 113, 118, 125, 126, 127, 133. *See also* difference
Amado, Jorge, 14, 59, 78, 87, 95–96, 169 n. 20, 170 n. 60, 174 n. 58; *Gabriela, Clove and Cinnamon*, 95–96; Rabassa's translations of works by, 147
ambiguity, 21, 43, 50–54, 92, 117, 127, 130. *See also* uncertainty
Americas, 94, 95, 97, 102, 103, 127, 129; literature of, 58, 87, 97, 99, 101, 102, 113, 133, 140; politics of, 52, 68, 70, 101, 102, 110–30, 133, 174 n. 58. *See also* Latin America, Latin American literature, United States
Andrade, Carlos Drummond de: Rabassa's translations of works by, 147
anthropology, 121, 128
Antunes, António Lobo, 14, 38, 59, 60, 84, 138, 140, 141, 144, 162 n. 33; Rabassa's translations of works by, 147
archive, 110, 119–30, 131, 133, 175 n. 84. *See also* collective memory
Argentina, 95, 116, 170 n. 57; literature of, 61, 85, 95, 116, 142
Arrojo, Rosemary, 22, 28, 132, 160 nn. 3 and 17
Asia, 94
Asturias, Miguel Ángel, 14, 59, 98, 100, 108, 169 n. 27; Rabassa's translations of works by, 147
author, 33, 34, 36, 37, 39, 41, 42, 50, 52, 55–56, 57, 61, 62, 66, 72, 73, 77, 79, 80, 81, 82, 131, 136, 139, 160 n. 23; function of, 22, 132; presence of, 22, 81
authorship, 20, 21, 22, 23, 28, 80, 160 n. 17. *See also* sacralized original

Babel, tower of, 20, 21, 40, 42
Bagby, Albert (translator), 87
Balcells, Carmen, 97
Barbosa, Heloisa, 173 n. 30
Barnstone, Willis (translator), 93
Barth, John, 100
Bellow, Saul, 140
Benedetti, Mario, 70
Benet, Juan, 14, 59, 60, 140; Rabassa's translations of works by, 147
Benjamin, Walter, 19, 20, 21, 30, 160 n. 8; "The Task of the Translator", 19–21
Blackburn, Paul (translator), 108, 165 n. 38
Blackburn, Sara, 14, 33, 48, 58, 61, 85, 93, 164 n. 83, 169 n. 27
body, 24, 52, 53, 127
Borges, Jorge Luis, 87, 98, 107, 113, 116, 117
Bourdieu, Pierre, 107, 133
Brazil, 64, 78, 91, 95, 114, 119, 138, 144; literature of, 59, 63, 78, 87, 91, 95, 96, 104, 107, 112, 113, 114, 117, 118, 142, 145–46, 169 n. 20, 170 n. 66

Cabrera Infante, Guillermo, 129
Caldwell, Helen (translator), 104
Camus, Albert, 73, 140
Cardenal, Ernesto, 96
Cardoso, Lucio, 145
Carvalho, Mário de, 14, 59; Rabassa's translations of works by, 147
Casa de las Americas, 103

Center for Inter-American relations, 44, 77, 105–7, 168 n. 144, 171 nn. 99 and 106
center-periphery relations, 94, 112, 113, 121, 123, 124, 170 n. 57
Cervantes, Miguel de, 72, 81; *Don Quixote*, 71, 72, 81, 139
Christ, Ronald (translator), 93, 99, 101, 105, 112
Cicogna, Enrico (translator), 74
Coindreau, Maurice-Edgar (translator), 73
cold war politics, 107, 133
collective memory, 124, 133. *See also* archive
Colombia, 70, 71, 122, 123, 136, 174 n. 58; literature of, 78, 85, 122, 123, 174 n. 58
coloniality, 28, 118, 121, 122, 124, 125, 133, 164 n. 89
Columbia College, 58
communication, 18, 25, 30, 34, 162 n. 24
Conrad, Joseph, 73
copyright, 25, 111, 159, n. 1 (ch. 1)
Cortázar, Julio, 38, 55, 57, 60, 61–70, 71, 74, 75, 77, 79, 82, 93, 98, 107–9, 111, 116, 136, 137, 138, 140, 142 143, 144, 164 n. 1, 166 nn. 68, 71 and 73, 166–67 n. 86; *Hopscotch*, 13, 58–64, 74, 76, 82, 84, 86, 92, 93, 100, 105, 108; *Rayuela*, 13, 14, 58, 61–64, 66, 75, 76, 83, 90, 93, 135; Rabassa's translations of works by, 147–48
Coutinho, Afrânio, 59; Rabassa's translations of works by, 148
Cronin, Michael, 28–31, 119, 128, 132
Cuba, 57, 68, 69, 70, 101–3, 109, 138; Cuban Revolution, 96, 101, 102, 109, 125; literature of, 63, 85
cultural appropriation, 52, 127
cultural practice, 43, 46, 50, 81, 129, 134
cultural production, 22, 25, 30, 46, 52, 101–4, 107, 111, 118, 125, 131, 133, 134, 171 n. 106, 175 n. 84
cultural studies, 22
cultural turn, 16, 21, 159 n. 5
Cunha, Euclides da, 145

Dalton, Roque, 70
Derrida, Jacques, 20, 21, 22, 23, 52, 129; "Des Tours de Babel," 20, 21
Dickens, Charles, 72, 145
difference, 19, 23, 46, 53, 56, 60, 62, 92, 111, 113, 126, 127, 129, 134, 160 n. 26. *See also* alterity
discourse, 26, 28, 33, 34, 39, 45, 53, 89, 92, 103, 119, 120, 122, 123, 126, 132, 160 n. 3; 174 n. 72
displacement, 26, 31, 34, 53, 85
domestication, 25, 84, 86, 90, 92, 112, 115; *See also* foreignization
Don Segundo Sombra, 95
Donoso, José, 14, 59, 99; Rabassa's translations of works by, 148
Dos Passos, John, 73, 140
Dostoyevsky, Fyodor, 143

editor, 13–14, 58, 65, 70, 72, 73, 75, 89, 91, 93, 96, 138, 141, 162 n. 41, 168 n. 163; editorial policy, 103
English language, 53, 60, 74, 77, 85, 89–93, 133, 143–44, 164 n. 89. *See also* language
English-language readership, 13, 30, 33, 44, 60, 64, 75–78, 86, 87, 89, 91, 92–93, 99–106, 108, 113, 114, 116, 117–19, 127, 131, 132, 143. *See also* United States readership
equivalence, 18, 19, 23, 28, 34, 36, 45, 46, 160 n. 3. *See also* fidelity
essentialism, 23, 116–17
Europe, 76, 94, 95, 97–98, 99, 102, 109, 121, 122, 124, 170 n. 57; literature of,14, 58, 59, 73, 111, 140; readership of, 76, 97–98, 115
Even-Zohar, Itamar, 112–13, 172 n. 9
exoticism, 96, 116–17, 120, 127

Fagundes, Lygia, 143
Faulkner, William, 73, 107, 140
fidelity, 16, 19, 23, 24, 43, 62, 74, 84–85, 87, 90, 92. *See also* equivalence
Fitzgerald, Francis Scott, 140
Flaubert, Gustave, 142, 145
foreignness, 21, 25, 26, 27, 45, 46, 48, 52,

53, 57, 86, 90, 106, 111, 112, 118, 126, 127, 128, 140
foreignization, 60, 84–85, 90, 91, 92, *See also* domestication
Foucault, Michel, 22, 133
França Júnior, Oswaldo: Rabassa's translations of works by, 148
Franco, Jorge, 59, 78, 137, 141, 173 n. 29; Rabassa's translations of works by, 148
Frank, Waldo, 94–95
Freud, Sigmund: *Civilization and Its Discontents*, 135–36
Fuentes, Carlos, 99, 109, 142

Gallimard (publisher), 98, 171 n. 74
García Aguilar, Eduardo: Rabassa's translations of works by, 148
García Márquez, Gabriel, 63, 70–75, 77, 84, 87, 92, 98, 100, 101, 107, 108, 109, 111, 113, 122, 123, 125, 127, 128, 135–37, 140, 141, 143, 144, 145, 167 nn. 98 and 118, 174 n. 58; *One Hundred Years of Solitude*, 13, 53, 59, 70–75, 76, 83, 84, 85, 86, 90, 91, 100, 101, 105, 110, 114, 120, 121, 122, 123, 124, 125, 126, 127, 128, 133, 164 n. 96, 174 n. 58; *Cien años de soledad*, 53, 70–75, 76, 85, 90, 98, 100, 105, 108, 121, 122, 124, 125, 127, 128, 138, 164 n. 95, 174 n. 58; Rabassa's translations of works by, 148
Garnett, Constance (translator), 143
Gide, André, 66, 137
Ginsberg, Allen, 96
global politics, 28, 29, 54, 104, 109, 117, 122, 125, 128, 134
globalization. *See* global politics
Goytisolo, Juan, 14, 59, 140; Rabassa's translations of works by, 148
Grossman, Edith (translator), 104
Grove (publisher), 107
Guimarães Rosa, João, 91, 142, 145
Gulliver's Travels, 34

hegemony, 51, 52, 108, 117, 118, 119, 126, 143, 164 n. 89, 174 n. 72
Hemingway, Ernest, 140

hemispheric exchange, 52, 94–109, 110–30, 133
Henry, Patrick, 32, 41, 135, 161 n. 1
hermeneutics, 19. *See also* textuality
heterogeneity, 81, 103, 115, 121, 172 n. 9
historicity, 25–26, 30, 46, 123–30, 131, 175 n. 84
Homer, 24
Houaiss, Antonio (translator), 144

identity, 18, 91, 124
ideology, 24, 25, 29, 45, 47, 81, 86, 92, 101, 102, 104, 108–9, 111, 117, 123, 124, 126, 174 n. 72
imperialism, 103, 123, 124, 125, 127
intelligibility, 40, 42, 53, 60, 86, 91, 113, 121
Irby, James (translator), 104
Isaacs, Jorge, 94

Jakobson, Roman, 18, 25
James, Henry, 145
Jameson, Fredric, 116
Joyce, James: *Finnegans Wake*, 60, 101, 138, 162 n. 33; *Ulysses*, 144

Kafka, Franz, 72

Lane, Helen (translator), 116
language, 41, 42, 67, 80, 81, 85, 108, 117, 118, 123, 124, 128, 141, 142, 145; arbitrariness and conventionality of, 34–37, 41, 50; function of, 34; materiality of, 33, 134. *See also* English language
Latin America, 52, 64, 76, 92, 94, 103, 109, 110–30; politics of, 68, 70, 101, 102, 103, 116, 117, 120, 122, 123, 124, 133; intellectuals from, 108, 109, 111,125, 175 n. 84; representations of, 110–30, 133, 175 n. 84
Latin American literature, 13, 14, 15, 30, 31, 52, 58, 59, 64, 71, 77, 78, 81, 83–109, 110–30, 131, 132, 133, 134, 135–46, 170 nn. 57 and 66, 171 nn. 74 and 80, 173 n. 29, 175 n. 84; exclusions of, 111–16, 120, 134; Latin American Boom, 14, 31, 58, 59, 83, 90, 91, 97–109, 110–19,

124, 128, 129, 132, 133, 139–40, 141–43, 173 n. 29, 174 n. 58; Latin American readership, 76, 94, 96, 101, 103, 111, 127; post-Boom literature, 106, 117, 141–42, 173 n. 29
Leopardi, Giacomo, 73
Levine, Suzanne Jill (translator), 31, 49, 56, 85, 94, 104, 105, 118, 128, 129, 162 n. 24, 165 n. 38, 171 n. 99
Lezama Lima, José, 13, 38, 60, 63, 64, 68–70, 74, 136, 137, 144; *Paradiso*, 59, 64, 68–70, 74, 84, 86, 90, 91, 92, 105, 137, 164 n. 1, 166–67 n. 86; Rabassa's translations of works by, 148
Lima Barreto, Afonso Henriques de, 78, 87, 146
linguistics, 19
Lins, Osman, 14, 59, 60; Rabassa's translations of works by, 148
literature: border-crossing of, 109, 112, 113, 119, 126, 129; canon of, 13, 14, 28, 83, 90, 91, 97–109, 111, 112, 115–20, 125, 128, 132, 133, 134, 173 n. 29; circulation of, 110, 111, 112, 119, 129, 132, 133, 173 n. 30; community of, 16, 110, 113, 115, 132, 160–61 n. 30; conventions of, 119, 125; criticism of, 19, 47, 59, 64, 66, 76, 83, 87, 95, 97, 100, 101, 103, 104, 107, 108, 109, 115, 123, 139; institutions of, 16, 30, 45, 92, 94, 96, 101–5, 110, 114, 115, 117, 118, 129, 131, 132, 144, 160–61 n. 30, 170 n. 57; internationalization of, 13, 30, 44, 68, 71, 75, 83, 92, 97–104, 106–13, 116, 125, 132, 142; marketplace of, 89–109, 111, 114, 117, 118, 128, 141, 144, 164 n. 89; patronage, 106, 107, 108, 131, 164 n. 89, 171 n. 106; reception of, 64, 71, 76, 90, 91, 94–109, 110–30, 132, 140; recontextualization, 52–54, 112, 116, 117, 120, 126, 127, 133; study of, 47, 48; system of, 45, 94, 97, 109, 111–14, 121, 172 n. 9; tradition of, 30, 47, 81, 88, 91, 92, 96, 97, 99, 100, 104, 109, 110, 111, 112, 113, 125, 131, 169 n. 20, 172 n. 9, 175 n. 84; Western, 13, 92, 99, 104, 107, 121

Lispector, Clarice, 59, 71, 75, 113, 114, 143; Rabassa's translations of works by, 149
Los Angeles Times, 75
lunfardo, 61

Machado de Assis, Joachim Maria; 13, 55, 59, 78, 84, 87, 117, 139, 142, 145, 146, 162 n. 36; Rabassa's translations of works by, 149
Macondo, 110, 119, 121, 123, 124, 126, 127, 169 n. 20
magical realism, 92, 100, 109, 113, 114, 115, 121, 122, 123, 125, 133
Malraux, André, 73
Martín Fierro, 95
Matto de Turner, Clorinda, 94
Melo, João de: Rabassa's translations of works by, 149
Mendoza, Mario, 173 n. 29
Mexico, 77, 95, 96, 136
modernity, 96, 121, 123, 127, 128
Monsiváis, Carlos, 68
Moraes, Vinicius de: Rabassa's translations of works by, 149
Mujica Láinez, Manuel, 14, 59; Rabassa's translations of works by, 149
Mundo Nuevo (literary journal), 103

nation, 29, 96, 109, 118, 120, 142, 164 n. 89
Neruda, Pablo, 111
New Directions (publisher), 107, 138, 145
New York Times, The, 75, 140
New Yorker, The, 108
Nida, Eugene, 18
Nietzsche, Friedrich, 34, 35
North America. *See* Americas, United States
North American readership. *See* United States readership
north-south exchange. *See* hemispheric exchange

Ocampo, Victoria, 95, 170 n. 57
Odyssey (literary journal), 13, 58, 78, 106;

Oliver Labra, Carilda: Rabassa's translations of works by, 149
Onís, Harriet de (translator), 96, 104
opacity, 33, 123. *See also* transparency
originality, 21, 22, 33, 35, 41, 76, 80, 100
Ortega y Gasset, José, 53, 135
otherness. *See* alterity

Padilla, Ignacio, 173 n. 29
Pantheon (publisher), 14, 107
Paz, Octavio, 96, 111
Peden, Margaret Sayers (translator), 85, 104, 105
PEN Association, 44, 71, 117
Piñon, Nélida, 143
Pires, Fernando: Rabassa's translations of works by, 149
Plumed Horn, The (literary journal), 96
Poe, Edgar Allan, 66, 137
poetry, 13, 38, 52, 70, 79, 93, 96, 106, 107, 108, 111, 137, 138, 142, 143
post-colonial discourse, 16
post-coloniality. *See* coloniality, post-colonial discourse
post-structuralism, 22, 35, 160 n. 26
power relations, 16, 26, 28, 29, 52, 71, 128, 134, 164 n. 89, 174 n. 72
Proust, Marcel, 70, 72
publishing industry, 25, 33, 63, 77, 89, 92–109, 111, 114, 115, 117, 118, 138, 141, 170 n. 60, 171 n. 106, 173 n. 31
Puerto Rican Traveling Theater, 59
Puig, Manuel, 106, 129, 173 n. 29

Rabassa, Gregory, 13–16, 30–31, 96, 98, 99, 104, 105–9, 113, 114, 119, 125, 126, 127, 129, 130, 131–34, 171 n. 99; accounts of translations by, 61–82, 136; agent, as, 30, 129, 131; articles and book chapters about, 159 n. 2 (Introduction); biography/sociography of, 44, 56–60, 70, 135–46, 159 n. 11; books about, 159 nn. 4-5; and the canon, 104–9; circulation and reception of translations by, 76, 83–94, 97–104, 108, 110–30, 141; criticism of translations by, 16, 83–94, 141; *If This Be Treason: Translation and Its Dyscontents*, 15, 32, 40, 42, 43, 46, 51–54, 55, 56, 79, 135, 138, 161 n. 2, 162 n. 41, 169 n. 20; interview conducted with, 135–46; legacy of, 13, 14, 16, 30, 34, 110–30, 131, 133, 160 n. 18; list of translations by 147–50; recognition of, 13, 33, 34, 71, 74, 93, 105, 108–9, 126, 129, 131, 132; relationship with authors, 55–6, 79–82, 108, 136–39; reviews by, 87–8, 144; reviews of translations by, 71, 83–6, 107, 108, 126, 168 n. 1; self-understanding of, 16, 32, 39, 44, 46, 57, 80, 132, 163 n. 75; theories of language, 30, 32–54, 57, 80, 87, 88, 132, 143–45, 169 n. 20; visibility of 13, 14, 16, 30, 34, 81, 93, 105, 131, 132, 164 n. 83; writings by, 131–32, 139, 162 n. 41, 169 n. 27
Rama, Ángel, 97
Reid, Alastair (translator), 48, 71, 93, 105, 171 n. 99
resistance, 29, 33, 50, 86, 88, 92, 124
Review (literary journal), 105
Ribeiro, Darcy, 59; Rabassa's translations of works by, 149
Robinson, Douglas, 23–24, 38–39, 80, 132, 160 n. 23
Rodó, José Enrique, 94
Rodoreda, Mercè, 87
Rodríguez Monegal, Emir, 103, 105, 145, 170 n. 66
Rosenthal, David (translator), 87
Roth, Philip, 140
Rulfo, Juan, 96, 142

Sábato, Ernesto, 116
sacralized original, 20, 21, 24, 80. *See also* authorship, fidelity, textuality
Sánchez, Luis Rafael, 59, 75–76, 84, 85, 136, 137; Rabassa's translations of works by, 149
Saramago, José, 140
Sarduy, Severo, 106, 173 n. 29
Sarlo, Beatriz, 170 n. 57
Sarney, José, 14, 138; Rabassa's translations of works by, 149
Sartre, Jean Paul, 140

INDEX 191

Scots verdict, 43, 51, 136
Seix Barral (publisher), 97, 108
Shakespeare, William, 126, 135
Shelby, Barbara (translator), 87
Simeoni, Daniel, 159 n. 11
social change, 94, 95, 101, 102, 103, 117, 122–24
social institution, 92
Sontag, Susan, 68, 100, 118, 164 n. 89
Spivak, Gayatri Chakravorty, 129
stylistics, 45, 47, 86, 89, 143
Sur (literary journal), 95, 170 n. 57

Teitelboim, Volodia, 59
textuality, 23–25, 38, 41, 46, 47, 49, 50, 53, 76, 80, 92, 120, 122, 127, 132, 160–61 n. 30 , 163 n. 69
Tolstoy, Leo, 143, 145
Torres, Ana Teresa, 113; Rabassa's translations of works by, 149
translatability, 18, 19, 21, 37, 38, 94, 144, 162 n. 33. *See also* translation
translation: as afterlife, 19, 20, 21; circulation and dissemination of, 26, 30, 45, 94–119, 120–30, 132, 133, 173 n. 30 and 31; and community, 26, 27, 81, 88–89, 92, 110, 120, 129, 131, 160–61 n. 30, 168 n. 163; criticism of, 48, 83–94, 101, 120–22, 141; ethics of, 24, 26, 46, 47, 92, 129–30, 132, 143; exclusions of, 111, 112, 113, 114, 115, 116, 118, 125, 134; fluency of, 33, 70, 84–85, 86, 89–94, 113, 141; ideology of, 24, 25, 26, 27, 28, 117–30; impossibility of, 18, 19, 37, 38, 50, 85, 130, 144–45; linguistics-oriented approaches to, 16, 17, 18, 160 n. 3; as mediation, 28, 29, 118–19; as negotiation, 25, 29, 30, 44, 45, 46, 52, 53, 56, 80, 90, 92, 115, 127, 127, 129, 131, 134, 141; norms and standards of, 22, 26, 31, 38, 41, 45, 86, 89, 90, 92, 112–13; philosophical approaches to, 19–21; postcolonial approaches to, 16; process of, 25, 33, 36, 43, 45, 46, 48–50, 53, 60–62, 67, 73–81, 86, 88–89, 92, 112, 117, 131–34, 137, 138, 141–45, 163 n. 69, 173 n. 30; as relation, 29, 128, 131;
reviewing, 84–85, 86–87, 88, 89, 92, 96, 101, 107, 108, 115; stigmatization of, 39, 40–43, 48, 135–36, 160 n. 17; strategy of, 33, 45, 84, 86, 89, 91, 92, 112, 160 n. 26; translational status, 109; as writing, 21–24, 30, 33, 36, 38, 39, 43, 44, 48, 50, 51, 53, 127, 131, 144. *See also* translatability, translator
translation studies, 15, 16, 20, 21, 46, 47, 49, 131, 132, 133, 159 n. 5, 160 n. 18;
translator: agency of, 27, 47; as agent, 27, 30, 34, 80, 104, 127, 129, 131; awareness of, 24, 27, 28, 29, 39, 46, 49, 51, 57, 67, 68, 80, 88, 108; biography/sociography of, 16, 133; consciousness of, 47, 48, 49, 57, 163 n. 69; ethics of, 16, 24, 27, 28, 29, 39, 44, 50–54, 92, 129–30, 132, 143; experience of, 26, 33, 34, 38, 44, 49, 56, 58, 66, 67, 70, 88, 92, 129, 133, 138, 144; image/figure of, 22, 24, 35, 37, 49, 73, 132; invisibility (*see* visibility); legacy of, 120, 129, 134; role and status of, 15, 19; 23, 24, 27, 31, 52, 56, 80, 92, 99, 104, 105, 109, 110, 119, 127, 129, 131, 132, 133, 134, 143; self-effacement of, 32, 33, 38, 43, 44, 46, 49, 50, 164 n. 83; self-reflection of, 15, 21, 27, 39, 49, 51–54, 131–32; self-understanding of, 22, 24, 27, 28, 39, 49, 52, 80; as subject, 17, 23, 25, 27, 30, 38, 45, 50, 127, 129, 131; subjectivity of, 20, 23, 24, 27, 39, 51; task and mission of, 17–22, 24, 30, 31, 39, 41, 73, 130; voice of (*see under* voice); visibility of, 16, 19, 21, 22, 25, 28, 30, 32, 34, 44, 47, 50, 81, 89, 105, 160 n. 18; writings of, 49, 131–32, 139. *See also* translation, translator-author relationship
translator-author relationship, 23, 24, 28, 39, 50, 55–56, 59–82, 132, 136, 139
transparency, 19, 45, 89. *See also* opacity
Trevisan, Dalton, 14, 59, 78; Rabassa's translations of works by, 149
truth, 21, 35, 56, 80, 120, 123, 126, 133

Unamuno, Miguel de, 81
uncertainty, 50, 54, 67, 123, 130, 132. *See also* ambiguity

Underdogs, The, 95
United States, 76, 94–100, 104–7, 109, 114, 124, 127, 140, 143, 144; literature of, 73, 89, 96, 100, 111, 116, 139, 140; policies of, 102, 107, 171 n. 106; politics of, 101, 102, 118, 124, 171 n. 106
United States readership, 31, 89, 94–97, 105, 106, 111, 113-16, 119, 140, 143, 170 n. 66, 173 n. 31. *See also* English-speaking readership
universality, 94, 103, 117, 119, 120
untranslatability. *See* translatability

Valenzuela, Luisa, 14, 59, 113, 137, 142, 143; Rabassa's translations of works by, 149
Vallejo, César, 96
Vargas Llosa, Mario, 14, 59, 77, 78, 100, 108, 109, 136; Rabassa's translations of works by, 149
Venuti, Lawrence, 18, 20, 22, 25, 27, 30, 32, 33, 34, 38, 44–48, 52, 81, 89–92, 107, 111–13, 132, 160 n. 26, 163 n. 69; canon of fluency, 26, 89–94; translator's visibility (*see under* translator)
Vilar, Irene, 113; Rabassa's translations of works by, 149–50
virtual image, 118–19, 126, 127

voice, 36, 37, 60, 80, 85, 87, 133; of translator, 23, 36, 49, 60, 132
Volpi, Jorge, 173 n. 29

Wall, Aroldo, 70
war, 54, 58, 95, 121, 124. *See also* cold war politics
Waste Land, The, 121
Weaver, William (translator), 45, 46, 52, 163 n. 69
Weinberger, Eliot (translator), 105, 171 n. 99
Willson, Patricia, 170 n. 57
Wilson, Edmund, 170 n. 66
wordplay, 57, 60, 62, 70, 77, 86, 136, 165 nn. 42–43
world literature, 92, 93, 97, 102, 109, 111, 116, 121, 125, 132, 171 n. 74
world system, 122
writing: materiality of, 36, 52, 127, 134, 139. *See also* authorship, language, textuality

Yourcenar, Marguerite, 66, 137

Zárate Moreno, Jesús: Rabassa's translations of works by, 150